Lonely Planet Publications
Melbourne | Oakland | London

S0-AWO-785

Martin Robinson

Seoul

The Top Five

1 National Museum of Korea
Discover the new shrine of Korean artistry (p62)

2 Gyeongbokgung
Enter the world of Seoul's Confucian kings (p49)

3 Itaewon
Party till dawn in Seoul's Sin City (p104)

4 War Memorial & Museum
Marvel at this splendid panorama of Korea's turbulent history (p63)

5 Dongdaemun market
Lose yourself in the mega-market that could clothe the world (p122)

Contents

Published by Lonely Planet Publications Pty Ltd
ABN 36 005 607 983

Australia Head Office, Locked Bag 1, Footscray,
Victoria 3011, ☎ 03 8379 8000, fax 03 8379 8111,
talk2us@lonelyplanet.com.au

USA 150 Linden St, Oakland, CA 94607,
☎ 510 893 8555, toll free 800 275 8555,
fax 510 893 8572, info@lonelyplanet.com

UK 72–82 Rosebery Ave, Clerkenwell, London,
EC1R 4RW, ☎ 020 7841 9000, fax 020 7841 9001,
go@lonelyplanet.co.uk

Printed by SNP Security Printing Pte Ltd, Singapore

The Authors

Martin Robinson

This is Martin's second edition of *Seoul*. For this guide he inspected over 100 Seoul hotels, ate in as many restaurants, and walked down almost every lane and alleyway in the city. Previously he spent two years in Korea teaching English, and also worked for the Jeollabuk-do governor's office.

Martin has travelled widely through Asia, and has written for magazines and newspapers. He's the author of a hiking guide to Jeollabuk-do province, and coordinating author of Lonely Planet's *Korea*. Born in London, he now lives in New Zealand – when he's not negotiating his way around the planet.

CONTRIBUTING AUTHORS

DONALD N CLARK

Donald N Clark is a professor of history and Director of International Programs at Trinity University in San Antonio, Texas. He is a specialist on Korean affairs, drawing on experience that began with his childhood in Seoul. Donald earned his PhD in East Asian History at Harvard University in 1978. He is the author of a number of books, including *Culture and Customs of Korea* (2000). His latest book is *Living Dangerously in Korea, 1900–1950* (2003). For *Seoul,* Donald wrote the History chapter.

THOMAS HUHTI

Studies for a major in linguistics took Thomas to Asia for half a decade as he attempted to suss out Mandarin and Thai. Not confused enough, he later spent two years studying in South Korea, oddly delighted by the grammatical complexities of its language and, more, touched by the graciousness of its people. Thomas hails from Wisconsin in the US and still walks its forests with his Labrador Bobo, when not travelling East Asia for Lonely Planet. Thomas wrote the City Life chapter.

PHOTOGRAPHER
Anthony Plummer

Growing up in Melbourne, Anthony unearthed a seething nest of travel and photo bugs. He has since dedicated years to soothing those itches, via the nunataks of Antarctica and the ashrams of India. But neither bitter Kyrgyz kumiss nor smooth Belizean Beliken beer could cure his hankering for a peripatetic life. Perhaps even stronger than the call of the road is Anthony's fondness for photography. His work has appeared in various Lonely Planet publications, as well as magazines and government and advertising publications.

MARTIN'S TOP SEOUL DAY

After a bagel breakfast at the Witch's Table, I drop into Seoul Selection to rent DVDs of the latest Korean movies, then stroll around the Insadong galleries for a modern-art fix. Development never takes a rest and I notice the Sex Museum, which used to be a guesthouse, has now morphed into a Chinese restaurant. For lunch I'll tuck into *wangmandu* (big dumplings) or ginseng chicken *juk* (rice porridge) followed by a fruit tea and rice cake in an atmospheric teashop. Next I jump on the subway to the wondrous COEX Mall, south of the river, to up my scores on the free PlayStation games and listen to the latest CDs at Evan. If I bump into someone we'll down a homebrew or two at O'Kim's Brauhaus. Friends text to say it's Daehangno tonight so I hop back on the subway and meet them sitting on the floor at Nolboojip listening to live *gayageum* (zither) music and praising the *dobu jjigae* (spicy tofu stew). Later we enjoy a blast of karaoke before listening to some decent singers at one of the live jazz venues. We'll then join the cheerful young crowd in Bier Halle until it's time to catch the last subway train home.

Introducing Seoul

Nothing is permanent in this fashion-filled, helter-skelter city that completely rebuilds itself every decade and vibrates with energy night and day. Every evening a tsunami of Seoulites sweeps into entertainment districts, where smoky barbecue restaurants, goblin-sized teashops, plush mugwort saunas, DVD mini-cinemas and more are stacked up 10-storeys high along narrow alleys. Seoul spreads a virtually unknown culture and cuisine at your feet.

Yes, the future has already arrived, but the past has not been completely uprooted – Seoul's mighty fortress wall and gates still stand, as do World Heritage palaces, royal shrines and tombs. A neighbourhood of *hanok* (traditional Korean one-storey wooden houses with tiled roofs), built by *yangban* (aristocrats), has miraculously survived the Korean War and the rush to bulldoze and modernise. Traditional cultural performances, feisty festivals, folk villages and folk museums allow visitors to peep into Seoul's feudal past when Confucian scholar noblemen in *hanbok* (traditional Korean clothing) wore black horse-hair hats and lorded it over their wives, concubines, peasants and slaves.

Some hotels still offer rooms where you can sleep on a padded quilt on an *ondol* (underfloor-heated) floor in a room furnished in *yangban* style. In traditional restaurants furnished like folk museums everybody sits on floor cushions, feasting on a table-top barbecue of beef, pork or chicken along with rice, seasoned soups and a multitude of piquant sauces and vegetable side dishes.

LOWDOWN

Population 10.7 million

Time zone GMT plus nine hours

Budget en suite room W35,000

Three-star room W90,000 upwards

Sauna sleepover W5000

Subway ticket W900

DVD room ticket W8000

Public museum admission up to W3000

Cup of coffee W500–W5000

Cup of beondegi (silkworm larvae) W1500

Packet of rice cakes W3000

The wide-ranging and healthy Korean cuisine is another of the city's attractions. Discover the delights of ginseng chicken, meat-and-lettuce wraps, spicy tofu soup, *hotteok* (sweet pita bread) and *omijacha* (berry) tea. Restaurants in every price range also offer Japanese, Western, Chinese and fusion food as well as the chance to sample special meals, such as royal court cuisine, which are hard to find outside Seoul.

The weather is at its best in spring, which is also festival time – Buddha's birthday celebrations and picnics under the cherry blossom make this a popular season to visit, but autumn with its transcendent tree tints, blue skies and music concerts is also highly recommended. Even the freezing winters are tempered by the *ondol*, while the hot and humid summers are made bearable by air-conditioning. Seoul hosts an endless stream of small festivals, so whenever you visit you can expect a special cultural event or two to be taking place.

Splashes of nature are beginning to appear out of the blue: Cheonggye stream, which used to be covered by a road, has been uncovered and reborn, and an instant woodland, Ttukseon Seoul Forest, has been planted on what used to be a racetrack and sports fields.

Thousands of expats live and work in Seoul – most enjoy their stay and a few never leave. Their main struggle is usually with the language as English is not widely spoken or understood. Seoul has its rough edges: traffic congestion, ugly high-rises, and not all the characteristics that have lead to the city's astonishing economic success are endearing. But as with working abroad anywhere, a positive attitude, adaptability and understanding are the keys to an enjoyable long-term stay.

Recommended excursions include touring the Demilitarized Zone (DMZ), which is a fascinating but stark reminder of the dangerous division of the country; walking around the rebuilt walls of Suwon's World Heritage fortress; and boarding a ferry to the beaches and seafood restaurants on unspoilt islands in the West Sea.

No other Korean city approaches the size and importance of rush-rush Seoul with its nearly 11 million residents and another eight million who live within commuting distance. It is the dynamic political, financial, educational and cultural hub of the world's 11th largest economy. Seoul is a 600-year-old capital, a complex, rarely explored Asian city that is a fascinating cultural *bibimbap* of rude energy, Confucian rules and democratic values, where Buddhists and shamanists rub shoulders with Christians and atheists.

ESSENTIAL SEOUL

- Gyeongbokgung (p49-50)
- National Museum of Korea (p62) and Seodaemun Prison (p62)
- Namdaemun market (p123) and Dongdaemun market (p122)
- War Memorial & Museum (p63)
- Nightlife in Hongik (p105) and Itaewon (p104)

City Life

City Life *Thomas Huhti*

SEOUL TODAY

Call it a geographic metaphor for Korean can-do, an El Dorado of some 'Korean Dream' of a better tomorrow. It's also, however, an unrivalled rat race, but one with style, grace and efficiency.

Economy, government, culture, education, health care, whatever – in South Korea it *all* starts here. About 10.7 million people live in Seoul proper, but the figure increases to 21 million-plus if you include its five satellite suburbs. Twenty-five per cent of Korea's population live in Seoul city and 47% live in Greater Seoul, the largest chunk of a nation's population in one city in the world. It is, indeed, the 'soul' of South Korea.

Each generation of Seoul's hardy citizens – many of them sucked in as youngsters from around the country – has contributed to its Herculean post–Korean War rebuilding project: from poverty amidst rubble to the centre of the world's 11th-largest economy (by GDP in 2004). So apt is the 'hurry-up culture' moniker you often hear that in 2005 South Korea officially chucked its longstanding tourism pitch of 'Land of Morning Calm' to tell it like it is: 'Dynamic Korea'. The efficient bustle of Seoul was a driving force behind this.

Yet what pains have come with the miracle. Sclerotic traffic patterns (don't even mention parking). Greenspace – what greenspace? A planned relocation of the capital. A sluggish but accelerating recovery from the 1997 economic crisis. Unnerving spikes in the cost of living, particularly housing.

And most telling: some Seoulites today do at times seem to be showing signs of an existential big-city angst and whether 'I' might not at times trump 'we' – a watershed event in a city that has long prided itself on clutching onto its past while hustling towards tomorrow.

Stroll the streets, though. Really *see* the city, this 'dynamic' street-by-street melding of history and modernity. You'll soon enough appreciate the population's admirable never-say-quit work ethic and unvanquishable faith in their future.

HOT CONVERSATION TOPICS

- President Roh's woes
- White-hot *hallyu* (Korean Wave) stars overseas
- The coaching merry-go-round of the Red Devils, Korea's national soccer team
- The meteoric rise and nearly immediate fall into disgrace of Hwang Woo-suk, 'father' of the world's first cloned dog Snuppy (true) and cloned human embryo (fabricated)
- Dokdo, the island chain hotly disputed by South Korea and Japan
- Young men dodging mandatory military service
- University entrance exam cheating
- Kim Il Sung's odd sleeping habits (one of many juicy titbits published in a 2004 bestseller)
- (Notice how North Korea and nukes weren't in that last one?)

CITY CALENDAR

Show up anytime in Seoul and you'll find a festival or celebratory blowout of some sort. Seoul has traditional cultural and religious festivals, yet you may be surprised by the many fêtes to the ultramodern city.

September's Chuseok (Thanksgiving) and April's Cherry Blossom Festival offer unparalleled weather. During Lunar New Year and Chuseok, transport tickets out of the city must be purchased well in advance (up to two months for some), and roads nationwide are utterly gridlocked. Most businesses, except essential services, shut down for at least the main celebration day.

Home-grown holidays and festivals follow the lunar calendar, while the rest follow the Gregorian (Western) calendar.

For a list of public holidays, see p167.

JANUARY/FEBRUARY

LUNAR NEW YEAR

Begins 17 February 2007, 6 February 2008, 26 January 2009. Seoul empties itself and the nation shuts down during this three-day holiday when Koreans return to their home town, visit relatives, honour elders and eat traditional goodies.

APRIL

CHERRY BLOSSOM FESTIVAL

Dates determined by nature, but generally early April, when the cherry blossoms go from first peek out to full colour riot within a week. Eating and drinking under the blossoms in Yeouido's Cherry Blossom Park (Map p210) is the best way to celebrate this festival, though groves of cherry trees are ubiquitous in Seoul.

WOMEN'S FILM FESTIVAL IN SEOUL

http://wffis.or.kr
This festival features over 100 films from 30-plus countries.

MAY

BUDDHA'S BIRTHDAY

For over a millennium, temples have honoured the Buddha's birth by adorning courtyards with resplendently coloured lanterns. The Sunday before Buddha's birthday, Seoul celebrates with a huge evening lantern parade – the largest in South Korea – by 100,000 Buddhists from Tapgol Park (Map pp202–3) to Jogyesa (Map p205). Upcoming dates are 24 May 2007, 12 May 2008, 2 May 2009.

HI SEOUL FESTIVAL

www.hiseoulfest.org
First week of May. This festival officially welcomes summer with nonstop citywide events – traditional performances, concerts, food fairs, fashion shows, tea ceremonies, parades, laser light shows, and more – all family-friendly and most free.

JUNE

DANO FESTIVAL

On 19 June 2007, 8 June 2008, 27 June 2009. Held according to the lunar calendar, this festival features shamanist rituals and mask dances in many locales. At Namsangol Hanok Village (Map pp206–7), you can ride a *geunettwigi* (a traditional Korean swing), gape at *ssireum* (traditional Korean wrestling) and get a traditional hair treatment with iris-infused water.

AUGUST

SEOUL FRINGE FESTIVAL

www.seoulfringe.net
International misunderstood geniuses in all artistic media converge on the trendy Hongdae area to flee the mainstream.

SEOUL INTERNATIONAL CARTOON & ANIMATION FESTIVAL

www.sicaf.or.kr
Half a million cartoon geeks pack auditoriums to see why Seoul is such a hot commodity in animation (fans of *The Simpsons* can thank Korean artists).

SEPTEMBER

CHUSEOK

Begins 5 October 2006, 24 September 2007, 13 September 2008, 3 October 2009. This is the Harvest Moon Festival, a major three-day holiday when families get together, eat crescent-shaped rice cakes and visit their ancestors' graves to perform *sebae* (a ritual bow).

Buddhist drummer at a performance to celebrate Buddha's birthday (opposite)

SEOUL NET & FILM FESTIVAL
www.senef.net

Open any cinematically-themed medium and you'll see how trendy Korean auteurs are. May through September you can peruse the online screenings; offline screenings are held the first week of September.

GUGAK FESTIVAL
www.gugakfestival.or.kr

Hip hop *gugak*? You'd be surprised how well traditional Korean music crosses over into a modern context at this annual 10-day Seoul-wide festival. From classy arts centres to basement grunge clubs, it does an amazing job of mixing traditional with trendy.

OCTOBER
HANGEUL DAY

This popular event is held every year on 9 October. The festival began in 1926 during the period of Japanese occupation as a means of maintaining Korea's cultural identity. Many of the historic attractions have hands-on demonstrations – it's great fun learning *hangeul* (the Korean phonetic alphabet) under the watchful scrutiny of local school children.

NOVEMBER
KIMCHI EXPO
kimchi.munhwa.com

Early November. It wouldn't be Korea without a *kimchi* fête, would it? Hundreds of purveyors and distributors show their stuff at this festival held at COEX (Map pp214–15); the public also gets an eye- (and mouth-) full of the national dish. Celebrity cook-offs, taste testing and lots of demos make for a super (and super hot) experience.

CULTURE

Seoul's frenetic pursuit of the future is eminently apparent: high-end fashion; up-to-ears debt for spiffier cars, flats, and up-to-the-nanosecond mobile technology; everyplace, everywhere wired to the outside world; a heads-down beehive pace on the streets.

Yet for all that, beneath the manic modernity Korea remains arguably the most Confucian nation in Asia, and here the past does smack quite hard at times into the present. Older generations and opinion pieces fret and grouse about the slow drift away from social mores. However, like nowhere else in Asia, younger generations of Koreans, particularly in Seoul, still feel (and do consider themselves devoted to) the firm pull of culture and tradition.

TOP FIVE BOOKS ON KOREA

- *The Koreans* by Michael Breen (updated 2004), written by a long-time Seoul expat journalist, remains the most accessible examination of Korea and its people in the modern era.
- *Native Speaker* by Chang-Rae Lee (1995) proves that an extraordinary novel – here, focusing on the changing family of the Korean-American diaspora – can rival any textbook.
- *Korea's Place in the Sun* by Bruce Cummings (1997) focuses on Korea's history since 1860.
- *Sourcebook of Korean Civilisation*, edited by Peter Lee (1993), is a fascinating book of themed original historical documents with a commentary.
- booksonkorea.org – not *a* book but over 1700 from the Korea Foundation, a phenomenal resource for titles on every piece of the Korean mosaic.

IDENTITY

The country's harmony and uniformity is often overstated, as family, clan, school, company, trade-union, religious, regional and social-class loyalties frequently cut across national unity. (And the world has little to rival the sight of Koreans when they do erupt.)

Seoul in the 21st century is a test tube of nascent Korean footloose-and-fancy-free cosmopolitanism. Seemingly every week a Seoul university or think-tank has a seminar on Korea's consistent erosion of trust in institutions, the increase in materialism, growing egalitarianism towards women, and ever more individualism. Sure, Seoul, more than other regions of Korea, is in flux.

That said, don't assume that that blond Seoulite you see has also bleached his or her traditional core values away. Korean culture can appear maddeningly inscrutable, at times contradictory.

MEET THE NEW BOSS(ES)

The neologism 386 Generation is generally applied to those Koreans who were born in the 1960s, participated in student protests in the 1980s, and are now entering positions of economic and political power. Having grown up essentially removed from the Korean War but during the rule of South Korea's dictatorial, development-minded governments, many still consider themselves to shoulder the responsibility of righting wrongs in the country's past and present and many are rising to positions of power in government and industry. Some see nothing wrong with those who refuse to forsake idealism for the status quo (read, money); others berate them for having been know-nothing hooligans – and borderline traitors – in the 1980s, and essentially hypocritical (preaching with one side of the mouth while being consumed by the monster 'machine' they once fought).

The 'P' generation, also coined by political scientists only very recently, is the up-and-coming wave of power; the 'P' stands for: (potential) power, passion, and – most important – participation, the latter of the Internet kind. Nowhere on the cyber planet is grass-roots activism as alive as with Korean youth. Organising and lobbying has never been so quick and effective in Korea – as exemplified by the social explosions following a South Korean speed skater's disqualification in the 2002 Olympics, the death of two Korean schoolgirls hit by a US military vehicle – even the presidential election. After president Roh Moo-hyun's election in 2002, the UK's *Guardian* newspaper dubbed him the world's first 'online president' and not necessarily for his cyber-skills!

Social Hierarchy

Korean relationships are complicated by a social hierarchy. Neo-Confucian ideals dictate that fathers, husbands, teachers, bosses and governments should be authoritarian rather than democratic, and this is changing, but only – grouse many youth – glacially. At the heart of this doctrine are the so-called Five Relationships, which prescribe behaviour between ruler and subject, father and son, husband and wife, old and young, and between friends.

All relationships require a placement in some sort of hierarchy, which ultimately dictates etiquette. The middle-aged male office worker jumping the queue at a store does not even register your presence because you have not been introduced and he has nowhere to place you on the scale of relationships. An introduction and an exchange of business cards would immediately place you into a category that would demand certain behaviour from him.

This notion of social status is one aspect of Korean culture that many foreigners find thorny. For short-term tourists, this is seldom a problem; since courtesy is highly valued and most Koreans are anxious to make a good impression, visitors are accorded considerable kindness and respect (and help). You should naturally return the favour – be polite and smile even when bargaining over prices in the markets. (Although even this depends on which country you are from – people from rich countries have a higher position in the social hierarchy than those from poorer countries.)

Han

Ask Korean friends to explain *han* (or its equally untranslatable cousins, *gibun* and *nunchi*) and expect widened eyes, a polite smile, and not much more than rising intonation indicating befuddlement. Even Korean texts spend pages hemming and hawing over this.

What is it? Carefully put, it's a deeply sublimated, at times achingly frustrating, spiritual-psychological stew of equal parts rancour and helplessness, with some lamentation thrown in. Textbook definition keywords include 'deprivation', 'discrimination', 'grief', 'grudge', 'heartburning' and 'deploring'.

The roots of *han* lie in the suppression of self by millennia of Confucian order, simmered in the overarching need to preserve group harmony (*gibun,* or 'feelings/state of mind/mood/face' and including but not limited to the individual; Koreans do this by an innate sense of comprehending subtle meaning called *nunchi*. Not to be understated as a major cause is Korea's grief-filled history of subjugation by outside cultures.

Han, this ember of the national soul, has long been the source of an ineffable 'Koreanness' in folk songs and literature. Indeed, Koreans can discuss an 'aesthetic of *han*'.

In the 1970s it became central to cultural analysis in virtually every field, particularly for psychologists, who now fret over how *han* is transforming the society. Lingering

GAY IN KOREA

In 2001 the country's National Security Act was modified to declare homosexuality 'dangerous to youth'. This could hardly have surprised Hong Seok-chun, a popular children's programme host, who in 2000 came out as gay, only to see his career end amidst intense public criticism (so bad his parents considered suicide). Amid the furore, his words: 'I expect our society will develop into a more generous society that will embrace these minorities with a warm heart.'

He may have been as prescient as he was hopeful. Seoul hosts semiregular gay film festivals and the Korean Queer Cultural Festival (www.kqfc.org) is an annual event. Two-thirds of Koreans recently polled believe homosexuality is wrong, but nearly the same number said Hong Seok-chun's public shaming was utterly wrong. Two years after his firing, the very network that fired him aired a documentary on his story – the highest-rated show that night.

Chingusai (www.chingusai.net), Korea's first gay rights organisation, is a good place to begin any investigation.

rage over Japanese colonialism in WWII (and newer anti-Americanism), the Korean War's unspeakable devastation to the family structure, and the country's light-speed modernisation have all led to a fracturing of the delicate internal 'balance.' The result – a looming society-wide rift; Seoul, walking the point into the future, sits at the epicentre.

Geomancy

Based on Chinese feng shui, geomancy *(pungsu)* is the art of remaining in proper physical harmony with the universe. If a Korean finds that their business is failing, a geomancer might be consulted. The proposed solution? Perhaps move the door to prevent good fortune disappearing through it, or relocate an ancestor's grave to placate a restless, unhappy spirit.

In this day of modern high-rises and housing estates, most Koreans have had to let much of this slide; however, the positioning of a relative's grave is still taken very seriously.

Fortune-telling

These days most people visit one of the city's street fortune-tellers for a bit of fun, but no doubt some take it seriously. For a *saju* reading of your future, inform the fortune-teller of the hour, day, date and year of your birth (if you know it); another option is *gunghap*, when a couple give their birth details and the fortune-teller pronounces how compatible they are. Expect to pay W10,000 for *saju* and double that for *gunghap*; you'll also need an English-speaking Korean to translate.

RELIGION

South Korea – even the urbane and sophisticated city of Seoul – seriously dents the myth that modernisation necessitates secularisation, that fashion precludes faith. South Korea has seen numbers of religious affiliation increase steadily since the 1960s; actual participation, except for Christianity, hasn't increased as much.

Shamanism

Shamanism lacks a body of written scriptures and is technically not an organised religion. Nevertheless, it remains fundamental to Korean culture.

Central to shamanism is the *mudang* (shaman) who nowadays is almost always female. Their role is to serve as the intermediary between the living and the spirit

A GIFT FOR GIVING *Martin Robinson*

During my first month of teaching English, I was showered with free meals and drinks, trips, and more. 'It's my treat,' all would say – and they meant it.

Gifts kept appearing on my desk. When a fellow teacher had a birthday, bought a new car, or returned from holiday, they often bought everyone a gift. One teacher had twins and bought everyone dog soup for lunch. When a foreign teacher in a nearby high school got sick, the teachers collected W300,000 for him as well as loading his hospital room with presents.

At Chuseok (Thanksgiving), gift-giving reaches fever pitch and the shops are filled with mountains of gift packages. One foreign teacher had to hire a taxi to transport all his gifts: 10kg each of pears and grapes, 1kg of *kimchi*, six pairs of socks, five tubes of toothpaste, a telephone card and a department store voucher!

Monk in shop outside Jogyesa (p53), near Insadong

world. Mediating is carried out through a *gut,* a ceremony that includes ecstatic dancing, singing and drumming.

Shamanism is often regarded as superstition today, yet official records show that 40,000 *mudang* are registered in South Korea (the actual figure could be closer to 100,000).

On Inwangsan (p78), a wooded hillside in northwestern Seoul, is a shamanist village where *gut* ceremonies are held.

Buddhism

Buddhism in Korea belongs to the Mahayana school and, since its arrival in AD 370, it has split into numerous schools. About 90% of Korean Buddhists belong to the Jogye sect, which has its headquarters in Jogyesa (p53) – a large temple located near Insadong. The sect claims to have 8000 monks and 5000 nuns, and is an amalgamation of two Korean schools of Buddhism: the Seon (better know by its Japanese name, Zen) school, which relies on meditation and the contemplation of paradoxes to achieve sudden enlightenment; and the Gyo school, which concentrates on extensive scriptural study.

The small Taego sect distinguishes itself by permitting its monks to marry, a system installed by the Japanese during their occupation of Korea.

Buddhism has coexisted closely with shamanism. Many Buddhist temples have a *samseonggak* (three-spirit hall) on their grounds, which houses shamanist deities. Some Buddhist monks also carry out activities associated with shamanism, for example, fortune-telling.

South Korea's growing concern about the environment and materialism is encouraging a revival of Buddhism. Visits to temples have increased, and more money is flowing into temple reconstruction. Approximately 25% of South Koreans are Buddhists (though not necessarily practicing).

Confucianism

Confucianism, properly speaking, is a system of ethics rather than a religion. Confucius (552–479 BC) emphasised devotion to parents and family, loyalty to friends, justice, peace, education, reform and humanitarianism. He also urged that respect and deference should be given to those in positions of authority – a philosophy exploited by Korea's Joseon ruling elite. Confucius firmly believed that men were superior to women and that a woman's place was in the home.

These ideas led to the system of civil service examinations (*gwageo*), where one gains position through ability and merit, rather than from noble birth and connections. Confucius preached against corruption, war, torture and excessive taxation. He was the first teacher to open his school to all students solely on the basis of their willingness to learn.

As Confucianism trickled into Korea, it evolved into Neo-Confucianism, which combined the sage's original ethical and political ideas with the quasi-religious practice of ancestor worship and the idea of the eldest male as spiritual head of the family.

Confucianism was viewed as being enlightened and radical when it first gained popularity, but during its 500 years as the state religion in Korea, it became authoritarian and conservative. It still lives on as a kind of ethical bedrock (at least subconsciously) in the minds of most Koreans, especially the elderly.

Visit the spirit shrines of the Joseon kings and their queens at the splendid Jongmyo (p50). A grand Confucian ceremony honouring them takes place there every year.

Christianity

Korea's first exposure to Christianity was in the late 18th century. It came via the Jesuits from the Chinese Imperial court when a Korean aristocrat was baptised in Beijing in 1784. The Catholic faith took hold and spread so quickly that it was perceived as a threat by the Korean government and was vigorously suppressed, creating the country's first Christian martyrs.

Christianity got a second chance in the 1880s, with the arrival of American Protestant missionaries who founded schools and hospitals and gained many followers.

Nowhere else in Asia, with the exception of the Philippines, have the efforts of Christian missionaries been so obviously successful. About 25% of Koreans are Christian, but their influence is greater than their numbers because members of elite groups tend to be Christian. Gaze out of any bus or taxi window as you cross the city at night and count the neon crosses!

The Catholic Cathedral (p55) in Myeong-dong is a national symbol of democracy and human rights, and the outspoken Cardinal Kim is the conscience of the nation.

Cheondogyo

Cheondogyo is a home-grown Korean religion containing Buddhist, Confucian and Christian elements that was started in 1860 by Choe Suun. Born in 1824, and the son of an aristocratic family, Choe Suun experienced a religious revelation and put his egalitarian ideas into practice by freeing a couple of his family's female slaves. The church was originally part of the Donghak (Eastern Learning) reform movement and embraced the idea of the equality of all human beings, a new concept in the conservative Neo-Confucian order of the time.

The church is still going and followers believe that god is within, and support humanist principles of peace and equality. The church headquarters, Cheondogyo Temple (p53), was built in 1921 near Insadong.

Religious Services

English-language Christian services are listed in the Saturday edition of the *Korea Times*. See p164 for details of Buddhist temple stays. The Korean Muslim Mosque (Map p209) in Itaewon has prayers in English and Arabic every Friday at 1pm.

LIFESTYLE

The pace here is still much more ant farm than spa – just spend a month in Seoul, then head for the countryside and compare! – though urbanites don't feel guilty about taking the kids to the park on a Saturday or hanging with chums. As nuclear rather than extended families are the norm, less time is also required for taking care of elders, but, like everywhere else on the planet, this free time gradually dwindles after marriage and even more later, in direct proportion to the number of kids one has.

The best thing for a Seoulite's lifestyle was the move in 2005 to an official five-day work week for many businesses and public offices. Official altruism played a part but really it is hoped that Koreans will dispose of more of their average salary of W2.3 million, thus jump-starting the economy.

Education

'A person without education is like a beast wearing clothes' is a proverb that nails Korea's obsession with education. Two or three degrees are the norm, preferably including one from overseas. However everyone incessantly complains about this manic pursuit and a few families are now encouraging a get-rich-quick attitude in their kids, unheard of earlier.

Seoul now has more than 40 universities – including the best, or at least most famous in Korea. To get into one of the top universities, high-school students go through examination hell, studying 14 hours a day, often in private cram schools at night. Almost from the cradle, mothers are preparing their offspring for those all-important exams that will determine their child's fate and status in life. An only-in-Korea phenomenon is a *girugi appa* (wild-goose father), a man who stays in Korea to work while the mother takes the children overseas to live (meaning, study).

There is an inexhaustible desire for studying English – see p174 for information on teaching English in Seoul.

MR & MRS SEOUL

Sweethearts since high school, he (30) and she (28) married three years ago, a bit younger than the median age for marriage (for women, in 2004 it finally reached 30). He, an IT office worker at a *jaebeol* (huge family-run corporation) subdivision and she, a schoolteacher, together earn around 4m won monthly (they both work – out of necessity, like most other couples). It's tight, but OK.

Two years later they had a son; they also hope to have a daughter – as do most couples (though over half of Korean women of childbearing age surveyed are 'unopposed to remaining childless').

Should they ever divorce, in 2005 the government began phasing out the family headship system, a legal framework heavily influenced by Neo-Confucianism in which the family name and legal authority went with first-born males, utterly disenfranchising women. (Sons other than the eldest were also a legal afterthought.)

No touchy-feely Mr Mom, Mr Seoul nevertheless defies the perpetuated stereotype of the 'Korean husband' (silent, domineering), at which young Koreans bristle; 'husband' and 'housework' aren't just words on the same page of a dictionary (though in social gatherings for school or work, young women still do all the work!).

Maternity leave of three months is legally guaranteed (a year is not uncommon). She is lucky – her school gives up to three years (not all paid). Luckily, her mother can watch the baby – many aren't so blessed. Free time? Ha!

The government faces serious family problems of its own: birth rates are the world's lowest (1.15%) while the population is ageing rapidly (life expectancy is 73.3 years for men, 80.4 years for women) and by 2010 it is estimated there will be a 128/100 ratio of men/women of 'peak marriageable age' (reread that part above about the family headship system for a partial explanation).

FASHION

Seoul has a thriving fashion industry which aims quite seriously to rival Tokyo in Asia (at present Andre Kim is probably the best-known designer abroad). The Seoul Fashion Design Center (www.fashionnet.seoul.kr) in Jung-gu is sponsored by the Seoul government. Seoul also hosts an annual Seoul Fashion Week in mid-April.

Hanbok

Hanbok, the striking traditional clothing that followed the Confucian principle of unadorned modesty, was as much a part of the local culture as *hangeul* and *kimchi*. Traditionally women wore a loose-fitting short blouse with long sleeves and a voluminous long skirt, while men wore a jacket and baggy trousers.

Hardly anyone wears *hanbok* now except at weddings or festivals. Waistcoats are still popular but only among hikers. Elderly men sometimes wear trilby hats, which are a kind of modern *hanbok,* while *ajumma* (older women) sport brightly-coloured baggy trousers with clashing multicoloured patterned blouses.

Fashion designers are reinventing *hanbok;* ramie (cloth made from pounded bark) is particularly fashionable. Everyday *hanbok* is reasonably priced, but the formal styles, made of silk and intricately embroidered, are objects of wonder and cost a fortune. *Hanbok: The Art of Korean Clothing* by Sunny Yang (1997) is an excellent primer.

SPORT

Soccer may soon (gasp) eclipse baseball as a national pastime following the heroic efforts of the South Korean team in the 2002 FIFA World Cup finals, which were cohosted by South Korea and Japan. The South Korean team reached the semifinals, defeating Poland, Portugal, Spain and Italy along the way. Keeping ahead of their Asian neighbours and rivals, Japan and China, is South Korea's aim in the future – and not just on the soccer field.

Yet, for now, baseball rules. Major League Baseball in North America has a handful of Korean players; watch the scurry in Seoul stop dead when their games are shown on public big screens.

Visit someone's home for a holiday, and grandfather may be watching *ssireum,* Korean-style wrestling, akin to Mongolian wrestling (never call it sumo). Wrestlers start off kneeling, then grab their opponent's piece of cloth, called *satba,* which is tied around the waist and thighs, and try to throw each other to the ground.

Taekwondo is an increasingly popular Korean martial art with millions of followers world-wide. In Korea all young men are taught taekwondo as part of their compulsory

DOS & DON'TS

Shoes Off

In temples, private homes, Korean-style restaurants, guesthouses and *yeogwan* (small family-run hotels) you should take off your shoes and leave them by the front door. Wearing socks is more polite than bare feet, particularly in temples.

Losing Face

It is important to bear in mind the Korean concept of *gibun* (face/harmony – individual *and* group). Great efforts are made to smooth over potential problems; if you say something silly, there will be, at the most, an embarrassed laugh before someone steers the topic on to safer ground. Arguments or any situation that leads to one party having to back down will involve a loss of face, and this is a huge no-no.

Keep it Neat

Here you are judged by your appearance, more so than in the West. Travellers who dress like slobs will be treated with less respect than someone dressed casually but neatly. This is particularly apparent in Seoul, and out-of-towners always dress up to come to the capital city.

Greeting

A short nod or bow is considered polite and respectful when greeting somebody or when departing, but don't overdo it.

Gift Giving

It's customary to bring along a small gift when visiting somebody at their home. It can be almost anything – flowers, chocolates, fruit, a book, a bottle of liquor, tea or something from your home country. It's also appropriate to have your offering gift-wrapped.

Your host may at first refuse it (so as not to look greedy). You should insist that they take it, and they should accept it 'reluctantly'. For the same reason, the recipient of a gift is not supposed to open the package immediately. Receive gifts using both hands.

Body Language & Respect

Don't use your forefinger to beckon someone. Put out your hand, palm *down* (palm up is for animals) and flutter all your fingers.

Don't force eye contact, which can make a Korean extremely uncomfortable; they will also likely angle themselves ever so slightly rather than face you directly (and don't cross your legs).

Embarrassed Smiles

A driver almost runs over you then stops and gives you a big grin. The driver is not laughing at you – it's a sign of embarrassment, a form of apology and a gesture of sympathy.

two years' military training. The headquarters and main hall for taekwondo competitions is Kukkiwon (p114).

See p112 for more details on other sports venues and schedules.

MEDIA

Korea leads the world in online access and citizen cyber-participation; Koreans also have some residual mistrust of news corporations, recalling that the large media conglomerates started under military dictatorships. This perhaps explains the monkey-wrench gang that is OhmyNews (www.ohmynews.com), a guerrilla news operation whose reader-journalists have been regularly scooping major news operations since its 2000 launch and is now considered a real-deal, albeit pesky, media player. President Roh Moo-hyun gave his first exclusive interview to these renegades.

For a run-down of all media in Seoul, see p169 for newspapers and magazines, p170 for radio stations and p171 for TV channels.

ECONOMY & COSTS

Seoul is home to the universities, scientists and companies at the forefront of Korea's expanding and enormous economy. The list of successful export industries led by Seoul-based *jaebeol* (huge family-run corporations) is a long one indeed. South of the Han River is Teheran St, which is Seoul's Silicon Valley, a fascinating place to get a gander at the remarkable cutting-edge position of Seoul in the world IT market.

Sounds great, yet Seoul has found itself mired in economic funks following the fiscal crisis of 1997, continuing *jaebeol* corruption and bankruptcy scandals, and government inertia. Economists fret over Seoul's dying (no hyperbole) middle class, which has shrunk nearly 10% to 15% since 1997. Pundits and politicians thus have even been known to quote that Clintonian nugget: 'It's the economy, stupid.'

Interminable 'reform plans' have become the butt of jokes; cynics insist any changes are charades. The government has tried to force *jaebeol* to have no more than 5% ownership from any one family and has indeed at least finally started a modicum of oversight (average debt-to-equity ratio of *jaebeol* is down from stratospheric levels of nearly 400% to 172%). Then again, now that Samsung's stock value has surpassed that of Sony – hugely symbolic, given anti-Japanese sentiment – even some vociferous protestors have fallen back in love with the *jaebeol*. Also, given that the top four *jaebeol* still account for nearly 60% of the nation's exports (Samsung itself over 20%) and 50% of foreign investment, how on earth can things change quickly?

The institutional disgust Koreans feel is also in part fuelling an enormous rise in Korean entrepreneurship; venture companies are proliferating like cherry blossoms in the spring!

GOVERNMENT & POLITICS

An unprecedented shift in local power came in 2002, when the national government – the erstwhile real power in Seoul – granted the city autonomy; the ruling party plans to divide Seoul further into five cities by 2012. Optimists say that the new direct election of the mayors and city councils will usher in a utopic level of civic participation.

The current mayor, Lee Myung-bak, is fascinating. Formerly the hard-nosed CEO of the Hyundai construction *jaebeol*, he is known as 'Bulldozer' – derisively for those who loathe him, glowingly for his supporters – for his physiognomy and his penchant for simply ramming through his policies (revamped bus systems and neighbourhood gentrification are two hot button issues), group opinions be damned.

The city government's website, www .english.seoul.go.kr, is well-designed and helpful.

ENVIRONMENT

During South Korea's economic rise, nature was an afterthought foundation for concrete and steel. Things began to improve in the 1980s – the city's standards exceed the

HOW MUCH?

Seoul is a big city in a developed country, yet you can actually get by on a low budget. Public transport, basic meals, admission prices and accommodation are all relatively cheap, although luxury hotels and famous restaurants are expensive. Allow around W90,000 for a two-star hotel room and three decent meals per day; for a four-star stay, this jumps to W300,000 (to infinity). The exchange rate is a key factor and the stronger the won is, the more expensive Seoul is for foreign visitors.

In Seoul, 'free' is often found only after 'duty', but it's not impossible to spend an admission-free day. Searching the keyword 'free' on the city's tourism website (www .visitseoul.net) or chatting with the staff at information centres will yield lots of ideas. See also p46.

2km taxi ride W1900

Apple W1000

Cinema ticket W7000

Litre bottle of water W1000

Litre of petrol W1500

Local beer in a bar W3000-W5000

One bowl of jjajangmyeon (noodles) W3500

Palace entry ticket Free-W3000

Souvenir T-shirt W6000-W12,000

Top-class dinner W50,000

national government's – but after 1997's economic crisis, standards were 'relaxed' to help rejuvenate development and the environment again swooned.

However, at least superficially, most foreigners find Seoul quite clean – litter (outside of stray cigarette butts) is fairly uncommon. Seoul's government has been quite consistent in efforts to reduce waste tonnage and increase recycling of organic and inorganic matter. The public has responded admirably – recycling has skyrocketed since 2000.

CLIMATE

Korea has four seasons and a notable feature is the summer and winter monsoons (seasonal winds). The city's most magnificent weather – crisp but comfy temperatures, little rain and an artist's palette of colours – is enjoyed from September to November.

During the winter, temperatures plummet to frigidity (and below) due to the icy Siberian winds blowing from the north, but at least it's dry; the worst of the cold is usually over by mid-March.

Spring temperatures are mild, but more prone to rain than autumn; then again, they do coax out those preternaturally lovely blossoms! Summers equal swelter – high temperatures and humidity – and occasional nearly biblical rains.

Destructive typhoons are also a possibility from late June through to September.

See p163 for climate charts, or log on to www.kma.go.kr for daily weather forecasts in English.

THE LAND

Seoul is in the northwestern corner of South Korea, 37° 30´ north of the equator. The city covers an area of 605 sq km and is 32km from Incheon, its airport and seaport on the West Sea. Seoul is surrounded by eight modest mountain peaks; Namsan, the proud sentinel, proudly overlooks the Han River, which cleanly bisects the city.

GREEN SEOUL

With the highest population density in the world (true, factoring in inhabited areas rather than area as a whole), there's only so much that can be green. Korea uses more energy per capita than any Asian nation and this doesn't seem to be ebbing. Korea's water consumption rate is the fastest growing in the world, worrying the UN of a looming water crisis. Air quality is generally decent, and natural gas buses are helping a great deal (the lion's share of air pollutants is from buses and trucks), but international pollution blowing in from China is gradually worsening.

URBAN PLANNING & DEVELOPMENT

Seoul has recently begun a massive, 25-neighbourhood 'urban renewal' project. In October 2005 the first link – the Cheonggye Stream Project – was opened. Connected to this is the equally new 1.15 million sq m Ttukseom Seoul Forest. Proponents insist this will improve water tributaries, provide much-needed greenspace chains for recreation and parks (a common complaint is that sure, Seoul has plenty of parks, they just aren't where anyone lives), and even moderate the city's radiant heat from buildings and concrete. Detractors roll their eyes at this and point out that for the sake of a few fountains, one of the funkiest

ENVIRONMENT

TECHNO-KONGLISH & MORE

Cypein (literally, 'cyworld-holic') A person who spends way too much time and money on the super-cool website Cyworld.

Dica Digital camera.

Henpon Shortening of 'hendepon', or mobile phone (get it, handphone?).

-jjang/yeolla- Like young folk everywhere, young Koreans adore/overuse the emphatic; the suffix *-jjang* (best) and prefix *yeolla-* (totally, er, *totally*) are ubiquitous (eg last year's craze in Korea was to attain *momjjang*, or 'knockout body').

Mini-hompi What everyone who is anyone has: a personal homepage.

Cheonggye stream (p19), Jonggak, at Christmas

extant 'real Seoul' neighbourhoods fell to the wrecking ball (and that the Cheonggye stream renovation actually worsened traffic).

Once again, Mayor Lee Myung-bak has 'bulldozed' in more than a few ambitious traffic plans: the city has put over 8000 natural gas–fuelled buses into service – a 20-fold increase since 2000 – and reorganised traffic flow (albeit not always successfully).

NATIONAL & PROVINCIAL PARKS

Straddling the northern border of Seoul is Bukhansan National Park (p81), a stunning area of steep granite peaks and cliffs, which also includes a 16th-century fortress and a number of Buddhist temples. Only 25km southeast of Seoul is Namhansanseong (p83), a provincial park that includes impressive 17th-century fortress walls that stretch for 9km, as well as fortress gates, Buddhist temples and a village of traditional restaurants.

Arts & Architecture

Arts & Architecture

CINEMA

Since the late 1990s, the fast-improving Korean movie industry has been producing an amazing 50 films a year and is providing a real challenge to the dominance of the commercial Hollywood blockbusters. Around 45% of the market is taken by locally produced films – a much higher percentage than most countries achieve. Protected by a quota system that forces each cinema to show Korean films on at least 146 days of the year (reduced to 73 days in July 2006), commercial success has been achieved by a string of action, drama and comedy films. Korean films have snapped up numerous festival awards, and the industry's profile was raised when the country's greatest film director, Lee Chang-dong, was made Minister of Culture. An excellent website (www.koreanfilm.org) covers all aspects of the industry and has reams of film reviews.

Korean films are not shown with English subtitles in cinemas, so the best way to see them is on DVD. Numerous DVD *bang* (rooms where you can watch DVDs) offer small private rooms with comfortable armchairs and a large screen, where you can watch Korean DVDs with English subtitles.

KOREAN WAVE

Hallyu (the Korean Wave) is the name given to the increasing popularity of Korean popular culture in other parts of Asia, from Mongolia to Malaysia. Korean TV dramas (broadcast with subtitles) such as *Winter Sonata* and *Daejanggeum* have gained millions of fans, while Korean movies, pop singers and fashion designers are riding on the Korean Wave along with Korean food, beauty products and electronics gadgets. This fad for all things Korean has led to more Asian tourists visiting Seoul to experience Korean culture at first-hand.

Dancer at Korea House (p101), near Myeong-dong

TOP TEN FILMS

- *The President's Last Bang* (2005) – Set in Seoul, this vivid and controversial satire directed by Im Sang-soo portrays the dramatic final day of military dictator Park Chung-hee, whose 18-year rule ended in 1979 when he was assassinated. In the confused aftermath, the conspirators find themselves being hunted down.
- *Marathon* (2005) – Based on a true story, a devoted Seoul mother battles prejudice and indifference as she struggles to bring up her autistic son. Funny, moving and well-acted, the movie is directed by Jeong Yun-chul and is full of unpredictable twists and turns.
- *Oasis* (2002) – Directed by Lee Chang-dong, brilliant acting and a tight script make this in-your-face movie about severe disability memorable and thought-provoking.
- *Peppermint Candy* (2000) – Also directed by Lee Chang-dong, this bleak, dramatic and sometimes brutal film turns time around to reveal how an innocent young man was corrupted by the military regimes that ruled the South after the Korean War.
- *JSA* (2001) – A taut and realistic thriller directed by Park Chan-wook depicting a dangerous friendship that develops across the Demilitarized Zone (DMZ) between soldiers from South and North Korea.
- *My Sassy Girl* (2001) – This role-reversal comedy directed by Kwak Jae-young involves a girlish boy and his bossy girlfriend.
- *Untold Scandal* (2004) – A historical drama directed by EJ Yong about a philandering Confucian nobleman and a young and virtuous Catholic woman, which has the idealised sets, intrigues and love-story theme typical of the genre that's currently wowing all of Asia.
- *Crazy Marriage* (2002) – Directed by poet Yu Ha, this light-hearted movie with a message reveals the ups and downs, in and out of bed, of a modern couple who enjoy breaking every Confucian rule.
- *The Way Home* (2002) – This unsentimental low-budget study of a rural grandma and her selfish and rude city-bred young grandson, written and directed by Lee Jeong-hyang, was a deserved but surprise hit with local audiences.
- *A Little Monk* (2003) – This poetic and sometimes humorous fable, directed by Ju Gyeong-jung, is about a nine-year-old boy growing up in a remote temple who longs for a mother. Every scene in the beautifully photographed film offers insights into the Buddhist philosophy of detachment.

DANCE & THEATRE

Modern dance is active in Seoul, with at least two annual modern dance festivals (p102). For the last 10 years Kim Young-hee has been a leading dancer, melding old and new styles. *Contemporary Dance Scenes of Korea* (2001) is a comprehensive, chronological study of Seoul's modern dance scene. For more information log on to www.korea.net and follow the link from the Culture section.

Korean folk dances include dynamic *seungmu* (drum dances), satirical and energetic *talchum* (mask dances) and solo improvisational *salpuri* (shamanist dances). Most popular are *samullori* dance troupes, who perform in brightly coloured traditional clothing, twirling a long tassel from a cap on their heads. Participants dance, twirl their heads and beat a drum or gong at the same time. See p100 for details on traditional dance venues. Every year, elegant court dances accompanied by an orchestra are performed in front of Jongmyo (p50) on the first Sunday in May.

Seoul also has a thriving avant-garde theatre scene based mainly around Daehangno (p100), where more than 50 small theatres put on everything from rock musicals and satirical plays to opera and translations of Western classics, all firmly aimed at a youth audience. The shows are all in Korean but drama fans should still enjoy the experience.

A NEW TRADITION

Samullori is a 'traditional' Korean farmer's dance that is popular with tourists who enjoy its party spirit, yet it has a very short history. *Samullori* was the name adopted by four musicians who formed a band in Seoul in 1978. They played four traditional Korean percussion instruments, the *kkwaenggwari* (small gong), *jing* (large gong), *janggu* (hour-glass drum) and *buk* (large barrel drum) and attempted to re-create traditional folk music and dances that had died out.

LITERATURE

Seoul has always been a city of poets – a tradition that goes back into the mists of time. Part of the Joseon government-service exam (*gwageo*) involved writing a poem. Perhaps if this tradition was revived, it would produce more imaginative civil servants.

During the term of the Joseon dynasty, literature meant *sijo*. short nature poems that were hand-written (using a brush and ink) in Chinese characters even after the invention of *hangeul* (the Korean phonetic alphabet) in the 15th century. Joseon kings were all poets. Folk tales reflect Joseon society from the point of view of the peasants and slaves. The goblins are cute – tall and skinny, they come out at night and have magic mallets that turn everything into gold. They generally reward good people and punish the bad, but being goblins, they can't always be trusted.

After 1945 there was a sharp turn away from Chinese (and Japanese) influence of any kind. Western ideas and ideals took

TOP FIVE NOVELS/NOVELLAS

- *A Dwarf Launches a Little Ball* by Cho Se-hui (1976) – A poetic novella about the victims of Seoul's urban redevelopment.
- *Appointment with My Brother* by Yi Mun-yol (2002) – The theme of two brothers divided by the DMZ and the complexity of North–South relations are explored in this brilliant novella.
- *Playing with Fire* by Lee Chong-rae (1997) – A powerful and dramatic revenge saga that begins during the Korean War but continues for generations. It grabs you on page one and never lets go.
- *My Innocent Uncle* by Chae Man-shik (1936) – A shocking colloquial short story about attitudes to Japanese colonial rule in Seoul.
- *Three Days in that Autumn* by Pan Wan-so (1988) – This original and forthright tale reveals the quirky life and views of a woman who becomes a backstreet abortionist in 1950s Seoul.

hold, and existentialism became the guiding cultural philosophy. Novellas came into vogue and an excellent series of these has been published in English (W5000 each). Korean writers are as talented as the film makers, but have not yet received the international recognition they deserve, partly because of some poor translations.

Log onto www.korea.net and click on 'Directory', 'Arts & Culture', 'Literature & Language' and 'Korea Literature Today' to access translated Korean poetry, novels and short stories. Other links go to traditional Korean folk tales and ancient legends.

MUSIC

Korean traditional music (*gugak*) is played on stringed instruments, most notably the *gayageum* (12-stringed zither) and *haegum* (two-stringed fiddle) as well as on chimes, gongs, cymbals, drums, horns and flutes. Court music (*jeongak*) is slow and stately while folk music such as *samullori* is fast and lively. Buddhist music (*bulgyo eumak*), mainly monks chanting, is another genre and cassettes and CDs of this music can be bought outside Jogyesa (p53).

Similar to Western opera is *changgeuk*, which can involve a large cast of characters. An unusual type of opera is *pansori*. It features a solo storyteller (usually female) singing in a strained voice to the beat of a drum, while emphasising dramatic moments with a flick of her fan. Only a few *pansori* dramas have survived so the repertoire is limited, but *Chunhyang*, the story of a faithful woman, is the most popular.

Western classical music is played in a number of concert halls in Seoul. Live jazz bars are common, and rock, punk, hip-hop, electronic and other genres all have their followers. Crying Nut is a sassy Seoul band that started off in a Hongik club and

TOP FIVE TRACKS

- *Gayageum Masterpieces* by Chimhyang-moo – quiet and relaxing raindrop sounds
- *Beautiful Things in Life* by Jeong Soo-nyun – haunting melodies played on the *haegum* (two-stringed fiddle)
- *The Fragrance of Bamboo* by Lee Saeng-kang – a retrospective album by a flute master
- *a day* by Cho Moon-young – crossover music including an Irish ballad played on a rarely heard 25-string *gayageum*
- *Seumusarui Eumakjeonji* – a sampler of modern Korean rock, pop, punk, ballads and rap

loves whipping up fast and furious punk riffs with the aid of an accordion. For something quieter Kim Hyun-chul is a jazz and ballad singer who often collaborates with Western musicians, while Jo Sung Mo is a long-lasting ballad singer with a unique voice.

Some unusual musical instruments are on view in the Museum of Korean Traditional Music (p65), next door to the Seoul Arts Centre. View www.ncktpa.go.kr for information on Korean percussion, woodwind and string instruments.

SCULPTURE, PAINTING & CALLIGRAPHY

Seoul has an active modern art scene, and local artists tend to follow Western trends while incorporating Korean motifs and themes. The best of them combine traditional techniques with a modern vision. The top Korean artist Paik Nam-june, who died in January 2006, has some excellent and imaginative installations in the National Museum of Contemporary Art (p65). Another icon of Korean modern art is Kim Tschang Yuel, who is obsessed with raindrops.

Stone Buddhist statues and pagodas such as the one in Tapgol Park (p52) are among the oldest artworks in Seoul. Cast bronze Buddhas were also common and some marvellous examples can be seen in the National Museum of Korea (p62). Zen-style, Buddhist art can be seen inside and outside Seoul's temples, Jogyesa (p53) and Bongeunsa (p58), as well as in the small Museum of Korean Buddhist Art (p51). Stone and wooden effigies of shamanist spirit guardians can be seen outside the National Folk Museum (p50) in the grounds of the main palace, Gyeongbokgung.

Chinese influence is paramount in traditional Korean painting. The basic tools (brush and water-based ink) are those of calligraphy, which influenced painting in both technique and theory. The brush line, which varies in thickness and tone, is the most important feature. The function of traditional landscape painting was to be a substitute for nature. The painting is meant to surround the viewer and there is no fixed viewpoint as in traditional Western painting. A talented artist who painted everyday scenes was Kim Hong-do (1745–1816). Court ceremonies, portraits, flowers, birds and the traditional symbols of longevity – the sun, water, rocks, mountains, clouds, pine trees, turtle, cranes, deer and a herb – were popular subjects. *Spirit of the Mountain* by David Mason (1999, W30,000) is an exhaustive study of the relatively unknown folk genre of shamanist art.

Calligraphy can be written in either traditional Chinese characters *(hanja)* or in *hangeul*. The Seoul Calligraphy Art Museum (p65) at the Seoul Arts Centre has examples of traditional and modern calligraphy. To buy some calligraphy head to Insadong (p52).

CERAMICS & POTTERY

Archaeologists have unearthed Korean pottery that dates back some 10,000 years, although it wasn't until the early 12th century that it reached a peak as skilled potters turned out wonderful celadon pottery with a green tinge.

Visit the National Museum of Korea (p62) for one of the best displays. Original celadon fetches huge sums at auction, but modern copies are widely available, particularly in Insadong (p52) and Icheon (p46).

The pottery business took a turn for the worse during the 13th-century Mongol invasion and the Koreans started to produce *buncheong* ware, which was less-refined pottery decorated with simple folk designs. But it was much admired by the Japanese, and during the Imjin War in the 1590s entire families and villages of Korean potters were abducted and resettled in Japan to produce *buncheong* for their new masters. Some are still there.

TOP THREE POETS

- Original poet So Chong-ju's *Unforgettable Things* (translated by D McCann) is a wonderful collection of poems that reflect the author's varied life and unusual philosophy.

- Environmentalist poet Kim Kwang-kyu's *Faint Shadow of Love* (translated by Brother Anthony) contains poetic protests about ecological degradation and sad reflections on people who have lost the dreams and idealism of their youth.

- Christian Buddhist Ku Sang's *Eternity Today* (translated by Brother Anthony) features poems that reflect and reconcile his philosophy of life.

ARCHITECTURE

Although Seoul is dominated by dull concrete-and-glass skyscrapers, there are a couple worth looking at. The gold-tinted 63 Building (p56) on Yeouido, and the downtown Jongno Tower (Map p205) are two of the more stylish ones with excellent views from the top floor.

The best examples of traditional architecture are found in Seoul's renovated palaces and temples. Their unique style is characterised by wooden structures set on stone foundations that are held together by notches rather than nails. A prominent feature are the roofs, which are made from heavy clay tiles with dragons or other symbols embossed on the end-tile. The strikingly bold, predominantly green and orange paintwork under the eaves is called *dancheong*. Ceilings are often intricately carved and coloured. Palaces were warmed during the bitterly cold winters by *ondol* (underfloor heating).

Carved lattice doors are something to look out for in the Buddhist shrines, and the outside walls are painted with murals of the Buddha's life or illustrate Buddhist parables about self-liberation. Inside the shrines are paintings of Buddhist heavens (and occasionally hells). By temple entrance gates are paintings or statues (sometimes both) of the fierce-looking guardians of the four directions who protect Buddhists from harm.

Seoul's great fortress gates, Namdaemun and Dongdaemun, are worth a look, but visit Suwon (p153) to walk around the most impressive fortress. Nineteenth-century Christian churches, built in an elegant West-meets-East fusion style, are among the few buildings to have survived the Korean War and subsequent modernisation – Myeong-dong Cathedral, Chungdong Methodist church and the Anglican church are all on Map pp206–7-00.

Namsangol Hanok Village (p55) and the Buckchon district (p77) in Seoul and the Korean Folk Village (p154) near Suwon have the best collections of *hanok*. The best-selling *Hanoak, Traditional Korean Houses* (1999, W30,000) is a fully illustrated book on the exterior and interior design of Korea's traditional one-storey wood-and-tile houses.

Joseon Royal Court Culture by Shin Myung-ho (2004, W28,000) gives the facts about the unique Confucian royal-court lifestyle. Based on primary sources, the superbly illustrated book gives a human context to the now bare and empty palaces.

OUTDOOR SCULPTURES

Seoul has more outdoor sculptures than any other city on the planet. Olympic Park (p59) has an ever-expanding collection of over 200 sometimes wacky modern sculptures created by artists from around the world, some bigger than a house. Plenty are clever and intriguing while others prompt thoughts of 'why?' or simply a chuckle. The east side of the main street in Daehangno (Map p208) is also lined with quirky modern sculptures. Every high-rise building must, by law, have a sculpture outside, so keep an eye out for them. The most amazing one is Hammering Man (p50), just off Sejong St.

Myeong-dong Catholic Cathedral (p55), Myeong-dong

Food & Drink

Food & Drink

HISTORY

Every spring the Joseon kings headed to Seonnongdan (p62), an altar where they prayed for a good harvest. After the ritual, a special beef and vegetable soup (*seolleongtang*) was served to the assembled peasants. *Seolleongtang* is still popular today.

When Japan abolished the Korean monarchy in 1910, the palace *tteok* (rice cake) makers were sacked, so they opened small shops around the Nakwon Arcade (Map pp202–3), just north of Tapgol Park, and sold their *tteok* to the public. The shops are still run by their descendants.

Budae jjigae or *Johnsontang* is a unique dish that originated in the hungry years after the Korean War when tins of ham, sausages and baked beans were bought on the black market around American army bases (such as Yongsan) and mixed with noodles and vegetable scraps to make a meal. Try it at Nolboo (p96) in Hongik.

The royal court was based in Seoul for over 500 years and royal cuisine dishes include *gujeolpan* and *sinseollo*. Generally the cooking style is less spicy than usual and requires elaborate presentation.

CULTURE

ETIQUETTE

The custom in Seoul is that the host pays for everything and if you are invited out by Korean colleagues or friends, you will find it difficult to pay the bill or even contribute towards it. Going Dutch is as rare as a W20,000 note. Arguing about who should have the honour of paying the restaurant bill is a common scene at the cashier's desk.

HOW KOREANS EAT

A traditional Korean meal (breakfast, lunch and dinner) typically consists of meat, seafood or fish, which is served at the same time as soup, rice and a collection of dipping sauces and *banchan* (side dishes, such as *kimchi*, shellfish, acorn jelly, quail eggs and cold vegetables). Meals are usually eaten communally, so side dishes are placed in the centre of the table and diners eat a bit from one dish, a bite from another, a little rice, a sip of soup and so on.

At some traditional restaurants, diners sit on cushions on the floor (the *ondol* heating system is beneath). Before stepping up, always remove your shoes. Nowadays most restaurants have a table-and-chairs option.

Nearly every restaurant in Seoul serves bottled or filtered water free of charge when you arrive.

STAPLES
BARBECUES

The many barbecue restaurants have a grill set into the tables, on which you cook slices of beef *(bulgogi)*, beef ribs *(galbi)*, pork *(samgyeopsal)*, chicken *(dak)*, seafood or vegetables. Often your server helps out with the cooking. The inexpensive *samgyeopsal* is like bacon and can be fatty. These meals are usually only available in servings of two or more.

Bulgogi, galbi and *samgyeopsal* are served with a bunch of lettuce and sesame leaves. Take a leaf in one hand (or combine two leaves for different flavours), and with your other hand use your chopsticks to load it with meat, side dishes, garlic and sauces. Then roll it up into a little package and eat it in one go.

AN INTRODUCTION TO KOREAN FOOD

Sampling all the quirky delights of Korean food and drink is one of the joys of visiting Seoul. *The Wonderful World of Korean Food*, published by the Korea Tourism Organisation (KTO), is a free booklet that provides an illustrated introduction to the food and snacks you are likely to come across.

BIBIMBAP

Bibimbap is a mixture of rice, vegetables and meat with an egg on top, which tastes much better than it sounds. Thoroughly mix it all together with your spoon before digging in. It comes with a generous dollop of *gochujang* (red chilli paste) so remove some if you don't want it too hot. *Bibimbap* is often served with bean sprout soup but don't mix that in too! *Sanchae bibimbap* is made with mountain-grown greens while *dolsot bibimbap* is served in a stone hotpot.

BREAKFAST

Traditional Korean breakfasts usually consist of soup, rice and *kimchi*. Western breakfasts are available in hotels, fast-food outlets, cafés and the ubiquitous bakeries, some of which have a few tables and chairs. Most convenience stores sell the basics – coffee, tea, sandwiches, fruit and pastries.

CHICKEN

Samgyetang is a small whole chicken stuffed with glutinous rice, red dates, garlic and ginseng and boiled in broth. *Dakgalbi* is pieces of spicy chicken, cabbage, other vegetables and finger-sized pressed rice cakes, which are all grilled at your table. *Jjimdak* is a spiced-up mixture of chicken pieces, transparent noodles, potatoes and other vegetables. Many informal *hofs* (pubs) serve inexpensive barbecued or fried chicken to accompany the beer.

DESSERTS

Desserts are not common in Seoul, but you may be served a piece of fruit, coffee or traditional tea at the end of the meal. Ice-cream parlours such as Baskin Robbins are everywhere, while the 'wellbeing' wave means that yogurt, fruit and red-bean concoctions are widely available at Red Mango and similar outlets.

Plate of bibimbap *(above)*

GIMBAP

This inexpensive item, Korean sushi, is popular for lunch, and is cold rice rolled in dried seaweed with strips of carrot, radish, egg and ham in the centre. 'Nude' *gimbap* has no dried seaweed wrap. A recent food fad are Californian-roll restaurants, which sell *gimbap* in fancy dress at three times the usual price. *Samgak gimbap* (three-sided *gimbap*) contains fillings such as marinated beef, tuna or *kimchi*, but is only sold at convenience stores.

HANJEONGSIK

Head to Insadong for a *Hanjeongsik* banquet for two or more people that includes fish, meat, soup, *dubu jjigae* (spicy tofu stew), rice, noodles, steamed egg, shellfish and lots of cold vegetable side dishes.

HOETJIP

Seafood *(haemul)* and fish *(saengseon)* are generally served broiled, grilled or in a soup, but raw fish has many fans. Visit Noryangjin fish market, or the West Sea islands to indulge in raw fish, blue crab and shellfish meals. *Haemultang* is a seafood soup that contains so much chilli that even Seoulites have to mop their brows.

JJIGAE

These stews are thicker than soups and served in a stone hotpot with plenty of spices. Popular versions are made with tofu *(dubu jjigae)*, soybean paste *(doenjang jjiggae)* and *kimchi*. *Beoseotjeongol* is a less spicy but highly recommended mushroom hotpot.

KIMCHI

Traditionally, *kimchi* was made to preserve vegetables and ensure proper nutrition during the harsh winters, but it's now eaten year-round and adds zest and a long list of health benefits to any meal. A side dish of the spicy national food is served at nearly every Korean meal whether it's breakfast, lunch or dinner. Although generally made with pickled and fermented cabbage seasoned with garlic and red chilli, it can be made from cucumbers, white radish or other vegetables. *Mul kimchi* is a cold gazpacho-type soup and not so spicy.

MANDU

An inexpensive and non-spicy favourite with visitors, these small dumplings (*wangmandu* are large ones) are filled with minced meat, seafood, vegetables and herbs. They are often freshly made to a special recipe by restaurant staff during quiet times. Fried, boiled or steamed they make a tasty snack or addition to a meal. *Manduguk* is *mandu* in soup with seaweed and makes a perfect light lunch.

VISITORS' FAVOURITE FOOD

- *Galbi* (beef ribs)
- *Bulgogi* (slices of barbecued beef wrapped in lettuce)
- *Bibimbap* (rice, egg, meat and vegetables with chilli sauce)
- *Dolsot bibimbap* (*bibimbap* in a stone hotpot)
- *Mandu* (filled dumplings)

NOODLES

Naengmyeon is chewy buckwheat noodles in an icy, sweetish broth, garnished with shredded vegetables and half a hard-boiled egg on top – add red chilli paste or *gyeoja* (mustard) to taste. It's popular in summer and can be eaten after a meat dish as a kind of dessert.

Japchae is a foreigner-friendly dry dish of transparent noodles stir-fried in sesame oil with strips of egg, meat and vegetables. *Kalguksu* is wheat noodles in a bland clam and vegetable broth.

Ramyeon is instant noodles often served in a hot chilli soup. Seoulites believe in fighting fire with fire and claim it's a good cure for hangovers.

SNACKS

Hotteok is a kind of pitta bread with a cinnamon and honey filling that comes in various shapes. *Delimanjoo* are freshly baked, custard-filled, machine-made minicakes that are sold in subway stations. Waffles, *churros* and red-bean paste snacks are also common snacks in Seoul.

In Insadong try *kkultarae*, fine threads of honey and cornflour wrapped around a nut sauce, and *daepae saenggang yeot*, a huge slab of toffee, which is shaved off in strips and served on a stick.

Savoury *tteokbokki* are finger-sized pressed rice cakes and other items in a sweet and spicy orange sauce. Other street-stall food includes marinated chicken kebabs, plain roasted potatoes, roasted honey-coated sweet potatoes and 20 types of hot dogs, including fishy ones. *Tteok* (pronounced 'dock'), rice cakes, are a bland, unsweetened and healthy alternative to sickly Western cakes.

Convenience stores offer cheap snacks such as a bowl of instant *ramyeon* noodles – just add hot water from the water-boiler and eat it at the stand-up counter. Other options include *gimbap*, *samgak gimbap*, egg salad or a sandwich. For dessert, buy fruit, pastry, ice cream or coffee. You can even buy alcohol – beer, wine and *soju* (local vodka).

SOUPS

Soups *(tang* or *guk)* are a Seoul speciality and vary from spicy seafood and tofu soups to bland broths such as *galbitang* and *seolleongtang*. *Gamjatang* is a spicy peasant soup with meaty bones and a potato. And a hint if a soup is too spicy – just tip in some rice.

FOR DAREDEVILS

- *Beondegi* (silkworm larvae)
- *Bosintang* (dog-meat soup)
- *Doganitang* (cow kneecaps soup)
- *Sannakji* (live baby octopus)
- *Yukhoe* (seasoned raw minced meat)

Street stall (p91), Insadong

VEGETARIAN OPTIONS

Seoulites love meat, fish and seafood and very few are vegetarian, although rice and vegetables make up a considerable part of their diet. Seoul's best vegetarian restaurants include Sanchon (p90), Dimibang (p89) and Sosim (p90) in Insadong and Pulhyanggi (p98) near Apgujeong. Department store food courts and Indian restaurants always offer some vegetarian meals.

It can be a struggle for vegetarians in ordinary restaurants, but you can order *bibimbap* or *dolsotbibimbap* without the meat (or egg), *beoseotjeongol, doenjang jjigae, dubu jjigae, jajangmyeon,* vegetable *pajeon* or *dotorimuk.* But check before you order that these meals don't have any meat, seafood or fish as fragments are sometimes used to add flavour. Some *gimbap* is vegetarian or ask for it without ham (or egg). If all else fails you can eat a meal of rice and vegetable side dishes.

DRINKS

Usually every diner is presented with good old H$_2$O *(mul),* bottled or filtered, when they first arrive. Beer, *soju* (the local firewater) and variously flavoured rice wines are often drunk with meals.

Medicinal tea may be served after the meal. *Nokcha* (green tea) is grown in the southern provinces. Other teas not made from the tea plant include *boricha* (barley tea), *insamcha* (ginseng tea), *omijacha* (berry tea) and *yujacha* (citron tea). For a country with a tea tradition, Korea has taken to coffee in a big way. Decaf drinkers may be out of luck but it never hurts to ask.

Cans of soft drinks include unique Korean choices such as *sikhye*, rice punch with grains of rice inside, and a grape juice that contains whole grapes. Health tonics, available in shops and pharmacies, are made with fibre blends, ginseng and other medicinal herbs, and are supposed to boost your virility, vitamin level and alertness, or cure (or prevent) a hangover.

For something alcoholic, popular Korean lager-like beer *(maekju)* brands are Cass, Hite and O.B. Imported bottled beers are widely available, and new microbreweries have widened the choice still further.

Soju, with an alcohol content over 20%, is often likened to vodka in that it's clear, nearly flavourless, has a kick and is cheap to produce. It comes in all sorts of flavours including lemon.

Makgeolli and *dongdongju* are fermented from rice and have a cloudy appearance. They taste something like fermented *lassi.* With a lower alcohol content than *soju,* they used to be popular with peasants and slaves, and were served in a kettle and drunk from bowls.

In recent years imported wine has caught on in a big way and can be found in Italian restaurants as well as department and convenience stores.

Seoulites consider it unhealthy to drink on an empty stomach, so most bars serve bar snacks *(anju)* such as nuts, dried squid, rice crackers or barbecued chicken. Some nightclubs serve large platters of *anju,* but they can cost an arm and a leg, and are a kind of cover charge.

Five-flavour tea and rice cakes

EAT YOUR WORDS
USEFUL WORDS & PHRASES

We'd like nonsmoking/smoking, please.

geumyeon seogeuro/heupyeon seogeuro juseyo 금연석으로/흡연석으로 주세요

Do you have an English menu?

yeong-eoro doen menyu isseoyo? 영어로 된 메뉴 있어요?

Do you have seating with tables and chairs?

teibeul isseoyo? 테이블 있어요?

Is this dish spicy?

i eumsik maewoyo? 이 음식 매워요?

Could you recommend something?

mwo chucheonhae jusillaeyo? 뭐 추천해 주실래요?

Excuse me! (please come here)

yeogiyo! 여기요!

Water, please.

mul juseyo 물 주세요

The bill/check, please.

gyesanseo juseyo 계산서 주세요

Bon apetit.

masitge deuseyo 맛있게 드세요

It was delicious.

masisseosseoyo 맛있었어요

I don't eat meat.

jeon gogireul anmeogeoyo 전 고기를 안 먹어요

I can't eat dairy products.

jeon yujepumeul anmeogeoyo 전 유제품을 안 먹어요

Do you have any vegetarian dishes?

gogi andeureogan eumsik isseoyo? 고기 안 들어간 음식 있어요?

Does it contain eggs?

gyerani deureogayo? 계란이 들어가요?

I'm allergic to (peanuts).

jeon (ttangkong)e allereugiga isseoyo 전 (땅콩)에 알레르기가 있어요

MENU DECODER
Chinese Dishes

bokkeumbap	볶음밥	fried rice
jajangmyeon/jjajangmyeon	자장면/짜장면	noodles in black bean sauce
tangsuyuk	탕수육	sweet and sour pork

Fish & Seafood

chobap	초밥	raw fish on rice
gwang-eohoe	광어회	raw halibut
jang-eogui	장어구이	grilled eel

jeonbok-juk	전복죽	rice porridge with abalone
kijogae	키조개	razor clam
kkotge-jjim	꽃게찜	steamed blue crab
modeumhoe	모듬회	mixed raw fish platter
nakji	낙지	octopus
odeng	오뎅	processed seafood cakes in broth
ojing-eo sundae	오징어순대	stuffed squid
saengseon-gui	생선구이	grilled fish
saeugui	새우구이	grilled prawns
samchigui	삼치구이	grilled mackerel
ureok	우럭	raw fish

Gimbap 김밥

chamchi gimbap	참치김밥	tuna *gimbap*
modeum gimbap	모듬김밥	assorted *gimbap*
samgak gimbap	삼각김밥	triangular *gimbap*

Kimchi 김치

baechu kimchi	배추김치	cabbage *kimchi*; the spicy classic version
kkakdugi	깍두기	cubed radish *kimchi*
mulkimchi	물김치	cold *kimchi* soup

Meat Dishes

bulgogi	불고기	barbecued beef slices and lettuce wrap
bulgogi jeongsik	불고기정식	*bulgogi* with side dishes
dakgalbi	닭갈비	pan-fried chicken
dakkochi	닭꼬치	spicy grilled chicken on skewers
dwaeji galbi	돼지갈비	barbecued pork ribs
galbi	갈비	beef ribs
jjimdak	찜닭	spicy chicken pieces with noodles
jokbal	족발	steamed pork hocks
moksal sogeumgui	목살 소금구이	barbecued pork
neobiani	너비아니	large minced patty
samgyeopsal	삼겹살	barbecued bacon-type pork
tongdakgui	통닭구이	roasted chicken

Noodles

bibim naengmyeon	비빔냉면	cold buckwheat noodles with vegetables, meat and sauce
bibimguksu	비빔국수	noodles with vegetables, meat and sauce
japchae	잡채	stir-fried noodles and vegetables
kalguksu	칼국수	thick handmade noodles in broth
kongguksu	콩국수	noodles in cold soy milk soup
makguksu	막국수	buckwheat noodles with vegetables
mul naengmyeon	물냉면	buckwheat noodles in cold broth
ramyeon	라면	instant noodle soup
udong	우동	thick white noodle broth

Rice Dishes

| bap | 밥 | boiled rice |
| bibimbap | 비빔밥 | rice topped with egg, meat, vegetables and sauce |

boribap	보리밥	boiled rice with steamed barley
dolsot bibimbap	돌솥비빔밥	*bibimbap* in stone hotpot
dolsotbap	돌솥밥	hotpot rice
dolssambap	돌쌈밥	hotpot rice and lettuce wraps
sanchae bibimbap	산채비빔밥	*bibimbap* made with mountain vegetables
sinseollo	신선로	meat, fish and vegetables in broth cooked at your table
ssambap	쌈밥	assorted ingredients with rice and wraps

Snacks

bung-eoppang	붕어빵	fish-shaped cake with red-bean filling
hotteok	호떡	pitta bread with sweet filling
tteok	떡	rice cake
tteokbokki	떡볶이	pressed rice cakes and vegetables in a spicy sauce

Soups

galbitang	갈비탕	beef-rib soup
gamjatang	감자탕	meaty bones and potato soup
haemultang	해물탕	spicy assorted seafood soup
kkorigomtang	꼬리곰탕	ox tail soup
manduguk	만두국	soup with meat-filled dumplings
oritang	오리탕	duck soup
samgyetang	삼계탕	ginseng chicken soup
seolleongtang	설렁탕	beef and rice soup

Stews

budae jjigae	부대찌개	ham-and-scraps stew
doenjang jjigae	된장찌개	soybean paste stew
dubu jjigae	두부찌개	tofu stew
nakji jeon-gol	낙지전골	octopus hotpot
sundubu jjigae	순두부찌개	spicy uncurdled tofu stew

Other

bindaetteok	빈대떡	mung bean pancake
donkkaseu	돈까스	pork cutlet with rice and salad (Japanese *tonkatsu*)
dotorimuk	도토리묵	acorn jelly
gujeolpan	구절판	eight snacks and wraps
hanjeongsik	한정식	Korean-style banquet
juk	죽	rice porridge
mandu	만두	filled dumplings
manduguk jeongsik	만두국정식	dumpling soup with side dishes
omeuraiseu	오므라이스	omelette with rice
pajeon	파전	green onion pancake
sangcharim	산차림	banquet of meat, seafood and vegetables
shabu shabu	샤브샤브	DIY beef and vegetable casserole
sigol bapsang	시골밥상	countryside-style meal
siksa	식사	budget-priced banquet
sujebi	수제비	dough flakes in shellfish broth
sundae	순대	noodle and vegetable sausage
sundubu	순두부	uncurdled tofu
twigim	튀김	seafood and vegetables fried in batter
wangmandu	왕만두	large steamed dumplings

Drinks

NONALCOHOLIC

cha	차	tea
daechucha	대추차	jujube (red date) tea
hongcha	홍차	black tea
juseu	주스	juice
keopi	커피	coffee
kolla	콜라	cola
mukapein keopi	무카페인 커피	decaffeinated coffee
mul	물	water
nokcha	녹차	green tea
omijacha	오미자차	berry tea
saenggang cha	생강차	ginger tea
saengsu	생수	mineral spring water
seoltang neo-eoseo/ppaego	설탕 넣어서/빼고	with/without sugar
sikhye	식혜	rice punch
ssanghwacha	쌍화차	herb tonic tea
sujeonggwa	수정과	cinnamon/ginger punch
sungnyung	숭늉	burnt-rice tea
uyu	우유	milk
uyu neo-eoseo/ppaego	우유 넣어서/빼고	with/without milk
yujacha	유자차	citron tea

ALCOHOLIC

dongdongju	동동주	fermented rice wine
insamju	인삼주	ginseng liqueur
maekju	맥주	beer
makgeolli	막걸리	unstrained rice wine
sansachun	산사춘	rice wine
soju	소주	vodka-like drink

History

History Donald N Clark

A CITY OF KINGS & NOBLES

It was King Taejo, founder of the Joseon dynasty, who moved Korea's government to the valley of Hanyang (later to become Seoul) in 1394. The valley was already known to be an auspicious location, with the Han River supplying Yin force and access to the sea, and the Pukhan mountain range supplying Yang energy and protection from the north. In the 6th century, the ancient Shilla kingdom had put an outpost here, near the boundary with the northern state of Goguryeo. Later, the kingdom of Goryeo had maintained a regional capital in the valley. Taejo's advisors needed a site for the new capital that possessed maximum potential for strong and effective rule. They considered several, but none could match Hanyang, the Yang side of the Han River.

For his palace, King Taejo used the principles of Chinese geomancy, or feng shui (*pungsu* in Korean), to find the focal point of the valley's Yang potential. He chose the foot of Bugak Mountain, a spot protected on the east by the dragon force along the ridge of Naktasan and on the west by the tiger force in Inwangsan Mountain. From this spot, Seoul's central axis – the main artery of its power then, as now – ran southward down the broad avenue now known as Sejong Blvd to Namsan (South Mountain), on the valley's opposite side. The city's walls followed these natural barriers, their heights marking the distances between the city's eight gates. In the heart of town, at what is now the Jonggak intersection, a great bronze bell was struck each morning and evening to signal the opening and closing of the city's gates. Beyond, in the mountains and on the coast, fortresses watched over the approaches to the city.

King Taejo named his palace Gyeongbokgung (Palace of Shining Happiness). The reference was to a line in the Chinese *Book of Songs:* 'May the king forever enjoy shining happiness in abundance!' For 200 years it stood as home to a succession of 14 dynastic rulers. Of these, the greatest was King Sejong (1418–50), a scholar-king of unmatched abilities who sponsored many cultural projects, consolidated border defences, and served as a model of Confucian probity. At his direction, court scholars devised the phonetic *hangeul* alphabet, a simple system of writing the Korean language that made it possible for anyone to learn to read. Though it took a while to catch on, King Sejong's alphabet is one reason why Korea enjoys universal literacy today. Present generations have acknowledged their debt to him by attaching his name to Seoul's main street, a university, a luxury hotel, and numerous other places and institutions.

The fortunes of Gyeongbokgung, however, were not always happy. In 1592 the Japanese warlord Hideyoshi invaded Korea on a quest to establish his hegemony on the mainland. The invading armies headed for Seoul and took the city in an orgy of fire and pillage. By the time they arrived, King Seonjo (1567–1608) was far from the palace, heading for the Manchurian border. No-one knows exactly who burned the Palace of Shining Happiness during the fighting. Some say it was the invaders; some say it was slaves who wanted to destroy the government's status records; others say that Seoul's own citizens put it to the torch to show their anger at having been left behind.

The hero of the war with Japan was a Korean admiral named Yi Sun-sin, whose statue stands on Sejong Blvd at the Gwanghwamun intersection, the city's main crossroads. While commanding Korean naval defences on the south coast, Admiral Yi outfitted quick, small boats with metal canopies over the decks to protect them from Japanese fire arrows. He used these to trick, lure, trap, ram, shoot and sink so many Japanese supply boats that he did decisive damage to Hideyoshi's campaign on the peninsula. The canopies inspired

AD 569	1394
Kingdom of Shilla establishes control over settlements in the Seoul area	Hanyang (Seoul) chosen as the capital of the new kingdom of Joseon

the term *geobukseon* (turtle boats) for Admiral Yi's fleet; and though he lost his own life in the Battle of Hansan Island, Yi Sun-sin is remembered still as Korea's greatest warrior.

After the Imjin War, as Koreans call Hideyoshi's failed campaign, Korea's kings reigned in Changdeokgung (Palace of Illustrious Virtue). It was built to the east, and was designed as the residential compound of the crown prince.

Gyeongbokgung was not rebuilt until the 1860s, when the Prince Regent Daeweongun nearly bankrupted the treasury by restoring it for his son, King Gojong (1864–1907). Gojong's reign saw the coming of the Japanese, the opening of contacts with the West, and a maelstrom of political conflict that culminated in Korea's subjection to Japan, first as a protectorate and then as a colony. Along the way Gojong lost his consort, Queen Min, who was assassinated by Japanese agents in 1895. No longer safe at Gyeongbokgung, he fled to the diplomatic district where Westerners could offer him quick sanctuary if he needed it; he eventually abdicated in 1907. His son, Emperor Sunjong, a hapless tool in the hands of Japanese 'advisors', oversaw the cession of Korea to Japan in 1910.

Old Seoul was the capital of a nation of villages spread across provinces whose main towns were centres for local judges and tax officials as well as regional farmers markets. Whatever its history, whether auspicious or tragic, Seoul was always Korea's cultural headquarters, not only the home of the royal family and the official *yangban* (aristocrat) class that supported the state and its monarch, but also the centre of Korea's commerce and communications and the pinnacle of its Confucian education system. Korean proverbs attest to the fact that anyone with any ambition needed to get to Seoul by all means. 'Even if you have to crawl on your knees, get yourself to Seoul!' was one. 'Send your ox to market but send your son to Seoul,' was another, as true today as it was in the days of King Sejong.

SEOUL IN MODERN TIMES

Seoul's modern history is a story of revolutionary change. The 20th century began with Korea's subjection to Imperial Japan. Gyeongbokgung, abandoned in the aftermath of Queen Min's murder, was completely stripped of its dignity. The Japanese removed its graceful gate and razed everything that stood in the front third of the palace grounds to make way for a huge Western-style colonial headquarters. Built in the shape of the character for 'sun', the great stone building with its two grand courtyards completely eclipsed the Korean throne hall, reducing what was left of Gyeongbokgung to a quaint Korean garden in the rear. To the south, across the valley on Namsan, a Shinto shrine for the worship of Japan's national deities was built. Downtown, neighbourhoods were slashed through to make new streets. Royal properties were hard hit. In one case the shrine complex memorialising Joseon's 27 kings was severed from the palace grounds by a new road. Not far away, another palace was turned into a zoo.

Koreans got their city back with the Allied victory in 1945, but there were even greater trials to come. The Allied decision to divide Korea in 1945 soon led to the creation of rival republics – Communist-backed in the north and US-backed in the south. Their two armies skirmished and then went to war, beginning with the North Korean leader Kim Il Sung's invasion of the south on 25 June 1950.

Seoul's sudden fall to the North Koreans caught the populace by surprise and sent the government of President Syngman Rhee fleeing southward, destroying the only Han River highway bridge and abandoning the remaining population to face the Communists. During their 90-day occupation of the city, the Communists arrested and shot many who had supported the Rhee government. More refugees fled the terror, adding to the chaos further south.

In September 1950, UN forces led by US and South Korean troops mounted a counterattack. After an amphibious landing at the port of Incheon, they fought their way into

History

SEOUL IN MODERN TIMES

1592	1910
Seoul falls to invading Japanese army during the Imjin War; Gyeongbokgung burned	Japan annexes Korea

Changing of the guard, Namdaemun (p55)

Seoul from the west and south. During days of bloody battles, whole city districts were bombed and burned in the effort to dislodge Kim Il Sung's Korean People's Army. When at last the UN forces succeeded in reclaiming the city for Syngman Rhee, much of it lay in smouldering ruins.

In January 1951 the Chinese People's Volunteers, who had entered the war and routed the UN forces up north, captured Seoul a second time for the Communist side. This time the invaders found a nearly empty city. Even after the UN regained control in March 1951, only a fraction of Seoul's population returned during the two years of war that raged along the battlefront until the armistice in July 1953. During that time Seoul's population lived with relatives in villages and in miserable camps in Busan and other safer cities.

The end of the monarchy, Japanese rule, and the ordeal of the Korean War completely distorted Korea's passage from a traditional Confucian agrarian society to a nation with modern laws and institutions. Japan exploited Korea's resources while keeping tight control over the people. Opportunities for Koreans remained scarce. There were schools, but only 20% of Koreans ever got to start elementary school. Western missionaries made up part of the shortfall with a network of schools including colleges such as Ewha and Yonhi (now Yonsei), but these were not enough to enable Koreans to rise above second-class citizenship in their own land.

THE LONG ROAD BACK

The Korean War created conditions for dictatorships in both the North and the South. In the city of Seoul, militarisation was obvious in the omnipresence of military personnel, vehicles, buildings and bases, both Korean and Allied, mostly American. The US took over the former Japanese army headquarters in the southern suburb of Yongsan and transformed it into their own headquarters, continuing to occupy the base even as the city spread around it and grew far to the south. Major roads and highways were constructed as MSRs (military

1945	1948
Korea liberated from Japanese rule	Republic of Korea founded; city officially named Seoul

supply routes) rather than as arteries for commerce or public transportation. Economic development took a back seat to national defence, and much of the aid that came from the outside world was for military projects.

As Seoul's population slowly returned to pick up the pieces, they found little to give them hope. Misery, hunger, disease and crime were elements of daily life for hundreds of thousands. On the slopes of Namsan a wretched village called Haebang-chon (Liberation Town) housed tens of thousands of war refugees, widows and beggars. Prostitutes lined up at the gates of the Yongsan military bases in a desperate effort to earn a few dollars. 'Slicky-boys' stole and a black market flourished. Unemployment sapped morale and diseases weakened even working people. Good education was so hard to get that Koreans compared college admission to 'plucking a star out of the sky'.

Desperate times begat every imaginable form of corruption. The Rhee regime, never democratic, rigged its own reelection several times until it was overthrown by a popular rebellion led by unarmed students. On 19 April 1960, the day of reckoning, thousands of high schoolers and collegians filled the streets of downtown Seoul and marched on Rhee's residence. As they advanced up Hyoja-ro (Filial Piety St) beside Gyeongbokgung, the police opened fire. By dusk nearly 200 people – both students and police – had been killed. Rhee's right-hand man committed suicide, as did his family. Rhee himself resigned a few days later and was spirited away to exile in Hawaii by the US Air Force.

During the year of democratic experimentation that followed Rhee's ouster, corruption and crime worsened while inflation raged. Student associations, emboldened by their eviction of Syngman Rhee, proposed solving the reunification problem by marching north to embrace their counterparts in North Korea. South Korean conservatives – property owners, anti-Communist refugees from the north, and the military – began fearing for their own future. On the morning of 16 May 1961, Seoulites awoke to news that army units had seized the main intersections of the city. Seoul fell under direct military rule and the civilian government was removed from power.

The coup leader, General Park Chung-hee, promised military efficiency to restore order. He proclaimed his intention to create a 'new Korean man', meaning one that was honest, hard-working and sacrificially devoted to the community. His junta went to work defining national goals and finding ways to achieve them. In some cases they followed patterns set by Imperial Japan, such as fostering big businesses (known in Japanese as *zaibatsu*) as engines of growth. Conglomerates such as Hyundai and Samsung were encouraged to emulate Japan's prewar *zaibatsu* (like Mitsubishi), using the same word, *jaebeol,* in Korean. The government put strict controls on workers rights and wages. General Park 'retired' from the army and ran for president, backed by a political party, an administration to do the party's bidding, and an internal police system that included a 'Central Intelligence Agency' capable of instilling terror in any aspect of the state system.

Leadership, efficiency and fear combined to deliver impressive results. The economy started to grow, and Korea's main patron, the US, which had been wary of Park at first, soon came around. US support for Park's programme was clearly visible in the twin buildings built largely by American aid funds on Seoul's Sejong Blvd – one for Park's Economic Planning Board, the other for the US Embassy.

By Park's third presidential term in the mid-1970s, Seoul was well on its way to becoming a major world city. Ambitious mayors, including one famously known as 'Bulldozer Kim', launched public works and expanded housing in the form of apartment towers to replace the shantytowns that had blighted the city since the war. The city spread in all directions, vaulting hills and even mountains and jumping the Han River to establish vast new bedroom districts of apartment buildings that seemed to line up like dominoes as far as the eye could see. Expressways and ring roads connected these communities. A network of subway trains was started, which has since grown to eight lines built over a quarter of a century (and more are under construction), carrying more than eight million people in and out of the city each day.

1950	1960–61
North Korean invasion; Communist occupation of Seoul (June–September)	Revolutionaries oust President Syngman Rhee and military junta installed under General Park Chung-hee

COMING INTO ITS OWN

Military rule continued after General Park's assassination in 1979, existing in various forms until 1993. Economic growth continued, as two generations of Koreans worked hard and sacrificed for the future. By the 1980s Koreans were hungry for notice and respect. Their products – textiles, shoes, electronics, and small cars and trucks – gained ground in the world market and Korea began showing signs of becoming wealthy. In the middle of the Han River, a large sandbar was transformed into a major business district (dubbed Seoul's Manhattan). More than 20 bridges were built across the Han, with a new one every year or two. The city's population had grown from 300,000 in 1953 to more than 11 million in 1990.

World sports gave Seoul its chance to showcase what the Korean people had accomplished since the war. The Asian Games came first, in 1986. Next came the 1988 Olympic Summer Games, for which the city built an impressive Olympic Park. In preparation, the Han River underwent a major facelift, with clean water and parks on both sides and an Olympic Expressway to whisk visitors from the airport to the stadiums. The games were a triumph for Korea, not least because they brought teams from Eastern Europe, the Soviet Union and China, creating contacts that blossomed before long into valuable trade and diplomatic relations.

Seoul's best coming-out party was the celebration that came with the 2002 FIFA World Cup championships, which Korea cohosted with Japan. Seoul built a magnificent stadium beside the Han River. World Cup mania gripped the city as soccer fans came from around the world. The Korean national team, entitled as hosts to one of the 16 slots in the first-round elimination, surprised everyone by advancing to the quarterfinals. 'Korea Team Fighting!' was the chant. Korean fans filled the stands wearing the team T-shirts emblazoned with 'Be the Reds!' in English. As the Korean team won once, twice, and then a third time, the country rang with the victory song 'Oh Pilseung (Victory to) Korea!' After a close victory over Spain, a million soccer fans massed in Seoul's City Hall Square for a rock concert and a wild celebration. It didn't matter that Korea was defeated by Germany in the semifinals. No Asian team had ever done what the Koreans did in the World Cup. The world had come to Korea and seen them triumphant. The effort, at long last, seemed worth it.

TRACING HISTORY IN SEOUL'S NEIGHBOURHOODS

The World Cup celebration has passed and Koreans have long since gotten back to work. But as they build their future, working out their differences with North Korea and adjusting to the emerging order in East Asia, the past still lingers on in the streets and neighbourhoods of Seoul. In Pukchon (Northtown), the neighbourhood between Gyeongbokgung and Changdeokgung, remain the traditional mansions, called *hanok,* of the Joseon-era noble families. Descendants of these *yangban* still live here, and there is hardly a corner, street or alley in the area that is not associated with a famous story from centuries past.

The Japanese colonial headquarters was torn down in the 1990s, but in the southern wards of the old city there are still relics of the Japanese colonial period. Along Namdaemun-no (South Gate St), which was the main thoroughfare of occupied Seoul, colonial landmarks are still in use: the original Mitsukoshi and Chojiya department stores are now the Shinsegae and the Midopa. The old Bank of Chosen is now the Bank of Korea. And the Japantown shopping districts of Meiji-machi and Honmachi are now Myeong-dong and Chungmuro.

Between these older districts, however, new Seoul is all about the future. From the Gwanghwamun crossing east along Jongno, and from City Hall Plaza east along Euljiro, rise the towers of Korea as a world economic power. These are still Seoul's most prestigious business addresses. Through the heart of this district, the clearing of a blighted expressway strip has enabled the city to uncover the Cheonggye stream that drains the valley of Seoul. Along its banks a river walk has been constructed. Decorative bridges have been built to span it. The beautification of the stream district marks a major achievement in environmental quality for Seoul's people, who are seeing their 'Clear Clean Stream' become one of the city's best attractions.

1988	2002
Seoul hosts the Olympic Summer Games	Korea cohosts the FIFA World Cup; Korean team does well and Seoul celebrates

Sights ∎

Sights

The main historical and sightseeing area of Seoul is the bustling downtown area of Gwanghwa-mun, which includes arty Insadong. To the north lies Bukhansan National Park. The fashion and shopping area of Myeong-dong, the traditional Namdaemun market and Namsan (South Mountain), with the landmark Seoul Tower perched on top), all lie to the south of downtown. To the east is a host of markets, including the busy Dongdaemun, and the student and theatre district of Daehangno. The tourist shopping and expat entertainment area of Itaewon, and the student neighbourhood of Sinchon/Hongik, with its bars, clubs and indie live music venues are both south of Namsan. The Han River winds through the city and midriver is the island of Yeouido (dubbed Seoul's 'Manhattan'), an important financial and administrative centre. South of the river, the upmarket Gangnam district includes Apgujeong with its brand-name boutiques and department stores, and top hotels. Further east is Jamsil, home to the giant COEX Mall and Conference Centre, the multifaceted Lotte World and Olympic Park.

ITINERARIES
One Day
Start at **Gyeongbokgung** (p49), Seoul's grandest palace that also contains two museums. Lunch in **Insadong** (p89) and explore the craft shops and private art galleries before sipping tea in a **teashop** (p107). Look round Seoul's major Buddhist temple **Jogyesa** (p53) and the nearby Buddhist shops before strolling to and around **Jongmyo** and **Changgyeonggung** (p50). Spend the evening in Daehangno – eat at **Nolboojip** (p94) then hit the bars or the **live jazz venue** (p108).

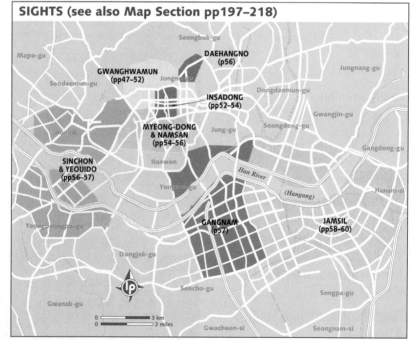

SIGHTS (see also Map Section pp197–218)

FOR CHILDREN

COEX Aquarium (p58) and **Sea World Aquarium** (p56) are the best. Near the COEX Aquarium is a zone with free PlayStation games, and near the Sea World Aquarium is an IMAX cinema.

Cycle (p115) along the Han River cycle path.

Everland (p155) has a popular Disney-sized amusement park as well as a world-class aquatic centre that's great fun in summer.

Lotte World (p59) is a mainly indoor Disneylandish amusement park with restaurants, a folk museum, scary rides and musical parades. The complex includes an ice-skating rink, cinemas, ten-pin bowling, fast food outlets and a swimming pool with slides.

Noraebang (karaoke rooms; p103) are fun even if you can't sing and will never make an *Idol* final.

Seoul Grand Park (p65) and **Children's Grand Park** (p61) both have large zoos. The former has a dolphin and seal show, while the latter has chimpanzee, parrot, seal and elephant shows. Both also have amusement parks with scary rides and fairground fun.

Ski resorts (p114) near Seoul provide skiing, snowboarding and sledding fun in winter.

Swimming pools (p115) open in July and August at hotels or in the parks along the Han River, or cool off at beaches on the **West Sea islands** (p150) off Incheon.

Three Days

Next day shop for clothing at bustling **Dongdaemun market** (p122), or health foods and ginseng tea at **Gyeongdong market** (p122), before touring the new **National Museum of Korea** (p62). Spend the evening among the ethnic restaurants, expat bars and nightclubs of **Itaewon** (p104).

Day three is the **Between the Palaces Walk** (p77) followed by a trip to the massive **War Memorial & Museum** (p63) and then back to **Deoksugung** (p54), a palace with art galleries inside and outside its walls. In the evening enjoy a fun live show at **Nanta Theatre** (p101) or something more traditional at **Chongdong Theatre** (p100).

One Week

On day four dive into the rugby scrum that is **Namdaemun market** (p123), followed by a visit to Myeong-dong's fashion boutiques and the **Catholic Cathedral** (p55). Look around **Namsangol Hanok Village** (p55) and walk or take the cable car up **Namsan** (p80) to the renovated Seoul Tower. In the evening, hang out with the students in **Hongik** (p105), enjoy some live bands and then go clubbing until dawn.

Next day start with another market – choose between **antiques** (p123), **electronics** (p123) or **fish** (p126), and then visit chilling **Seodaemun Prison** (p62). Hike up **Inwangsan** (p78) to a sha-manist shrine and Seoul's fortress wall. At nightfall, relax in a sauna (p116), a pool hall, a DVD *bang* (a room where you can watch DVDs) or a game café.

On day six join a tour round **Changdeokgung** (p48), a palace with a World Heritage secret garden, followed by a **cycle ride** (p115) along and across the Han River to the **World Cup Stadium** (p64) with its mall, cinemas and parks. In the evening enjoy a **Han River cruise** (p57) followed by a buffet dinner in the **63 Building** (p97) on Yeouido.

There is no rest even on your seventh day, so take the subway south of the Han River to **Olympic Park** (p59), the **COEX Mall** (p58) and the **royal tombs** (p60). Spend the evening in **Lotte World** (p59) or listen to live jazz or rock in smart **Apgujeong** (p110).

There is plenty more to see and do, including all the **excursions** (p147). Check out the Activities listing (p112) for other options.

CLOSED ON MONDAY

Most palaces and major museums are closed on Monday, but Gyeongbokgung, Jongmyo, Chang-gyeonggung and Namsangol Hanok Village close on Tuesday and the Agriculture Museum closes on Sunday. Some public art galleries as well as the Buddhist temples are open every day.

ORGANISED TOURS

If you join a tour, ensure it has an English-speaking guide. Tours usually include lunch and shopping stops. View www.triptokorea.com or www.startravel.co.kr for examples of tours and prices, and visit the KTO tourist information office (Map pp202–3) for tour leaflets. An **Icheon Ceramics Village tour** including a pottery class costs W75,000 to W120,000, and an all-day **Ganghwado tour** (W120,000) are a good idea as both these places are difficult to access using public transport. In winter numerous package tours to **ski resorts** (one day/overnight W75,000/270,000) are available.

Hyundai Asan has been operating overland tours (W230,000 to W350,000) to the scenic **Geumgangsan** (spelt Kumgangsan in the North) mountains inside North Korea since 2003. Coaches leave from the northeastern province of Gangwon-do in South Korea, cross over the highly fortified Demilitarized Zone (DMZ) and drive through North Korea to Geumgangsan. Phone ☎ 3702 2344 for more information or find a travel agent that handles these tours. A new tour to **Gaeseong** (spelt Kaesong in the North), a historic town just over the border and much nearer to Seoul, may be available.

ABC TOURS

☎ 363 9877; www.abckoreatour.com
This new tour company specialises in backpacker tours to Gyeongju and Andong (W75,000).

IT'S FREE!

- Look around some great **markets** (see the boxed text, p124)
- Wander around the traditional houses in **Namsangol Hanok Village** (p55)
- Check out the Buddhist temples **Jogyesa** (p53) and **Bongeunsa** (p58)
- Go on a **walking tour** (p76) or a **hiking trip** (p81)
- Enjoy traditional music and dance on weekend afternoons at **Seoul Norimadang** (p102)
- View art and crafts in **Insadong** (p119)
- Explore **Olympic Park** (p59), including the sculpture garden and Mongchon Museum
- Visit the brand new **Agriculture Museum** (p54)
- Log on to the **Internet** (p167) at KTO or the many other free providers
- Watch ice-skaters at **Lotte World** (p59)

PANMUNJEOM TRAVEL CENTRE
Map pp206-7

☎ 771 5593; www.koreadmztour.com; 2nd fl Lotte Hotel; subway Line 2 to Euljiro 1-ga, Exit 8
In this tour to the DMZ, you'll have a once-in-a-lifetime chance to question a defector from North Korea with help from an interpreter. The tour costs W58,000, but doesn't include a cross into the DMZ at Panmunjeom.

ROYAL ASIATIC SOCIETY KOREA
BRANCH Map pp202-3

☎ 763 9483; www.raskorea.org; ☺ 10am-noon & 2-5pm Mon-Fri; Room 611, Korean Christian Bldg; subway Line 1 Jongno 5-ga, Exit 2
Founded in 1900 the society is still very active with over 1000 local members, and organises tours to all parts of South Korea, usually at weekends. Log onto their website for the busy schedule. Nonmembers can always join in and all tours are led by English speakers who are experts in their field. The tours are reasonably priced, costing from W6000 to W50,000 to nonmembers, who pay a bit more than members. Membership costs W40,000 for a calendar year or W20,000 after 1 July. Free lectures are organised twice a month.

SEOUL CITY TOUR BUS

☎ 777 6090; www.seoulcitytourbus.com; adult/child day pass W10,000/8000; ☺ Tue-Sun
Comfortable and colourful tour buses run between Seoul's top tourist attractions north of the Han River every 30 minutes and you can hop-on and hop-off anywhere along the two routes – downtown (9am to 9pm) and around the palaces (9am to 5pm). Bus times and routes can change so check the schedule. Ticket holders are entitled to considerable discounts on tourist attractions along the route. Take the tour bus if your time is limited and you want to see as much as possible. The routes cover the palaces, Insadong, Namdaemun and Dongdaemun markets, Itaewon and Namsan. You can buy the tickets on the bus, which can be picked up outside Deoksugung.

UNITED SERVICE ORGANIZATIONS
Map pp200-1

USO; ☎ 795 3028; www.uso.org/korea; ☺ 7am-5pm Mon-Sat; subway Line 4 & 6 to Samgakji, Exit 11
The US military's entertainment wing organises tours for American troops but

LOST IN SEOUL

Most streets in Seoul have no name, or if they do, there is no street name sign and hardly anyone knows its name (*no* or *ro* means road, while *gil* is a lane). Using street names and consecutive numbers is a Western idea that has not been adopted, so the traditional system is still used. Thus Seoul is divided into 25 large districts (*gu*) and 522 smaller neighbourhoods (*dong*). Every building has an official number, but they are assigned as they are built, so building No 27 could be next to building No 324. Thus, an address like 104 Itaewon-dong, Yongsan-gu, means building No 104 in the Itaewon neighbourhood of the Yongsan district. However, you could wander around Itaewon for hours in search of this building with no hope of finding it, even with the help of a Korean friend. This is the time to make a phone call to the place you are looking for and get directions.

This guide gives street names where useful, indicates the nearest subway station and which exit to take, and gives directions to places that are tricky to find. But you're still going to get lost sometimes unless you're a human compass. Don't worry about it and don't be afraid to ask. Seoulites get lost too and know what it's like. Try to navigate around Seoul using landmarks rather than street names and numbers, just as the locals do.

Writing down the name and address of your destination in *hangeul* (the Korean phonetic alphabet) can be helpful for taxi drivers or if you need to ask a shopkeeper or a passer-by for directions. Many larger buildings have names – knowing the name of the building is more useful than knowing the number. Always check the neighbourhood map on the wall at every subway exit to orientate yourself before venturing out.

civilians from any country are welcome to join in. Twice a week the USO runs the best tours to the DMZ and Panmunjeom (p147). Other all-day tours include the historical and unspoilt island of Ganghwado (US$24) and white-water rafting excursions (US$35). In winter, skiing trips are organised. On the USO premises is a US-style diner and a travel agency, Apple Tours (p173).

GWANGHWAMUN

Although their size and splendour have been greatly reduced by wars, fires and Japanese colonial policy, Seoul's royal palace compounds contain a variety of restored buildings that offer visitors glimpses of Korea's fascinating feudal past. The palaces followed Confucian ideals of frugality and simplicity, which makes them unique, but don't expect the opulent grandeur of Western palaces.

Today the large palaces are deserted but the maze of corridors, courtyards, buildings and gardens used to be thronged with hundreds of government officials and scholars, eunuchs and concubines, soldiers, servants and slaves. The grand formal buildings, where government business was carried out, contrast with the smaller, more informal living quarters, divided into male and female sections as dictated by Confucian principles. In the warmer months, free concerts and historical re-enactments are held in the palaces, some of which are popular backdrops for wedding photos and videos. Admission

prices are a bargain – all seven palaces can be visited for less than W10,000.

ADMIRAL YI SUN-SIN'S STATUE
Map pp202-3
Sejongno; subway Line 5 to Gwanghwamun, Exit 4
This statue is a downtown landmark. Seoul-born Yi Sun-sin (1545–98) designed a new type of metal-clad warship called *geobukseon* (turtle boats), and used them to help achieve a series of stunning victories over the much larger Japanese navy that attacked Korea at the end of the 16th century. A *geobukseon* replica can be seen in the War Memorial and Museum (p63). A greatly admired hero, he is also featured on the W100 coin.

BUKCHON MUSEUM Map pp202-3
☎ 747 3957; adult/child W2000/1000;
🕙 10am-7pm Mar-Oct, 11am-6pm Nov-Feb;
subway Line 3 to Anguk, Exit 3
This *hanok* (traditional Korean one-storey wooden house with a tiled roof) is packed with curios and collectables, but is more of a shop than a museum as everything is for sale. Entry is free if you make a purchase, or buy a W3000 cup of homemade tea.

TRANSPORT
An alternative to walking and the subway is provided by the Seoul City Tour Bus (opposite). Taxis are inexpensive and don't expect a tip, but finding an available one can take time.

TOP THREE IN GWANGHWAMUN

- Gyeongbokgung (opposite)
- Changdeokgung Biwon (below)
- Jongmyo (p50)

BUKCHON CULTURE CENTRE
Map pp202-3

☎ 3707 8388; admission free; ◐ 9am-6pm
Mon-Fri; subway Line 3 to Anguk, Exit 3
A small exhibition about *hanok* in Bukchon,
housed appropriately in a Bukchon *hanok*.

CHANGDEOKGUNG Map pp202-3
Palace of Illustrious Virtue; ☎ 762 8262;
adult/teenager W3000/1500; ◐ closed Mon;
subway Line 3 to Anguk, Exit 3
You can't look around this World Heritage palace on your own, but must join a
90-minute tour. Tours run by an English-
speaking guide are available at 11.30am,
1.30pm and 3.30pm.

Changdeokgung was originally built
in 1405 as a secondary palace, but when
Gyeongbokgung (Seoul's principal palace)
was not rebuilt after its destruction in the
1590s, Changdeokgung became the primary palace until 1896, a period of nearly
300 years. Like all Joseon palaces, it has a
mountain behind it and a small stream in
front – good feng shui. The palace has large
public halls and smaller private ones that
are divided into 'his' and 'her' sections.

The modern world appears in the form
of electric lights that were installed in 1908
in some buildings, and a restored Daimler
and Cadillac in the garage. Buildings of
note are the main hall, the **blue-tiled royal
office** and **Nakseonjae** (originally built by King
Heonjong for one of his concubines, Lady
Kim), which was home to descendants of
the royal family up until 1989.

But the highlight is the **Biwon** (Huwon),
the rear, secret garden. In the midst of
trees is a large lily pond surrounded by
little pavilions. This tranquil garden is more
nature than garden and was where the
Joseon kings relaxed, studied and wrote
poems. The large two-storey building was
the royal library (its nameboard written by
King Jeongjo means 'Gather the Universe')
with books on the lower floor and study
and discussion rooms upstairs. A smaller
pavilion, Yeonghwadang, was where the
king or officials sat when overseeing the
all-important civil service examination,
gwageo (see the boxed text, below).

Behind the secret garden is **Yeongyeongdang**, built in the 1820s in the style of a rich
nobleman's house, complete with a library,
servants quarters and a two-hole toilet.

CHEONGWADAE Map pp202-3
Blue House; ☎ 737 5800; www.president.go.kr;
subway Line 3 to Gyeongbokgung, Exit 5
The Blue House is Korea's answer to
America's presidential residence the White
House. Back in 1968 a squad of 31 North
Korean commandos was caught just 500m

EXAMINATION HELL

It's not just recently that Korean students have had to study 12 hours or more every day to squeeze themselves into
a high-status job. In the past *yangban* (aristocratic) sons had to torture their brains learning Chinese characters and
memorising Confucian classics in order to pass through the very narrow *gwageo* gate, the examination that gave
them access to the all-important government jobs. From over 10,000 hopefuls, only the top 30 or so were offered
high-ranking posts.

The kings took a personal interest and role in the exam and the final stage was held in the secluded Biwon garden
and lasted from 8am until sunset. The scholar King Sejong even set some of the questions: Are identification tags a
good idea? How should a census be organised? Should the number of slaves be limited? Students who passed returned
to their hometown in triumph like an Olympic gold medallist.

The civil exam had the highest status because Joseon society valued the scholar above the soldier (with unfortunate
consequences when samurai-dominated Japan attacked in the 1590s). For military protection, the kings relied on
regional superpower, China, to help them when necessary. But there was a military exam, *mugwa*, which included
horse-riding and archery (a high-status sport that kings took part in and in which Koreans excel today). The third exam,
japgwa, was for technical specialists such as doctors, astronomers, lawyers, linguists and accountants. Their status was
low, but they were far better off than the artisans who were slaves and could never escape their low-born status.

Detail of painting at Changdeokgung (p48), Gwanghwamun

from the Blue House on a mission to assassinate President Park Chung-hee. The threat from the North has diminished but still remains, so security is tight. To see Cheongwadae, visitors must join a tour (Korean language only; passports required), which is free and lasts 80 minutes, but does not venture inside any important buildings and only visits the palatial grounds and Chilgung – small locked shrines that contain the spirit tablets of seven royal concubines whose sons became kings during the Joseon dynasty.

Tour times vary and you must pre-book online and pick up your tickets at the **ticket booth** (🕑 9am-3pm tour days) in Gyeongbokgung. A tour bus takes you the short distance from the car park to Cheongwadae.

GYEONGBOKGUNG Map pp202-3

Palace of Shining Happiness; ☎ 732 1931; adult/ youth/child under 6 W3000/1500/free; 🕑 9am-6pm Wed-Mon Mar-Oct, 9am-5pm Wed-Mon Nov-Feb; subway Line 3 to Gyeongbokgung, Exit 5
Originally built by King Taejo, the founder of the Joseon dynasty, the grandest of Seoul palaces served as the principal palace until 1592, when it was burnt down during the Japanese invasions. It lay in ruins for

nearly 300 years until Heungseon Daewongun, regent and father of King Gojong, started to rebuild it in 1865. King Gojong moved in during 1868, but the expensive rebuilding project nearly bankrupted the government.

On 8 October 1895, Queen Myeongseong (also known as Queen Min) was killed in her bedroom by Japanese assassins who then burnt her body. It is said only one finger survived the fire. Four months later King Gojong fled from the palace to the nearby Russian legation building and never returned.

During Japanese colonial rule, most of the palace was destroyed. The Japanese governor general's ugly office block was built inside the walls, but was demolished in 1996, and work on restoring the palace to its former glory is likely to continue for decades.

Two of the grandest architectural sights in Seoul are here. The first is the two-storey, ornate **Geunjeongjeon**, the main palace building where kings were crowned, met foreign envoys and conducted affairs of state. It is best viewed from the imposing second entrance gate, Heungnyemun, which is guarded by soldiers in Joseon uniforms. With its double-tiered stone platform, flagstone courtyard and surrounding open-sided corridors, Geunjeongjeon is an impressive sight. Then walk left to **Gyeonghoeru**, a large raised pavilion resting on 48 stone pillars and overlooking an artificial lake with two small islands, which is almost as grand a scene. State banquets were held inside.

Behind these imposing structures are smaller meeting halls, and behind them are the king's living quarters with a master bedroom the size of a ballroom, surrounded by eight small rooms that were used by ladies-in-waiting, concubines, servants, slaves and guards. Altogether the palace had up to 3000 staff, including 140 eunuchs, to serve the royal family.

On the right is **Gyotaejeon**, the separate but large living quarters for the primary queen, and behind that is a terraced garden with *ondol* (underfloor heating) chimneys decorated with longevity symbols. Also on the eastern side is **Jaseondang**, the quarters for the Crown Prince, who spent his mornings, afternoons and evenings reading, studying and listening to lectures. But at night he could relax with his wife and his concubines who were graded into four ranks (the king naturally had more and they were graded into six ranks). One canny Crown Prince tutor married the Crown Prince off to his daughter and put his family members into top government positions.

At the rear of the palace King Gojong built an ornamental pond with an attractive hexagonal pavilion on an island, where a heron can sometimes be spotted.

An audio guide is available (W2000) and gives brief comments. More useful are the free guided tours (in English) that begin at 9.30am, noon, 2pm and 3pm from the ticket gate near Gwanghwamun, the front entrance gate. From 1 March to 31 December the **changing of the guard ceremony** takes place on the hour from 10am until 3pm daily except Tuesday.

The **National Folk Museum** (☎ 3704 3114; www.nfm.go.kr; admission free with entry to the palace) takes at least an hour to walk around. This major museum, built in 1939, has modern displays in three large sections and uses models to illustrate the official version of Korea's history, culture and traditional lifestyle. You have to visit museums in North Korea to learn about cruel slave masters and the exploitation of the peasants. Clothing revealed your status in the 'good old days'.

A glance at somebody's clothes, shoes and hat and you could tell exactly where they stood in the fixed Confucian hierarchy, which stretched from the king at the top of the pyramid to the slaves, low-born and untouchables at the bottom. It has a fun hands-on section for children and an audio guide (in English) is only W1000 but doesn't add much to the exhibit labels.

The new **National Palace Museum** (p52) is in the front courtyard.

GYEONGHUIGUNG Map pp202-3
Palace of Shining Celebration; ☎ 724 0274; admission free; ☼ 9am-6pm Tue-Sun; subway Line 5 to Gwanghwamun, Exit 6
This detached palace was completed in 1623 and used to consist of a rabbit warren of courtyards, buildings, walls and gates that spread over a large area. But it was destroyed during the Japanese annexation (1910–45) when a Japanese school was established here. Only the main audience hall, **Sungjeongjeon**, and the smaller royal bedchamber behind it have been restored along with a few paved courtyards, walls and corridors. The entrance gate, **Heunghwamun**, has toured around Seoul including a stint outside the Hotel Shilla, but was moved to its present site in 1988.

STATUE OF HAMMERING MAN
Map pp202-3
Subway Line 5 to Gwanghwamun, Exit 6
The moving metallic shadow of a hammering man towers five storeys above the street. Funded by a local insurance company, the superman of a blacksmith has been silently hammering since 2002.
It was made out of 50 tons of steel by American artist Jonathon Borofsky whose art is humanist but mechanical, monumental but intriguing, simple but thought-provoking. Is work just a meaningless ritual that we allow to dominate our lives?

JONGMYO & CHANGGYEONGGUNG
Map pp202-3
☎ 765 0195/762 4868; adult/child W1000/500; ☼ 9am-6pm Wed-Mon Mar-Oct, 9am-5.30pm Wed-Mon Nov-Feb; subway Line 1, 3 or 5 to Jongno 3-ga, Exit 11
Surrounded by dense woodland are the impressive buildings of **Jongmyo** (www.jongmyo.net), which house the spirit tablets of

the Joseon kings and queens and some of their most loyal government officials. Their spirits are believed to reside in a special hole bored into the wooden tablets.

Near the entrance is a square pond (representing the earth) with a round island (representing the heavens). The main shrine, **Jeongjeon**, originally constructed in 1395, is a very long, stately and austere building with a large stone-flagged courtyard in front of it. Inside are 49 royal spirit tablets in 19 small rooms but they are usually locked. On the right-hand side of the main entrance is **Gonsindang**, which houses the spirit tablets of 83 meritorious subjects who served their kings well and were rewarded with their spirit tablets sharing the royal compound – the highest honour they could hope for. On the left side are shrines to Chilsa, the seven gods who aid kings.

The smaller shrine, **Yeongnyeongjeon** (Hall of Eternal Peace), originally built in 1421, has 34 spirit tablets of lesser kings in six rooms. These include four ancestors of King Taejo (who founded the Joseon dynasty in 1392) who were made kings posthumously. An English-speaking guide may be available at 10am and 3.30pm (free, one hour).

On the first Sunday in May the peaceful atmosphere is shattered by the crowds who come to watch the World Heritage ceremony, **Jongmyo daeje**, when a grand royal procession precedes a seven-hour Confucian ritual that is performed by the many living descendants of the royal family, who pay homage to their distant ancestors. The royal spirits are welcomed and praised, fed with offerings of cooked meat and rice wine, entertained with solemn music and dance, and then respectfully farewelled. During the Joseon dynasty the ritual was performed five times a year and led by the king. Nowadays it usually starts at 3pm at Yeongnyeongjeon, with the royal procession at 5pm and the ceremony at the main hall starting around 8pm.

From Jongmyo walk over the footbridge to **Changgyeonggung** (Palace of Flourishing Gladness). An English-speaking tour guide should be available at 11.30am and 4pm at the main gate. This palace was originally built in the early 15th century by revered King Sejong for his parents. Like all the palaces it was destroyed twice by the Japanese – first in the 1590s and then during the colonial period from 1910 until

1945, when the palace suffered the ultimate indignity of being turned into a zoo. Only a fifth of the palace buildings survived or have been rebuilt so far. The oldest surviving structure is the 15th-century **stone bridge** over the stream by the main gate.

The main hall, **Myeongjeongjeon**, with its latticework and ornately carved and decorated ceiling, dates back to 1616. The stone markers in the courtyard show where the different ranks of government officials had to stand during major state ceremonies. The smaller buildings behind the main hall were where the kings and queens lived in their separate households.

Near the ponds, the Joseon-dynasty government service examination *(gwageo)* is re-enacted every October. Behind the ponds is a **botanical glasshouse**, which was completed in 1909 and is still full of plants. It takes 25 minutes to walk from here back down to the entrance to Jongmyo. In the small park at the entrance to Jongmyo, especially during the summer, a crowd of pensioners gathers to discuss politics, play *baduk* (Asian chess), picnic, chat, nap and even dance.

KOREAN COMFORT WOMEN PROTEST Map pp202-3
Outside Japanese Embassy; ☽ noon Wed; subway Line 3 to Anguk, Exit 6

Every week a handful of elderly Korean comfort women, who were forced into prostitution during WWII, gather outside the Japanese embassy. Together with their supporters they wave placards and shout slogans. One of them, Hwang Geum-joo, says she will never give up: 'Our numbers are dwindling every year, but we are still full of anger and they should apologise for what they did to us!' The protest started in 1992 but the ladies are still waiting for a heartfelt apology and compensation for their suffering.

MUSEUM OF KOREAN BUDDHIST ART Map pp202-3
☎ 766 6000; adult/student W5000/3000; ☽ 10am-6pm Tue-Sun; subway Line 3 to Anguk, Exit 3

The permanent exhibition is displayed in one section, and 50m down the street is the second section which hosts changing exhibitions. The entry price includes admission to both. The permanent exhibition is small but the paintings and carvings, many 200 years old, suggest that Korean Buddhist art is undervalued by the global art scene. The **Yeonam teashop** (☎ 742 999; tea with museum entry W4000; ☻ 10am-7pm) has homemade teas – hibiscus petal tea is worth trying.

NATIONAL PALACE MUSEUM

Map pp202-3

☎ 3701 7500; www.gogung.go.kr; adult/child W2000/1000; ☻ 9am-6pm Tue-Fri, 9am-7pm Sat & Sun; subway Line 3 to Gyeongbokgung, Exit 5

This spacious new museum is in the front courtyard of Gyeongbokgung, but is run separately. It closes on Monday while the palace closes on Tuesday. English descriptions are brief but an audio guide is W1000. The museum provides the usual uncritical look at certain aspects of the lives and significance of the 27 Joseon kings, including scientific inventions and Jongmyo ritual metalware. Displays highlight the wonderful artistic skills of the Joseon era – royal seals, illustrations of court ceremonies, and the gold-embroidered *hanbok* (traditional Korean clothing) and exquisite hairpins worn by the queens and princesses.

SEJONG GALLERY Map pp202-3

☎ 399 1111; Sejongno; admission free; ☻ 10am-5pm; subway Line 5 to Gwanghwamun, Exit 8

It's worth popping into this gallery, which is divided into three sections: on two floors in the building south of the main theatre and in the subway station behind. It exhibits changing modern art shows.

SEOUL MUSEUM OF ART ANNEXE

Map pp202-3

☎ 2124 8800; http://seoulmoa.org; admission free; ☻ 10am-6pm Mar-Oct, 10am-5pm Nov-Feb; subway Line 1 or 2 to City Hall, Exit 2

Two large hangar-like structures make up this unusual art gallery.

SEOUL MUSEUM OF HISTORY

Map pp202-3

☎ 724 0114; www.museum.seoul.kr; adult/student/child W700/300/free; ☻ 9am-9pm Tue-Fri & Sun, 10am-7pm Sat & holidays Mar-Oct, 9am-8pm Tue-Fri & Sun, 10am-6pm Sat Nov-Feb; subway Line 5 to Gwanghwamun, Exit 7

Opened in 2002, this museum is disappointing with a mishmash of disorganised

displays, many of which are so dimly lit that they are hard to see. It focuses on Joseon-era Seoul when the city was called Hanyang or Hanseongbu and was confined to north of the Han River. Downstairs is a café (drinks and snacks W1000 to W4000) and special exhibitions are put on which may be more worth a visit.

TAPGOL PARK Map pp202-3

Admission free; subway Line 1 or 5 to Jongno 3-ga, Exit 1 or 5

'Tapgol' means 'pagoda', which refers to the 10-tier, 12m-high stone pagoda in the park that is all that remains of Wongaksa, a temple that stood here but was destroyed in 1515. Constructed in 1471, the pagoda is adorned with wonderful Buddhist carvings, but unfortunately the ugly protective glass box around it spoils its ancient beauty and charm.

Opened in 1897, Tapgol was Seoul's first Western-style park and is a symbol of Korean resistance to Japanese rule. On 1 March 1919, Son Byeong-hui and 32 others signed and read aloud a Declaration of Independence. Many of them were high-school teachers, 16 were Cheondogyo followers, 15 were Protestant Christians and two, including poet-monk Young-un, were Buddhists. All were arrested and locked up in the notorious Seodaemun Prison (p62). A torrent of protest against Japan followed in Seoul and throughout Korea, but the *samil* (1 March) movement was ruthlessly suppressed. Hundreds of independence fighters were killed and thousands arrested. Ten murals in the park depict scenes from the heroic but unsuccessful struggle.

INSADONG

The small, compact Insadong district is one of the few parts of Seoul to retain an atmosphere of the past. The narrow alleys are packed with 50 art galleries (most of them small), as well as traditional restaurants and teashops selling a wide range of Korean food and drinks. Craft shops sell fans, handmade paper boxes, masks, lacquerware, pottery and antiques.

BOSINGAK Map p205

Jongno; subway Line 1 to Jonggak, Exit 4

Situated in Jongno (Bell St), Seoul's main street during the Joseon period, this pavilion

TRANSPORT

Take the subway to Anguk or Jonggak and after that walking is the only way to get around this small district.

houses a modern version of the city bell, which was originally forged in 1468. The bell is rung only at New Year, when crowds gather here to celebrate. In Joseon times, the great bell was struck 28 times every night at 10pm to ask the heavens for a peaceful night and to signal the closure of the gates and the start of the nightly curfew, which was enforced by club-wielding watchmen. It was struck 33 times for the 33 Buddhist heavens at 4am, which signalled the start of the new day when the gates were reopened. It also sounded when fire broke out.

CHEONDOGYO TEMPLE Map p205

☎ 732 8991; subway Line 3 to Anguk, Exit 6

On the outside the headquarters of this Korean fusion religion is a handsome baroque-style, red-brick and stone church with a tower and spire, but inside it looks like a plain meeting hall with a piano but no altar, statues or paintings. It was completed in 1921 and was used as a centre of opposition to Japanese rule.

JOGYESA Map p205

☎ 725 6641; www.jogyesa.org/english; Ujonggungno; ⏲ 4am-9pm; subway Line 3 to Anguk, Exit 6

The largest Buddhist shrine in Seoul, **Daeungjeon** was built in 1938, but the design followed the late Joseon-dynasty style. Murals of scenes from Buddha's life and the carved floral latticework doors are two of its attractive features. You can follow the tradition of lighting a candle or incense stick and then walking around the **seventiered pagoda** to make a wish. Jogyesa is the headquarters of the Jogye sect, the largest in Korea, which emphasises Zen-style *(Seon)* meditation and the study of Buddhist scriptures as the best way to achieve enlightenment.

Behind the main shrine is the modern **Amitabha Buddha Hall** where funeral services are held. The statues are the 10 judges who pass judgement along with the Amitabha Buddha, 49 days after someone's death, to decide if they go to heaven or hell.

The **belfry** houses a drum to summon earthbound animals, a wooden fish-shaped gong to summon aquatic beings, a metal cloud-shaped gong to summon birds and a large bronze bell to summon underground creatures. They are banged 28 times at 4am and 33 times at 6pm.

New Year bell at Bosingak (p52), Insadong

The **Information Centre for Foreigners** (☎ 732 5292; ✆ 9.30am-6pm) can provide a guide and help with booking a **temple stay** (p164).

Around the temple are shops that sell Buddhist images, beads, candles, incense, music, paintings, lanterns and clothing.

KNIFE GALLERY Map p205
☎ 735 4430; Eoreumgol-gil; admission W1000; ✆ 10.30am-8pm; subway Line 3 to Anguk, Exit 6
In a basement is a weird and wonderful global collection of swords and knives along with other army equipment.

UNHYEONGUNG Map p205
Cloud Hanging Over the Valley Palace; ☎ 766 9090; www.unhyeongung.com; Samilno; adult/youth W700/300; ✆ 9am-7pm Tue-Sun Mar-Oct, 9am-5pm Tue-Sun Nov-Feb; subway Line 3 to Anguk, Exit 4
The modest and plain natural-wood design of this minor palace reflects the austere tastes of Heungseon Daewongun (1820–98), King Gojong's stern and conservative father whose policies included massacring Korean Catholics, excluding foreigners from Korea and closing Confucian schools. Gojong was born and raised here until 1863 when he ascended the throne aged 12 with his father acting as regent. Rooms are furnished and mannequins display the dress styles of the time. An hour-long re-enactment of the marriage of King Gojong to Queen Myeongseong (Queen Min) is held here, where the actual event took place in 1867 when he was 15 and she 16.

MYEONG-DONG & NAMSAN

Myeong-dong is a compact, traffic-quiet zone packed with fashion stores that attract mainly young shoppers. Nearby Namdaemun market attracts all types. It's a 15-minute walk south to either Namsan-gol Hanok Village or the cable car to the summit of Namsan.

AGRICULTURE MUSEUM Map pp200-1
☎ 2080 5727; admission free; ✆ 9am-6pm Mon-Sat; subway Line 5 to Seodaemun, Exit 5
A brand new museum that has imaginative displays such as glass floors, a mock-up of a painted tomb, and a traditional village complete with voices. It's a worthy effort

but has no chance of persuading the young generation to become farmers, so the outlook for the industry is bleak despite the upbeat tone of the museum.

ANGLICAN CHURCH Map pp206-7
☎ 738 8952; subway Line 1 or 2 to City Hall, Exit 3
An imposing Renaissance-style church, built in the shape of a cross with Korean-style tiles on the roof – it's a fine example of architectural fusion. Work on the church began in 1922 but the full design was not completed until 1996.

BANK OF KOREA MUSEUM Map pp206-7
Currency Museum; ☎ 759 4888; admission free; ✆ 10am-5pm Tue-Sun; subway Line 4 to Hoehyeon, Exit 7
It is worth a quick visit to see the old coins and banknotes as well as the grand hall of the chateau-like Bank of Korea building (constructed in 1912 by the Japanese) where the exhibition is displayed.

DEOKSUGUNG Map pp206-7
Palace of Virtuous Longevity; ☎ 771 9951; adult/youth/child W1000/500/free; ✆ 9am-6pm Tue-Sun Mar-Oct, 9am-5.30pm Tue-Sun Nov-Feb; subway Line 1 or 2 to City Hall, Exit 2
Originally an aristocratic villa, Deoksugung became a palace in 1593 when King Seonjo moved in (after all of Seoul's other palaces were destroyed during the Japanese invasion). Despite two kings being crowned here, it became a secondary palace until 1897 when King Gojong moved in after leaving the nearby Russian legation. Although he was forced to abdicate 10 years later by the Japanese, Gojong carried on living here in some style until he died in 1919. He lost his kingdom but he kept his harem. His son, Sunjong, reigned as a puppet emperor until 1910 when he too was forced to abdicate by the Japanese, who then annexed Korea, bringing the Joseon

TRANSPORT
Walking to Myeong-dong and Namdaemun market from Gwanghwamun is possible, but you can take a taxi or use the subway. If you don't fancy walking up 262m-high Namsan take the cable car or hop onto the frequent and handy yellow No 2 bus.

dynasty to an undignified and abrupt end after more than 500 years.

The palace contains small gardens and ponds amid an extraordinary mixture of architectural styles that include a grand wooden audience hall in traditional Korean style and a fusion-style tea pavilion, **Heong-gwanheon**, which has pillars, a veranda and metal railings decorated with deer and bats – both auspicious creatures. This is where King Gojong drank the soothing beverage while discussing current affairs and poetry with his visitors. The stone mythical creatures in the main courtyard are *haetae*, who are supposed to protect the palace from fire but in 1904 they must have fallen asleep because most of the palace burnt down.

King Gojong's living quarters, **Hamnyeongjeon**, was where he died in 1919, an event which sparked off nation-wide protests against Japanese rule. Two large Romanesque buildings now house art galleries – **Seokjojeon** (built between 1900 and 1909) houses art and craft exhibitions (usually free admission), while the other houses the **National Museum of Contemporary Art Annexe** (☎ 779 5310; www.moca.go.kr; admission around W2000). With four large galleries on two levels, the exhibitions vary but concentrate on pre-1960 modern art. Tea or coffee in the café is W2000.

The **changing of the guards** (☒ 10.30am, 2pm & 3pm Tue-Sun 15 Feb-31 Dec) is an impressive ceremony that involves 50 participants, who dress up as Joseon-era soldiers and bandsmen. It takes place either around the main entrance gate or over the road on Seoul Plaza.

MYEONG-DONG CATHOLIC CATHEDRAL Map pp206-7
☎ 774 1784; subway Line 4 to Myeong-dong, Exit 9
This elegant brick Renaissance-style cathedral was constructed between 1894 and 1898 by Chinese bricklayers. Inside, the traditional vaulted ceiling and stained-glass windows contrast with the modern air-conditioning and the TV screens that help worshippers at the back see what is going on. The cathedral provided a sanctuary for student and trade-union protestors during the long period of military rule after the Korean War, and is a national symbol of democracy and human rights. English-language Sunday worship takes place at 9am in the Cultural Centre.

NAMDAEMUN Map pp206-7
Great South Gate; Sungnyemun; subway Line 1 or 4 to Seoul Station, Exit 3
The Great South Gate of Seoul fortress was originally constructed in 1398, rebuilt in 1447 and has often been renovated since then. Designated as National Treasure No 1, it's an impressive sight, especially when floodlit at night, and is a reminder of the once-mighty Joseon dynasty. The soldiers in Joseon uniforms that guard the gate (☒ 10am-4pm Wed-Mon) march around every 30 minutes, but are there for photographic rather than defence purposes. The famous day-and-night Namdaemun market (p123) that starts at the gate is also centuries old.

NAMSANGOL HANOK VILLAGE
Map pp206-7
☎ 2266 9101; admission free; ☒ 9am-8pm Wed-Mon May-Sep, 9am-6pm Wed-Mon Oct-Apr; subway Line 3 or 4 to Chungmuro, Exit 4
Five differing *yangban* (aristocratic) stone, wood and tile houses from the Joseon era have been moved here from different parts of Seoul. The architecture and furniture are austere and plain, and conjure up the lost world of Confucian gentlemen scholars who wielded calligraphy brushes rather than swords. Scenes from the drama movie *Untold Scandal* were filmed here. Weavers, calligraphers and kite-makers can be spotted at the weekend and the occasional festival livens the place up.

One *hanok* has become the **Dasahon Restaurant** (meals W4000-8000; ☒ 9am-8pm Wed-Mon), which serves up *bibimbap* (rice, egg, meat and vegies with chilli sauce), noodles and traditional liquor in a yesteryear atmosphere. A pleasant park and Time Capsule Square adjoin the village. The time capsule of 600 items was buried in 1994 and will be opened in 2394.

RODIN GALLERY Map pp206-7
☎ 2259 7781; www.rodin.co.kr; adult/child W5000/3000; ☒ 10am-6pm Tue-Sun; subway Line 1 or 2 to City Hall, Exit 8
This unusual glass pyramid building has two large sculptures by French sculptor Rodin on permanent display plus changing contemporary art exhibitions in another two galleries.

SEOUL MUSEUM OF ART Map pp206-7

☎ 2124 8800; adult/youth/child W700/300/free; ⊙ 10am-10pm Mon-Fri, 10am-7pm Sat & Sun Mar-Oct &10am-9pm Mon-Fri, 10am-6pm Sat Nov-Feb; subway Line 1 or 2 to City Hall, Exit 2

Ultra modern, bright galleries hide behind the brick-and-stone façade of the 1927 Supreme Court building. Opened in 2002, displays in this major public gallery change regularly and are generally worth visiting.

SEOUL TOWER Map pp206-7

☎ 772 1626; adult/youth/child W7000/4000/3000; ⊙ 9am-midnight; subway Line 1 or 4 to Seoul Station, Exit 10

Take the cable car, yellow bus No 2 or walk up from Seoul subway station (p80) to reach this recently revamped Seoul icon. The observation deck is located at the top of the tower along with a revolving grill-restaurant and a Korean restaurant.

DAEHANGNO

This student hang-out is thronged with young people and features many small theatres, a performance park, outdoor restaurants, plenty of bars and a live jazz venue. Street sculptures can be found all the way along the eastern side of the main street, Daehangno.

LOCK MUSEUM Map p208

☎ 766 6494; admission W5000; ⊙ 10am-8pm Tue-Sun; subway Line 4 to Hyehwa, Exit 2

For people who like visiting unusual, small museums, up on the 4th floor is a well-lit display of antique locks. In the same rusty-looking building are two (free) exhibition halls that usually display metalwork.

MARRONNIER ART CENTRE Map p208

☎ 742 2274; admission free-W3000; ⊙ 11am-8pm Tue-Sun; subway Line 4 to Hyehwa, Exit 2

Avant garde art of all shades is assembled here in three small galleries to the north of Marronnier Park.

TRANSPORT

Take a subway (or taxi) – don't try to walk here from downtown.

MUSEUM OF KOREAN STRAW HANDICRAFTS Map p208

☎ 743 8787; admission W3000; ⊙ 10am-5pm; subway Line 4 to Hyehwa, Exit 4

The masks, human figures, torches, bird catchers, bags, mats, cradles, chicken nests, rope, egg holders, and human and cattle shoes are all made of straw.

SINCHON & YEOUIDO

Yeouido (known as Seoul's Manhattan) is a 3km long and 2km wide island in the Han River where skyscrapers house the headquarters of many media, finance and insurance companies. The Stock Exchange and the National Assembly are on the island, but the gold-tinted 63 Building is the main tourist attraction. Along the southeastern side of the island Cherry Tree Park is popular in mid-April when the cherry trees blossom, but it's nothing special during the rest of the year.

63 BUILDING Map p210

☎ 789 5663; www.63city.co.kr; ⊙ 10am-9pm; subway Line 5 to Yeouinaru, Exit 4

The 63 Building, the tallest and most stylish skyscraper in Seoul, is not as popular as it used to be. It's a 15-minute walk from the subway, and has three major attractions. **Sea World Aquarium** (adult/teenager/child W10,500/9500/9000; ⊙ 10am-8.30pm) has penguins, reptiles and seals as well as turtles, sharks and other fish. The **IMAX giant screen cinema** (adult/teenager/child W7000/6500/6000; ⊙ 10am-9pm) provides headphones with an English-language version. The **Observation Deck** (adult/teenager/child W6000/5500/5000; ⊙ 10am-9pm) is up on the 60th floor. A ticket for all three costs W19,000/17,500/16,000. The best dining is at **Plaza Fountain Buffet** (p97).

EWHA WOMANS UNIVERSITY MUSEUM Map p210

☎ 3277 3151; admission free; ⊙ 9.30am-5pm Mon-Sat, closed 1-31 Aug & 21 Dec-1 Mar; subway Line 2 to Ewha Womans University, Exit 2

This modern museum in Sinchon has three floors of displays that vary but usually include traditional *hanbok,* centuries-old pottery, the history of the university and student art.

TRANSPORT

Take the subway to both Sinchon and Yeouido, although you can arrive at the latter on a Han River ferry.

HAN RIVER FERRY Map p210

☎ 785 4411; adult/child W9000/4500;
🕐 11.30am-10.30pm; subway Line 5 to Yeouinaru, Exit 3

The five ferry piers are at Yeouido (Map p210), Yanghwa (Map pp198–9), Nanji (Map pp198–9), Ttukseom (Map pp214–15) and Jamsil (Map pp214–15). You can take one-hour trips to any of the piers or take a round trip back to where you started. The boats run all year, hourly from June to August, but every one or two hours during the rest of the year. **Evening cruises** (adult/child W13,000/6500) have a buffet and live music and leave from Yeouido pier.

JEOLDUSAN MARTYRS MUSEUM & CHAPEL Map p210

☎ 323 1950; museum admission by donation;
🕐 10am-noon, 1-5pm Tue-Sun; subway Line 2 or 6 to Hapjeong, Exit 7

Jeoldusan means 'Beheading Hill' and this site is where up to 2000 Korean Catholics were executed in 1866 following a decree, signed by Regent Heungseon Daewongun (King Gojong's father), to kill all Catholics. The victims' bodies were thrown into the nearby Han River and today, less than 40 of their names are known. A memorial to the martyrs, a garden overlooking the river, a small museum, a stark memorial chapel and a statue of the first Korean priest, St Andrew Kim Daegeon (1821–46) make up the site.

The **museum** has very little in English but has relics of the many Catholic martyrs, and downstairs are miniature models of scenes from the early church together with souvenirs of Pope John Paul II's visit here in 1984. Steadfast early Christian converts faced waves of government persecution, but refused to recant their new faith. Inside churches, *yangban* nobles and ordinary folk sat together as equals in the sight of God, which challenged the rigid Confucian hierarchy of Joseon society. Many faced cruel tortures before they were executed.

Visit on a Sunday afternoon to attend the 3pm service at the stark white modernist **chapel** – the beautiful voices of the choir and packed congregation is a highlight. Female worshippers still wear a white veil on their heads. The chapel is open every day.

From the subway exit, take the second turning left and follow the covered railway line for 700m – it's less than 10 minute's walk. On the way back take a look at the well-kept **Foreigners Cemetery** (🕐 9am-5pm) where early Protestant missionaries are buried.

NATIONAL ASSEMBLY Map p210

☎ 788 3804; subway Line 5 to Yeouinaru, Exit 1

The pillared building with a green roof was completed in 1975. Free tours (Korean language only) take only 15 minutes although they can take longer if the country's 299 elected representatives are in session. Full meetings are held in February, April and June, and from September to December.

GANGNAM

Gangnam is a modern business district south of the Han River, which is more noted for its numerous bars and restaurants than for its tourist sights.

MUSEUM OF KOREAN EMBROIDERY Map p211

☎ 515 51114; 4th fl Sajeon House; admission free;
🕐 9am-4pm Mon-Fri; subway Line 7 to Hak-dong, Exit 10

Only a small amount is on show, but it includes exquisite examples of a neglected female craft. In the 'good' old days nearly everything was embroidered – clothes, shoes, boxes, pillow-ends, screens, pin cushions, toys and thimbles. Delicate patchwork *pojagi* (wrapping cloths) had many uses and some were made out of silk or ramie (cloth made from pounded bark). Items are not described but illustrated books on Korean embroidery (in English) are on sale.

TRANSPORT

Use the subway to travel to and around Gangnam.

JAMSIL

Jamsil is a modern area of offices and apartments south of the river, but also contains an ancient Buddhist temple and some 500-year-old royal tombs. The COEX Mall, Lotte World and Olympic Park are the other major attractions. Teheranno is the heart of Seoul's thriving IT industry.

BONGEUNSA Map pp214-15

☎ 511 6070; www.bongeunsa.org; subway Line 2 to Samseong, COEX Exit

Just north of the COEX Mall, the shrines and halls of this Buddhist temple are spread among a forested hillside and have a quieter, more secluded atmosphere than Jogyesa in Insadong, although somewhat marred by the car park. Founded in AD 794, the buildings have been rebuilt many times over the centuries. The oldest hall is **Panjeon**, constructed in 1856, which houses over 3000 150-year-old woodblocks with Buddhist scriptures and art carved into them.

Near the entrance on the left is a small hut where an English-speaking volunteer guide may be available. On the right is a charity shop, **Beautiful Store** (🕙 10.30am-6pm Tue-Sun). Entry to the temple is through **Jinyeomun** (Gate of Truth), protected by four fierce guardians. Beyond the gate you can write your name, address and wish on a roof tile in return for a W10,000 donation.

The main shrine **Daewungjeon**, last renovated in 1982, has lattice doors and is ornately decorated inside and out with Buddhist symbols and art designed to express Buddhist philosophy and ideals. Behind are smaller shrine halls and a large outdoor standing statue – the Maitreya (Future) Buddha.

COEX MALL Map pp214-15

☎ 6002 5312; www.coexmall.com; 🕙 10am-10pm; subway Line 2 to Samseong, COEX Exit

This vast underground mall is Seoul's top entertainment and retail zone with a maze of shops and food courts, a department store, luxury hotels, a handful of bars and nightclubs, a popular cinema multiplex, a free PlayStation games zone and the COEX conference centre.

The **COEX Aquarium** (☎ 6002 6214; adult/teenager/child W14,500/12,000/9500; 🕙 10am-8pm) is the largest in Seoul with 40,000 fish and other sea creatures in 90 tanks. You can see live coral, sharks, turtles, rays and evil-looking piranhas swimming around in large tanks. Exquisitely beautiful small creatures such as pulsating jellyfish, glass fish and sea horses are also on display. Next door, one wall of the Deep Blue restaurant is a huge aquarium tank.

The small **Kimchi Museum** (B2; adult/child W3000/1000; 🕙 10am-5pm Tue-Sat, 1-5pm Sun) is unique – the only museum dedicated to pickled cabbage and its health benefits.

Explex (admission free; 🕙 noon-9pm) has free Internet (30 minutes) and board games, while at the popular **PC Zone** (per hr W2000; 🕙 10am-10pm) you'll have to pay to play.

Play **four-ball** or **pool** (per 10 min W2000; 🕙 10am-11pm) in the U-Mille zone or play the latest PlayStation games for free in the **Seejong Game Zone** (opposite Bandi & Luni's). Sing along in the **Karaoke Room** (per hr per room W15,000; 🕙 11am-11pm) or record your own song onto CD for W4000 at Netian Music next door. Watch a movie in the **DVD Room** (per 2 people W15,000; 🕙 10am-11pm), play board games in **Jumanji Board Game Café** (☎ 6002 3838; 1st/next hr W3000/2000; 🕙 10am-10pm) or try out the latest iPod gadgets and laptops at the Apple Experience Centre. Join the crowds at **Megabox** (☎ 6002 1200; W8000; 🕙 8am-5am), which has 17 cinema screens.

Three of the best stores are **Bandi & Luni's** (☎ 6002 6090; 🕙 10am-10.30pm), which has Seoul's best selection of books and magazines in English, **Evan Records** (☎ 6002 1000; 🕙 10.30am-11pm) where you can listen to the latest releases, and **COEX Duty Free** (☎ 3484 9777; 🕙 10am-7.30pm) where you can shop till you drop.

Hyundai Department Store Food Court (meals W3000-12000; 🕙 10.30am-8pm) has something for everyone at reasonable prices, which means it's always busy. Try the Asian-Spanish fusion paella or the very English *tunggamja* (roast spuds).

TRANSPORT

Subway trains and taxis are the best way to get around, although cycling along the Han River is good exercise.

Carousel at Lotte World (below), Jamsil

LOTTE WORLD Map pp214-15

☎ 411 4921; www.lotteworld.com; ⊙ 9.30am-11pm; subway Line 2 or 8 to Jamsil, Exit 3

A huge complex that includes an amusement park, cinema multiplex, department store, folk museum, shopping mall, ice-skating rink, hotel and countless restaurants.

Lotte World Adventure & Magic Island (adult/teenager/child day pass W30,000/26,000/23,000; ⊙ 9.30am-11pm) is a mainly indoor Korean version of Disneyland, complete with a monorail train, 'flying' balloons, 3-D films, musical shows, parades and thrill rides that go down very fast, or round and round and up and down very fast. The scarier the ride, the longer the queue on busy days. The new Atlantis flume/rollercoaster/ghost train ride starts with a bang and doesn't let up. The main section is indoors but Magic Island is outside in the middle of Seokcho lake. The carousel has been popular with dating couples since it starred in the TV drama series *Stairway to Heaven*.

The all-year indoor ice-skating rink (B3 fl; adult/child per session W11,000/10,000, skate hire W3200; ⊙ 10.30am-9.30pm) is the best in Seoul. Each day is divided into six sessions (check for times as they vary). The bowling alley (B3 fl; adult/child W3000/2800, shoe rental W1200; ⊙ 9am-midnight) has 16 lanes. The pool & four ball hall (B3 fl; pool/four ball per hr

W10,800/9600; ⊙ 10am-10pm) is next to the bowling alley.

The swimming pool (1st fl; adult/child W8000-10,000/7000-8000; ⊙ 1pm-7pm Mon-Fri, 6am-8pm Sat & Sun) has a king slide, which costs W500 (W1000 in July and August), and a cave sauna (adult/child W4500/3500; ⊙ 6am-8pm).

The Folk Museum (3rd fl; adult/teenager/child W4500/3000/2000; ⊙ 9.30am-11pm) uses imaginative techniques like moving waxworks, dioramas and scale models to bring scenes from Korean history to life. The price is included in the day-pass ticket for Lotte World Adventure & Magic Island.

A cinema multiplex (per person W7000; ⊙ shows 10.30am-9pm) is next to the department store (⊙ 10am-8pm), which has the usual high quality but reasonably priced food court. Other eating options include the popular Marché (p98), Korean restaurants, a food court on B3 floor, Pizza Hut (pizzas from W12,000; ⊙ 11am-10pm) and Sizzlers (buffet salads & desserts W22,000, with steak W33,000; ⊙ 11am-10pm). The Edinburgh Pub Restaurant (fusion meals W7000-20,000, beers W3000; ⊙ 11am-11pm) has wood panels and tartan-clad staff.

OLYMPIC PARK Map pp214-15

subway Line 8 to Mongchontoseong, Exit 1

This very large park with lakes and pheasants is best visited by bicycle (p115) but the park itself has none for hire. The park contains the **sports stadiums** built for the 1988 Seoul Olympics – the indoor swimming pool (sometimes open to the public), tennis courts, three gymnasiums and the open-air **velodrome** (admission free; ☉ 2-9.30pm Fri-Sun Jul & Aug) where in summer months thousands gamble on the short cycle races.

The **Olympic Museum** (☎ 410 1051; adult/teenager/child W3000/2000/1000; ☉ 10am-5.30pm Tue-Sun) has screens showing the exciting highlights of the long ago 1988 Seoul Olympics, together with a brief history of the Olympics. Downstairs are sports games (W500 coins needed for some) and upstairs is a 10-minute simulated ride with moving seats (☉ 10.30am, 11.30am, 1pm, 2pm, 3pm, 4pm and 5pm), unrelated to the Olympics.

Two hundred large **sculptures** are scattered around the park. Designed and made by artists from around the world, the collection was started during the 1988 Seoul Olympics, but has been growing ever since. Most of the artwork is puzzling even after you have read the artists' descriptions of their work.

The new **Seoul Olympic Art Museum** (☎ 410 1062; adult/teenager/child W3000/2000/1000; ☉ 10am-9pm Mar-Oct, 10am-6pm Nov-Feb) puts on unusual, thought-provoking multimedia exhibitions.

A massive Baekje-dynasty earth fortification, **Mongchontoseong**, built in the 3rd century AD, runs through the park. The small **Mongchon Museum** (☎ 424 5138; admission free; ☉ 10am-9pm Mar-Oct, 10am-8pm Nov-Feb) has some precious golden relics of the Baekje kings and an unusual seven-pronged sword.

On warm evenings and weekends hundreds of young people go to the park to rollerblade around the plaza, play roller-blade hockey and do skateboard tricks, while members of the older generation play badminton, jog, eat ice cream, picnic under the trees, or exercise tiny dogs.

A **car-tram** (adult/teenager/child W1000/700/500; ☉ 10.35am-6pm or 7.20pm) runs around a 3km loop approximately every hour.

Food is very limited inside the park – a basic **snack bar** (Gongwon Maejeom Seunek; 공원매점스넥; *ramyeon* W1500; ☉ 6am-10pm) is near the World Peace Gate. Otherwise head to the classy restaurants in Olympic Parktel or bring a picnic.

SEOLLEUNG PARK ROYAL TOMBS
Map pp214-15

Samneung Park; ☎ 568 1291; adult/teenager W1000/500; ☉ 6am-5.30pm Tue-Sun Mar-Oct, 6am-4.30pm Tue-Sun Nov-Feb; subway Line 2 or Bundang Line to Seolleung, Exit 8

The spirit tablets of the Joseon kings and queens are in Jongmyo, but their tombs are scattered all over Seoul. The tombs are elaborate but mostly underground, and were the scene of rituals to remember the dead who were officially mourned for three years according to Confucian rules. The tombs of **King Seongjong** (ruled 1469–94), his third wife, **Queen Jeonghyeon Wanghu**, and his second son, **King Jeongjong** (ruled 1506–44), are in this park. King Seongjong is remembered as a prolific author and father (he had 28 children by 10 concubines), while King Jeongjong ruled for a long time but was a weak king.

The entranceway to the tombs is marked by a red spirit-gate with spikes on the top, and a small hall used for ceremonies to honour the dead. The tombs are guarded by larger-than-life stone statues of warriors and government officials along with smaller statues of horses, tigers and imaginary animals that look like sheep. The stone lanterns, pillars and pathways are there to guide the spirits back home. From subway Exit 8 walk straight ahead for 500m (five minutes) and the entrance is on the right.

TTUKSEOM RIVERSIDE PARK
Map pp214-15

subway Line 7 to Ttukseom Resort, Exit 2 or 3
In the park is a popular outdoor **swimming pool complex** (☎ 3780 1750; adult/teenager/child W4000/3000/2000; ☉ 9am-7pm Jul & Aug), a bicycle rental stall (W3000 per hour, ID required) and a pier where the Han River ferries stop (p57).

OTHER NEIGHBOURHOODS NORTH OF THE RIVER

The major sights outside the downtown area should not be missed and can be easily and quickly reached by subway. These neighbourhoods are uninspiring conglomerations of shops and apartments, so once you've seen the sight, head back to the subway.

TRANSPORT

The subway is the best way to visit the following sights and you can always take a taxi in cases where a short walk is required from the subway exit.

CHILDREN'S GRAND PARK Map pp198-9

☎ 450 9311; adult/teenager/child Apr-Jun, Sep & Oct W1500/1000/free, Jul & Aug, Nov-Mar W900/500/free; ☽ 9am-10pm Mar-Oct, 9am-6pm Nov-Feb; subway Line 7 to Children's Grand Park, Exit 1

Ask for a free map at the entrance to this large shady park with a rose garden, flower beds and fountains that has plenty to keep children busy and occupied. An **amusement park** (rides W2500) has 30 fear-factor experiences for all ages, but some of the **zoo** animals – which include lions, tigers, elephants and bears – live in enclosures that are small by modern standards.

A glasshouse **botanical garden** has cacti up one end, a tropical jungle and bonsai trees at the other end and a small **folk museum** upstairs. A **wetland eco area** has a boardwalk, and nearby **pony rides** (W3000) and **camel rides** (W4000) are other options. The 30-minute **Anistory Show** (adult/teenager/child W5000/4000/3000; ☽ 11am, 1pm, 3pm, 5pm & 7pm) is fun and features a cute parrot, a chimpanzee act and eager performing seals. The 30-minute **Elephant Theme Show** (adult/child W6000/5000; ☽ 11.30am, 1pm, 3pm & 5pm) has nine elephants that play soccer and basketball and also features six Laotian female dancers.

DONGDAEMUN Map pp200-1

Great East Gate; Heunginjimun; subway Line 1 or 4 to Dongdaemun, Exit 6

Seoul's Eastern fortress gate, Dongdaemun, dates back to the 14th century, but the existing structure was built in 1869 and had to be renovated after being severely damaged during the Korean War when Seoul changed hands four times. Dongdaemun market (p122) starts at this gate.

HONGNEUNG ARBORETUM & SURROUNDS Map p216

☎ 961 2651; cnr of Hoegiro & Hongneung-gil; admission free; ☽ 9am-5pm Sun; subway Line 6 to Korea University, Exit 3

Winding footpaths turn this 38-hectare arboretum, established in 1922 and packed with many varieties of trees and plants, into a pleasant maze that is popular with dating couples, nature lovers and keen photographers. It is only open on Sunday and picnics are not allowed. On the right is the **Forestry Museum** (☎ 961 2873; admission free; ☽ 10am-5pm Tue-Fri & 10am-1pm Sat Mar-Oct, 10am-4pm Tue-Fri & 10am-1pm Sat Nov-Feb), which has an original design containing exhibits on native trees and their uses, but little English description.

From the subway exit take the first road on the right (Hoegiro), walk under the expressway and 600m from the subway exit is the arboretum entrance on the left facing Hongneung-gil.

Opposite the arboretum entrance is the rather neglected **King Sejong Memorial Museum** (☎ 969 8851; admission free; ☽ 9am-6pm Tue-Sun. It has a few galleries devoted to paintings, books, *hangeul* typewriters and musical instruments, but there are no English descriptions. In the garden are some tomb statues and a huge slab of rock carved with praise of King Sejong and his primary wife, Queen Soheon.

Walk 100m down Hongneung-gil to reach the entrance to two **royal tombs** (adult/teenager W1000/500; ☽ 9am-5.30pm Tue-Sun). **Yeonghwiwon** is the tomb of Lady Eom (1854–1911), the favourite concubine of King Gojong after the assassination of Queen Min. **Sunginwon** is the tomb of Yi Jin who died in his first year in 1922 and was Lady Eom's first grandson, the son of King Gojong's fourth son whom the Japanese made Crown Prince. See opposite for more information about royal tombs.

Carry on walking down Hongneung-gil to reach Cheongnyangni station (Line 1, Exit 2), which is only 600m from the tombs.

TOP FIVE OUTSIDE THE CITY CENTRE

- National Museum of Korea (p62)
- War Memorial & Museum (p63)
- Seodaemun Prison (p62)
- World Cup Stadium & Mall (p64)
- Seoul Grand Park (p65)

NATIONAL MUSEUM OF KOREA
Map pp198-9

☎ 2077 9000; www.museum.go.kr; adult/child W2000/1000; ⏰ 9am-6pm Tue-Fri, 9am-7pm Sat & Sun; subway Line 1 or 4 to Ichon, Exit 2

This grand, marble-lined, modernist building cleverly channels plenty of natural light to show off Korea's ancient treasures. The museum took eight years to construct, finally opening in October 2005. Walking past the reflecting pond by the entrance, the west wing of this spacious museum has a hands-on, fun-filled, young children's section and houses the 800-seat Yong (Dragon) theatre which has hosted concerts, musicals and even a circus. In the east wing are the main galleries together with a large shop, café with views and a restaurant.

The national treasures on the first floor are accessed from the Path of History and span thousands of years with outstanding Buddhist pagodas and sculptures, ancient maps and royal artefacts from the Three Kingdoms and Joseon periods. The second floor has calligraphy and other art and the donations gallery includes items from Japanese collectors. The third floor displays Buddhist sculptures, metalwork and the wonderful and celebrated pale-green celadon ceramics. Another gallery puts Korean art into the context of other Asian art with works from China, Japan, Southeast Asia and some surprising ones from Central Asia. Volunteer and audio guides are available.

SEJONG UNIVERSITY MUSEUM
Map pp198-9

☎ 3408 3077; admission free; ⏰ 10am-noon, 1-3pm Mon-Fri; subway Line 7 to Children's Grand Park, Exit 6

The best of the university folk museums, Sejong has a superb collection, especially the well-displayed *hanbok* that takes up an entire floor and includes outstanding royal clothing. Rarely visited, the museum should be much more popular – the furniture chests, palanquins, shamanist items, and the wooden, leather and silk shoes for the different social classes all present vivid images of the feudal past. English descriptions are poor, but the objects are worthy of the poem that praises the museum as 'a place of wisdom, beauty and virtue' where you can 'listen to the thousand-year-old ancestors whispering quietly'.

SEODAEMUN PRISON Map pp200-1

☎ 303 9750; adult/teenager/child W1500/1000/500; ⏰ 9.30am-6pm Tue-Sun Mar-Oct, 9.30am-5pm Tue-Sun Nov-Feb; subway Line 3 to Dongnimmun, Exit 5

The prison is a stark reminder of the sufferings of Korean independence fighters who challenged Japanese colonial rule (1910–45). It contains an entrance gate, two watchtowers, a wooden execution house, interrogation cells and eight of the original 18 red-brick prison buildings. Built to house 500 prisoners, up to 3000 were packed inside during the height of the anti-Japanese protests in 1919.

Altogether 40,000 freedom fighters passed through the entrance gate and at least 400 died or were killed inside, including Ryu Gwan-sun, an Ewha high-school student, who was tortured to death in 1920. You can see photos and videos of the harsh conditions and go inside the bleak cells of one block. Overcrowding, lack of food, beatings and torture were daily facts of life, and the interrogation cells give a vivid and nightmarish demonstration of what went on there.

The independence fighters were brave but too few to threaten Japan's brutal rule, which attempted cultural genocide – banning the Korean language and forcing Koreans to adopt Japanese names (12% refused). An English-speaking guide (☎ 017-750 8323) is usually available on Wednesday and Thursday and is useful as not everything is translated into English.

Next to the prison is **Dongnimmun Park**, the main feature of which is an impressive Western-style granite archway. Built by the Independence Club in 1898, it stands where envoys from Chinese emperors used to be officially welcomed to Seoul. This ritual symbolised Chinese suzerainty over Korea, which ended when King Gojong declared himself an emperor in 1897. The two stone pillars in front of the gate are all that remain of Yongunmun, the gate near Mohwagwan, the Guest Hall for Cherishing China, where Chinese envoys stayed on their regular visits to Seoul.

SEONNONGDAN Map pp200-1
Subway Line 1 to Jegi-dong, Exit 1

The altar is not worth visiting (it's usually locked anyway) except for one day in April (which varies with the lunar calendar) – the re-enactment of the ceremony when Joseon kings came here to pray for a good harvest.

Entrance to execution building, Seodaemun Prison (left)

A royal procession heads to the altar where food offerings are laid out in special brass containers. Musicians in red robes play traditional instruments, and after the Confucian ceremony the onlookers tuck into *seolleongtang* (beef and vegie soup, originally served to peasants) and *makgeolli* (fermented rice wine) free of charge, just as in Joseon days. From the subway exit, walk straight until you reach the notice board where you turn right. Fork right and the altar is a 300m (five-minute) walk on the right.

TTUKSEOM SEOUL FOREST Map pp200-1

☎ 3708 2588; admission free; ۞ 24hr; subway Line 2 to Ttukseom, Exit 8

This new park, a 12-minute walk from Ttukseom station (but don't confuse it with Ttukseom Resort station), is a pleasant area to walk or cycle around and enjoy a picnic or a beer in natural surroundings. The area used to be a hunting ground in Joseon times, then became a horse racing track and sports fields, but is now a regenerating forest. Among the trees and lakes are fountains, a poetic photographic exhibition on the theme of trees, and a mirror pond.

The **bicycle rental stall** (per hr W3000; ۞ 9am-10pm) behind the visitors centre at the entrance is useful if you plan to explore the further reaches of the park. The **Turri curry restaurant** (☎ 465 1194; meals W5000-9000; ۞ 10am-2am) serves Korean-style curries on a big plate and you can sit outside on a shady deck overlooking a carp-filled pond. Just a 10-minute walk from the visitors centre it's also a relaxing spot to enjoy a beer (W2700).

WAR MEMORIAL & MUSEUM Map pp200-1

☎ 709 3139; www.warmemo.co.kr; adult/child W3000/2000; ۞ 9.30am-6pm Tue-Sun; subway Line 4 or 6 to Samgakji, Exit 12

This huge museum documents the history of warfare in Korea and has a specially good section on the Korean War. It takes at least three hours to look round everything so arrive before 3pm. Only snacks are available. To try to cover this museum and the National Museum of Korea in one day is too exhausting.

Downstairs are paintings and panorama displays illustrating many fierce battles fought against invading Mongol, Japanese and Chinese armies, which focus on Korean victories. Many items are only vaguely dated, but there is a replica of one of Admiral Sun-sin's famous turtle warships.

THE FORGOTTEN WAR

During the Korean War (1950–53) 21 countries took part in the UN operation to save South Korea after it was attacked by the North, including five countries which sent medical teams. North Korean and Chinese troops suffered huge casualties, estimated at 215,000 and 400,000 killed respectively. Civilian casualties on both sides added up to two million. It was a massive conflict involving millions of troops and many desperate battles, yet it is often referred to as the 'Forgotten War' – the name of a book (and film) on the Korean War. Few people know much about the war, and many Korean War veterans feel that they have been forgotten. The Republic of Korea lost 152,279 killed in action, America 33,642, UK 1086, Turkey 724, Canada 516, Australia 332, France 269, Colombia 213, Greece 186, Thailand 130, Netherlands 124, Ethiopia 122, Philippines 112, Belgium 106, New Zealand 43, South Africa 35, Luxembourg 2 and Norway 2.

Upstairs in the museum, black-and-white documentary film footage, photos, maps and artefacts give an insight into the dramatic events of the Korean War (1950–53). The surprise 4am attack from the North (spearheaded by 240 Russian-made tanks), the build-up of UN (mainly American) forces in Busan, the daring amphibious landing at Incheon, the sweep north followed by the surprise Chinese attack all took place in 1950. It was followed by fiercely fought but fruitless battles, and a two-year stalemate that was finally ended by an armistice in 1953. On the left of the museum entrance are the names of UN soldiers killed during the war (see the boxed text, above).

Other displays cover Korea's involvement in the Vietnam War, where 4700 Koreans died. The Combat Experience Room is just that and lasts five minutes (every 30 minutes from 9.30am to 4.30pm).

Outside is more military hardware including a B52 bomber (the wings are so long that they need landing wheels on the tips), Russian-made tanks, a Cobra helicopter and missiles. Children love climbing on or into them.

Every Friday at 2pm from March to June and in October and November a military band performs, and a marching parade culminates in an awesome display of military precision and weapon twirling by an honour guard made up from the army, navy and air forces.

WORLD CUP STADIUM & MALL
Map pp198–9

☎ 2128 2002; subway Line 6 to World Cup Stadium, Exit 1

Costing US$151 million, the spectacular 64,000-seat World Cup Stadium was built to stage the opening ceremony and some of the matches of the 2002 World Cup soccer finals, which Korea cohosted with Japan. Under the stadium is CGV (☎ 1544 1122), a five-screen cinema multiplex that shows films from 10am to after midnight. Also in the mall are lots of small shops, a food court (meals W3000-9000), Starbucks (drinks W4000) and Carrefour (☺ 9.30am-midnight), a giant hypermarket with food and household goods on the lower floor. Around the stadium are large parks that have been cleverly reclaimed from landfill sites and returned to a natural state. To arrive by bicycle see p115.

OTHER NEIGHBOURHOODS SOUTH OF THE RIVER

Seoul's southerly neighbourhoods are dormitory suburbs with little of interest except for the Seoul Arts Centre and the major zoo, amusement park and art gallery complex built amid forested hillsides near the horse-racing track.

AMSA-DONG PREHISTORIC SETTLEMENT SITE Map pp198–9

☎ 3426 3867; adult/teenager/child W500/300/free; ☺ 9.30am-5.30pm Tue-Sun Mar-Oct, 9.30am-4.30pm Tue-Sun Nov-Feb; subway Line 8 to Amsa, Exit 1 (bus or taxi), Exit 4 (walking)

It's a 20-minute walk – just go straight from subway Exit 4 – or else catch a bus (No 02 or 05; W500; every 10 minutes) or taxi (W2000) to reach Korea's largest Neolithic site. Set in a park frequented by woodpeckers, you can see a thatched village of pit houses and look around the exhibition

TRANSPORT

Take the subway to the nearest stop, but then you may need to take a shuttle bus, normal bus or taxi.

Interior of Opera House, Seoul Arts Centre (right)

SEOUL ARTS CENTRE Map pp198-9

☎ 580 1300; www.sac.or.kr; subway Line 3 to Nambu Bus Terminal, Exit 5

The centre is a 600m, 10-minute walk from the subway or else you can take the frequent shuttle bus (W500). This huge arts complex includes an **Opera House**; the **Music House**; the **Hangaram Art Museum** (☎ 580 1234; admission W3000-10,000; ⏲ 11am-7pm, closed last Mon of each month), which contains three major galleries that host changing exhibitions; the **Hangaram Design Art Museum** (☎ 580 1490; www.designgallery.or.kr; admission around W3000; ⏲ 11am-7pm, closed last Mon of each month), which has worthwhile design-oriented exhibitions; and the **Seoul Calligraphy Art Museum** (☎ 580 1282; admission free-W5000; ⏲ 11am-7pm Tue-Sun).

Also part of the complex is the **Korea Film Archives**, with a cinema that sometimes shows programmes of classic Korean movies with English subtitles. The archives has film magazines from around the world and a library of books, videos and DVDs. Upstairs is an **arts library** with more books, CDs, videos and DVDs.

Clustered together next door is the **National Centre for Korean Traditional Performing Arts** (see p101) and the **Museum of Korean Traditional Music** (☎ 580 3300; admission free; ⏲ 9am-6pm Tue-Sun), which exhibits unusual musical instruments including *eo* (a wooden tiger with 27 indentations on its back that is played by passing a stick over them), *chuk* (a wooden box that is hit with a stick), *pyeongyeong* (16 stone chimes) and *pyeonjong* (16 bronze bells). Mainly Korean instruments are on show at this old-fashioned museum.

centre that has been built over the site. The 6000-year-old artefacts include pottery with comb designs – the Neolithic stone culture seems to have been remarkably uniform on different continents.

NATIONAL MUSEUM OF CONTEMPORARY ART Map pp198-9

☎ 2188 6000; www.moca.go.kr; adult/youth/child W700/300/free; ⏲ 10am-6pm Mar-Oct, 10am-5pm Nov-Feb; subway Line 4 to Seoul Grand Park, Exit 2

This large and impressive art gallery is spread over three floors and also has sculptures in the garden. The outstanding exhibit is 'The More the Better' – a 1988 installation of 1000 flickering TV screens piled up into a pagoda shape by leading Korean artist, Paik Nam-june. The gallery of figurative art includes Kim Tschang-yeol's famous drops of water while the circular international gallery has a sequinned Buddha. Make of that what you will. Other styles include abstract, minimalist and pop art, but the landscape art section is the most impressive.

Overall, the art is slightly disappointing considering the gallery is the national showcase for modern Korean artists. There always seems to be underused or wasted space, and galleries don't show the development of particular artists. The café (drinks W1500 to W2000) has a pleasant balcony area. See right for the next-door zoo and amusement park.

SEOUL GRAND PARK Map pp198-9

☎ 500 7114; www.grandpark.seoul.go.kr; adult/teenager/child Apr-Jun, Sep & Oct W3000/2000/1000 & Nov-Mar, Jul & Aug W1500/1200/700; ⏲ 9.30am-9pm Mon-Thu, 9.30am-10pm Fri-Sun; subway Line 4 to Seoul Grand Park, Exit 2

Walk straight ahead from the subway Exit 2 for five minutes and you come to a large glass building. Here you can either take a **tram train** (adult/teenager/child W600/500/400), turn right to catch the **sky chairlift** (adult/teenager/child W4500/3000/2500) or walk (10 minutes) to the entrance of **Seoul Grand Park**. Another 15-minute walk takes you to the National

Museum of Contemporary Art or to Seoul Land Amusement Park.

The excellent and extensive zoo (Seoul's best) is set among forested hillsides and families picnic along the shady banks of a stream that runs through the park. You can hike along a number of marked trails that stretch for 2km to 6km. The zoo is home to a long list of exotic creatures, including the popular African ones. A huge aviary contains cranes, swans, pelicans and other large birds, and an indoor botanic garden houses a forest of cacti, numerous orchids and carnivorous pitcher plants. Ants and swimming beetles are on display in a 'miniature creature' exhibit. An entertaining **dolphin and seal show** (adult/child W1000/300) is held at 11.30am, 1.30pm, 3pm and 4.30pm in summer but only at 1.30pm and 3pm in winter.

SEOUL LAND AMUSEMENT PARK
Map pp198-9

☎ 504 0011; www.seoulland.co.kr; adult/teenager/child W12,000/8000/7000, day pass W26,000/22,000/18,000; ⊗ 9.30am-10pm; subway Line 4 to Seoul Grand Park, Exit 2

Keep the children happy all day at Seoul's biggest and best amusement park with five themed areas, special events (the Sky Pirates show with stuntmen leaping from high-up into a small pool is heart-stopping and spectacular) and adrenalin rides – the Sky-X bungy swing, the shot drop and the two rollercoasters are wicked. See p65 for Seoul Grand Park, the extensive zoo next door, and earlier in this section for the adjacent National Museum of Contemporary Art.

1 *Cheonggye stream (p19)*
2 *Yeouido, with 63 Building (p56)
on the right* 3 *Jongno Tower
(p26), Insadong* 4 *World Cup
Stadium (p64)*

1 *Jogyesa (p53), Insadong*
2 *Pagoda in Tapgol Park (p52), Gwanghwamun* **3** *Changdeokgung (p48), Gwanghwamun* **4** *Bosingak (p52), Insadong*

正八品
正九品

eyongbokgung (p49),
anghwamun **2** Palace
rd at Deoksugung
4), Myeong-dong
aper lanterns celebrating
dha's birthday (p9)

1 *Street-stall food (p91), Insadong*
2 *Herbs, spices and tea at Gyeongdong market (p122)*
3 *Noryangjin fish market (p126), south of Yeouido* **4** Gujeolpan, *a royal dish served at Korea House (p92), near Myeong-dong*

1 *Traditional dancer at Sanchon restaurant (p90), Insadong*
2 *Gogung restaurant (p89), Insadong* 3 *Rice cakes at Jilsiru Tteok Café (p89), Insadong*
4 *Namdaemun market (p123), near Myeong-dong*

1 *Galleria department store (p127), Gangnam* **2** *Noraebang (karaoke; p103) performance, Gangnam* **3** *Musicians at Once in a Blue Moon (p110), Apgujeong*

1 *Mr Guitar at Marronnier Park (p101), Daehangno* **2** *Nightlife in Seoul (p104)* **3** *Dancers at Korea House (p101), near Myeong-dong* **4** *Party-goers at Bahia nightclub (p111), Hongik*

1 *Traditional teashop (p107), Insadong* 2 *Namsan Hanok Village (p55), near Myeong-dong* 3 *The changing of the guard at Deoksugung (p54), Myeong-dong*

Walking Tours

Walking Tours

URBAN WALKS

Walking around Seoul is generally not that great. Hurry-hurry pedestrians who knock into you, numerous intersections that slow progress and an unattractive urban landscape that's a jungle of tile-covered concrete, glass, signage, power lines, neon and traffic, mean that taking the subway or a taxi or is the best way to get around (except for short distances). An exception is the walk along the newly revealed and beautified Cheonggye stream that used to be covered by a road but now runs for nearly 6km through the heart of Seoul from Sejongno to beyond Dongdaemun market. It features fountains, Joseon stone bridges and massive tile artworks. The first two easy downtown walks below explore interesting neighbourhoods near palaces, while the other two head uphill for a magpie's-eye view of the city.

AROUND DEOKSUGUNG WALK

Take subway Line 1 or 2 to **City Hall station** and leave by Exit 1. Turn right and then go left along Deoksugung wall. It's a pleasant walk with shady trees and little traffic. After five minutes, **Seoul Museum of Art 1** (p56) on the left is worth a visit. The nearby **Chungdong Methodist Church 2** was built in 1898 and is the oldest Protestant church in Seoul.

Carry on straight ahead and on the right is **Chongdong Theatre 3** (p100), which puts on traditional music, song and dance shows. The well-known **Todam Teashop 4** (p107) has a rustic interior and sells lots of teas including alcoholic ones and *sipjeon daebotang,* a tea with 13 medicinal ingredients.

Continuing along the road, turn right at the sign for a short detour to **Nanta Theatre 5,** (p101), where the long-running musical *Nanta* has proved popular. At the end of the road is a white tower, which is all that remains of the **Russian Legation Building 6** where King Gojong sought refuge for a year in 1896.

Back on the main road is a budget restaurant **Gimbapgwamandusai 7** (p92) and the **Star Six Cinema** and the **Tokebi Storm Theatre 8** (p102). Turn left at the main road for a short detour to the brand new **Agriculture Museum 9** (p54). Walk back to the cinema and cross over the main

Seoul Museum of Art (p56)

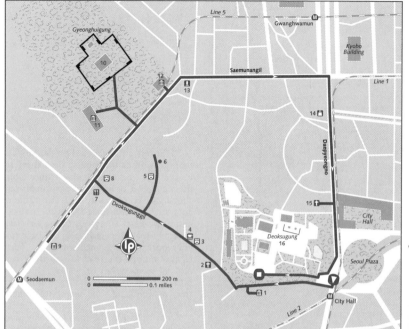

road to Heunghwamun, a traditional gate, in front of **Gyeonghuigung 10** (p50), a palace (admission free) that has been only partially rebuilt. On the left is the **Seoul Museum of Arts Annexe 11** (p52).

Next door is the **Seoul Museum of History 12** (p52), which focuses on Joseon-dynasty Seoul but will only interest die-hard history buffs. From here cross over the road to the moving giant statue of a **Hammering Man 13** (p50). Walk down to Sejongno and turn right for **Donghwa duty-free shop 14** (p119). Also on the right is the **Anglican Church 15** (p54), one of Seoul's few Renaissance-style Asian fusion buildings. Finally, if you have the energy, take a look round **Deoksugung 16** (p54) or leave it for another day.

WALK FACTS

Start Subway Line 1 or 2 to City Hall station, Exit 1

End Deoksugung

Distance 2km

Time 3 hours

Fuel stop Todam Teashop, Gimbapgwamandusai Restaurant

BETWEEN THE PALACES WALK

This walk is shaded by trees most of the way, avoids crossing major roads and covers a conservation area that is filling up with intriguing shops, galleries and small museums (although many close on Monday). It's like Insadong but more upmarket and less swarming with tourists.

Leave Anguk subway station via Exit 1 and turn right along the main road until you reach **Dongsipjagak 1**, an old Joseon-era watchtower. Turn right and pop into **Seoul Selection Bookshop 2** (p119) and **Beomyeonsa 3**, an unusual Buddhist temple with a shrine on the 3rd floor of a modern concrete building. Further on are **Gallery Hyundai 4**, **Jewel Button 5** (p119), **Kumho Museum of Art 6** and **Kukje Gallery 7**.

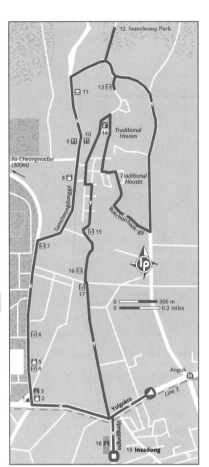

WALK FACTS

Start Subway Line 3 to Anguk station, Exit 1

End Insadong-gil

Distance 3½km

Time 3 hours

Fuel stop Samcheong-dong Sujebi, Solmoemaeul, Sipjeon Daebotang Teashop

At the fork either take a short detour (less than 1km) by carrying on straight ahead to look at the presidential Blue House from the main road, or fork right past small craft shops such as **Gypsy 8** (p119), and restaurants such as **Samcheong-dong Sujebi 9** (p88) and **Solmoemaeul 10** (p88). **Sipjeon Daebotang Teashop 11** (p107) specialises in red-bean *juk* (rice porridge) and medicinal teas. Turn right and cross the road to visit the green oasis of **Samcheong Park 12**, where a short 15-minute loop walk takes you through attractive woodland. The spring water here is popular.

Cross back over the road to look round one lady's magnificent obsession, the one-room **Owl Museum 13** with 2000 owl objects at the last count. Then walk down the hill to Bukchonhanok-gil on your right. Follow this alley through a quiet neighbourhood of traditional *yangban* (aristocrat) houses hiding behind high walls. At the end of the alley (building number two faces you) turn left and walk uphill. At the top is a splendid **viewpoint 14** of tiled rooftops that hasn't changed much in the past 100 years. The *yangban* monopolised this auspicious suburb between the palaces while the poor lived in thatched houses south of Jongno.

At the next junction turn right, and then left at the red-brick public bath chimney. Turn left again at the end of this alley and on your left is the new **World Jewellery Museum** (**15**; adult W5000; 10am-7pm Tue-Sun), which proves with some well-lit displays that small is beautiful. Further on is the **Tibet Museum** (**16**; adult W5000; 10am-7pm), which has a small but interesting collection of Tibetan items and Chinese teapots.

At the crossroads is **Art Sonje Centre 17**, another well-known art gallery with an Indian restaurant inside. At the main road, turn left for Anguk subway station or cross over the road to visit **Jogyesa 18** (p53) and **Insadong 19** (p52).

INWANGSAN SHAMANIST HILLSIDE WALK

On this short, but uphill, walk you can see Seoul's most famous shamanist shrine, visit small Buddhist temples and see part of the Seoul fortress wall. The walk only takes an hour if you just want a quick look but it's sensible to take longer and soak up the unique atmosphere.

From subway Exit 2 turn down the first small alley on your left. Walk uphill past the golf driving range and grocery shops for 10 minutes, and you should see a colourful **temple gateway 1** on your left. Walk through it to the large notice board.

Turn left to walk around the **village 2** where small Buddhist temples and traditional wooden houses cling to the rocky hillside, suspended high above the concrete city. The temples have colourful murals on the outside walls of birds and blossom, and wind chimes clink in the breeze.

Back on the main path, a bronze bell marks the entrance to **Bongwonsa 3**, the largest of the temples. The paintings on the entrance gate doors depict the guardian kings of heaven who protect Buddhists from evil and harm. The shrine hall has five golden Buddha statues and a side shrine for the three main shamanist deities – Sansin (mountain god), Dokseong (river god) and Chilseong (the seven stars of the Big Dipper). Buddhism and shamanism have coexisted peacefully in Korea for over 1500 years.

Carry on up the steps to Seoul's most famous shamanist shrine, **Guksadang 4**. It was originally built on Namsan by order of King Taejo, the founder of the Joseon dynasty, who established Seoul as Korea's capital. But in 1925 Guksadang was demolished by the Japanese, so Korean shamanists secretly rebuilt it on Inwangsan. The shrine is small but many of the paintings inside are historic and valuable, and the altar is often loaded with offerings of food for the spirits – rice cakes, fruit, meat and a pig's head. Shamanists believe that the dead still need food and drink. Natural springs in the area provide fresh water.

Walk left and up some steps to the extraordinary **Zen rocks** (Seonbawi) **5**, which look like a Salvador Dali painting – two large rocks have been so eroded that they look like two robed monks. At the altar in front of the rocks, women still come to pray for a son.

The hillside above is full of eroded rocks that create an eerie atmosphere. In front of small crevices are candles, incense sticks and offerings of sweets for the spirits. Climb up the hill for 10 minutes and you reach an **exercise trail 6** and after another 10 minutes you reach an outdoor altar with a small **Buddha rock carving 7** on the left. Turn right here to see other makeshift altars including a **Sansin statue 8**. Carry on to look at the renovated **Seoul fortress wall 9** before heading back to Guksadang.

People have been visiting this sacred area for thousands of years. One rock embodies the spirit of a famous general, while another is where children's spirits shelter. Shamanists perform their ceremonies under the

WALK FACTS

Start Subway Line 3 to Dongnimmun station, Exit 2

End Dongnimmun station, Exit 2

Distance 2km, or 5km if you climb Inwangsan

Time 1½ hours, or 3 hours if you climb Inwangsan

Fuel Stop Take a picnic

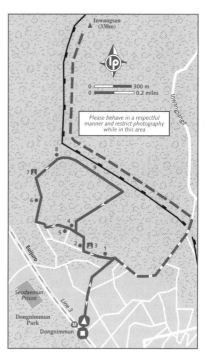

Please behave in a respectful manner and restrict photography while in this area

A shamanist deity

SHAMANIST CEREMONIES

Ceremonies called *gut* usually take place outdoors. They involve contacting departed spirits, which are attracted by music, chanting, waving flags and lavish offerings of food and drink. During some *gut* drums beat and the *mudang* (female shamanist priest) dances herself into a frenzied state that allows her to communicate with the spirits and be possessed by them. Another *gut* helps to guide the spirit of a recently departed person to find peace. Resentments felt by the dead can haunt and plague the living and cause them all sorts of misfortune, so upset or angry spirits need placating. For shamanists death does not end relationships, they simply take another form. Smartly dressed couples come to Guksadang shamanist shrine to ask for good fortune with a business project, make contact with a deceased relative or cure an illness (see p12).

shade of the trees – an old lady is bowing and waving five different coloured flags to attract the spirits, and a young girl is drumming and meditating. You can sense the ancient atmosphere here, even though the traffic and the modern world is only a 20-minute walk away. All visitors should treat the area and the people with respect, and remember that taking a photograph could interfere with an important ceremony.

At the temple gateway you can walk on and hike along the other side of the fortress wall up to the top of Inwangsan. Slogging up the steps takes less than an hour. The walk can also be combined with a visit to Seodaemun Prison (p62), which is on the other side of the main road.

NAMSAN & SEOUL TOWER WALK

It's uphill all the way but the view from the top is worth the climb.

Take subway Line 1 or 4 to Seoul Station and leave by Exit 10. Walk up the steps and turn right towards the Hilton Hotel, then take the first left towards the **multistorey car park** 1. From there turn right up the steps and into and through the small hillside park. At the **Millennium Seoul Hilton** 2 (p136), go right and walk round to the front of the hotel. Cross the road, bear left, cross the second road, and go up the steps into the park.

Walk past the children's playground and the old men playing Korean chess, cross the road and go up more steps. Keep going straight and cross another road. Go up yet more steps. Here you will see a **statue of Kim Koo** 3 (1876–1949), a Korean independence fighter who led a very eventful life. Ahead is a **statue of Lee Si-yeong** 4 (1869–1953), another independence movement leader. Cross the road and up more steps. On the left is **Seoul Science Park** (5; admission free; 🕙 10am-5pm Mon-Fri), a rabbit warren of a children's science museum. On the right is the **Ahn Junggeun Museum** (6; adult W1000; 🕙 9am-5pm Mon-Fri), which displays the life of another independence hero.

Seoul Tower (right), Namsan

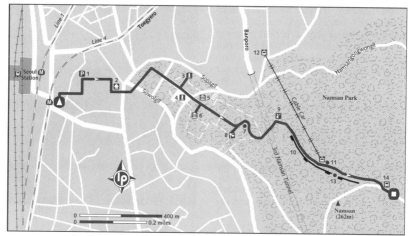

From here walk to the **indoor botanical garden** (7; adult/teenager/child W500/300/200) and on the right is a **mini zoo** (8; admission free), with some birds and animals in cages.

The walk up Namsan begins to the left of the indoor botanical garden. On the way is a **lookout deck** 9, part of the **Seoul fortress wall** 10 and some Joseon-era **signal beacons** 11. If you don't want to walk up, take the **cable car** (12; adult/child one way W4800/3000, return W6300/4000; ⏰ 10am-11pm). It takes less than 30 minutes to walk up the steps to **Seoul Tower** 13 (p56).

WALK FACTS

Start Subway Line 1 or 4 to Seoul station, Exit 10

End Seoul Tower; yellow bus No 2

Distance 1½km

Time 1-2 hours

Fuel stop Seoul Tower restaurants or take a picnic

Just 50m past the Seoul Tower is the stop for **yellow bus No 2** (14; W500, every 10 minutes, 8am to midnight), which runs to Namsangol Hanok Village, the National Theatre of Korea and back to Seoul Tower. Pick up the yellow No 2 bus by Exit 4 of Chungmuro station (Line 3 or 4) if you want to take the bus up to Seoul Tower and then walk down.

MOUNTAIN HIKES

One of the main reasons that Joseon's first king selected Seoul as his capital was that the city is surrounded by mountains. Back in those early days defence was the primary consideration and besides Seoul's long fortress wall, other fortresses were built in the mountains to the north at Baekundae (now part of Bukhansan National Park) and to the south in Namhansan. These days the fortresses attract hikers who come to see these historical monuments and enjoy a day in the forest-covered mountains that are located so conveniently close to Seoul. Fresh air, natural surroundings, countryside food and outdoor exercise combine to lure jolly crowds into the mountains every day of the year. If your energy flags, take a shot of the hiker's friend, pine-needle *soju* (vodka), and it should power you to the top.

BUKHANSAN NATIONAL PARK

Straddling the northern border of Seoul is this **national park** (Map p216; ☎ 909 0497; www. npa.or.kr; adult/teenager/child W1600/600/300; ⏰ 7.30am-6pm). Seoul is lucky to have such a great hiking area that can be reached so easily by subway. The park features forests, rivers, Buddhist temples and many rocky peaks over 700m. Hiking is such a popular activity in Seoul that it is best to avoid weekends and the hordes of well-equipped hikers toiling to the summits. Seoulites are the world's best-dressed hikers – check out those red waistcoats, black ninja outfits and Darth Vader sunvisors. Basic hiking huts *(sanjang)* are available. The national park receives over four million visitors annually and to reduce environmental damage, footpaths are closed in rotation, but alternative routes are always open. The ticket booths sell a detailed hiking map (mostly in Korean) for W1000. The following all-day hikes are recommended, the first in the north of the park and the second in the southern section.

Baekundae (opposite), Bukhansan National Park

Dobongsan Hike

This is the most popular hike and is easy to reach as it is within walking distance of the subway station. The hike is cool and shady but moderate fitness is required.

Take subway Line 1 or 7 north to Dobongsan station (don't get off at the previous station, Dobong). Follow the nattily dressed Korean hikers across the main road and up through the long lines of hiking-equipment shops and food stalls. The best restaurants are near the ticket office under the trees and overlooking a stream, and one sells four-colour tofu. It's a 15 minute walk to the ticket office.

Dobongsan has three peaks clustered together – Seoninbong (선인봉, 708m), Manjangbong (만장봉, 718m) and Jaunbong (자운봉, 739m) – so follow signs that indicate any of these peaks.

On the main path, follow the sign to Jaunbong, 2.7km away. Five minutes past the spring, turn right, following the sign to Manjangbong. Keep a look out for woodpeckers and squirrels.

About an hour from the subway station, you arrive at **Dobong Hut** 1. Bear right following the sign to Mangwolsa, then follow the signs to **Jaunbong** 2. Go past the police rescue post and up the final steep and rocky stretch to the top, which is between two rocky peaks. It's here that the adventure really begins as you scramble down a ravine (helped by metal cables), then up and along a rocky ridge and finally through some narrow crevices.

Follow the signs to the mountain temple, **Mangwolsa** 3 (망월사), and then continue down to the road, bearing left as you enter the town to reach Mangwolsa subway station for the trip home.

WALK FACTS

Start Subway Line 1 or 7 to Dobongsan station

End Mangwolsa subway station

Distance 10km

Time 5 hours

Fuel stop Restaurants near the ticket office

Baekundae Hike

Leave Gupabal station by Exit 1, walk straight for 100m to the bus stop and take bus No 704 (W900, 10 minutes, every 15 minutes) to the Bukhansanseong bus stop. Get off with the other hikers, walk straight and then turn right and the ticket office is 500m from the bus stop.

The park's highest peak, Baekundae (836m), is 4km or two hours away. A five-minute walk brings you to the **fortress wall** 1 and **Daeseomun gate** 2. The wall is 9.5km long and was made of earth in the Baekje dynasty. It was rebuilt with 13 gates and stone blocks in 1711 during the reign of King Sukjong and encircled 12 Buddhist temples and numerous wells.

Fifteen minutes after leaving the gate the road crosses a bridge. Fork left following the sign to Baekundae – keep a look out for little striped squirrels. Spring water is available at **Yaksuam** 3, a hermitage which you reach 45 minutes after leaving the road. Past Yaksu-am there are stairs up to another fortress gate and then you use metal cables to haul yourself up bare rock to **Baekundae peak** 4. Surrounded by granite cliffs and with a 360-degree view, it's a top-of-the-world feeling.

The easiest option is to return the same way, but it's more interesting to turn left on the stairs and walk along a scenic, rocky route to **Yongammun** 5, another fortress gate 35 minutes away. Then walk along the remains of the wall to **Dongjangdae** 6, a command post, and on to **Daedongmun** 7, which is 40 minutes from Yongammun.

At Daedongmun, walk down to the toilets and take the path that follows the river bed. There is no sign but the track is clear. The path goes through an attractive valley and passes three small temples, **Taegosa** 8, **Yonghaksa** 9 and **Beobyongsa** 10, to the beginning of the road, which you reach after 45 minutes. From here it is another 40 minutes back to the bus stop.

Palgakjeong (11; Map p216; ☎ 354 4440; meals W6000-11,000; 10am-9.30pm), a large restaurant at the Baekundae entrance, has plenty of indoor and outdoor seats. The side dishes are above average and the *sanchae bibimbap* (rice topped with egg, meat, mountain vegies and a chilli sauce) is crunchy and has a distinctive flavour. The free *sikhye* (rice punch) is good too. The *seonggeguk* is clam and seaweed soup.

WALK FACTS

Start Subway Line 3 to Gupabal station, Exit 1 & bus No 704 to Bukhansanseong bus stop

Finish Bukhansanseong bus stop

Distance 9km short route, 12km loop route

Time 6-7 hours

Fuel stop Palgakjeong

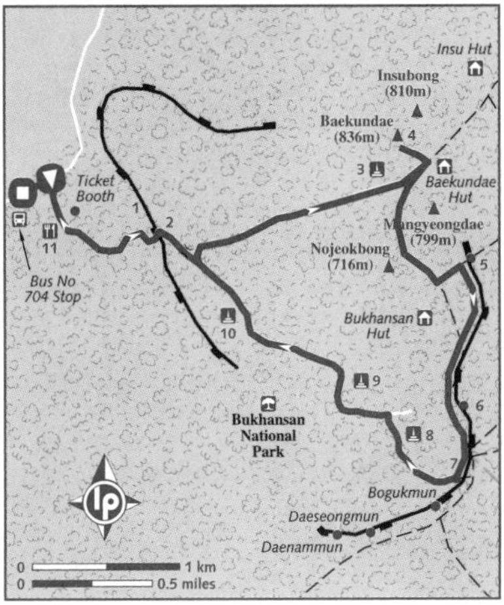

WESTERN NAMHANSANSEONG HIKE

This relatively easy hike in Namhansanseong Provincial Park, 20km southeast of the city centre, follows part of the ancient fortress wall, which is 3m to 7.5m high and stretches 9.6km (although the inner circle is only 6.5km). Completed in 1626, Namhansanseong guarded the southern entrance to Seoul, while Bukhansanseong guarded the northern approaches. It was garrisoned by tough Buddhist monks who were soldiers rather than pacifists in those days. In 1636 King Injo fled to this fortress when the Manchus invaded from China. After a siege of 45 days the king surrendered and his son was kept hostage in China for eight years.

WALK FACTS

Start Subway Line 8 to Namhansanseong

End Jungro Village; bus No 9

Distance 4½km

Time 2 hours

Fuel Stops Nammun Gadeun, Jangseong

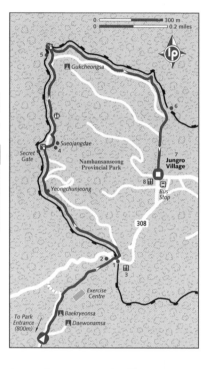

To get there, leave Namhansanseong station by Exit 1. Take any bus the short way up the road to the park entrance (Namhansanseong *ipgu*) because it's a 30-minute walk.

At the entrance is a large **handicraft shop** (☎ 749 7976; ☺ 9am-6pm Tue-Sun) on the right. An uphill walk for 30 minutes along a concrete path takes you past small temples, stone pinnacles and an exercise centre to **Nammun 1**, the South Gate. The fortress **ticket office** (**2**; adult/teenager/child W1000/600/300; ☺ 7am-8pm Apr-Oct, 9am-7pm Nov-Mar) has a free map in *hangeul* (Korean phonetic alphabet) only. Near the gate is **Nammun Gadeun (3;** ☎ 031-743 6608; meals W5000-8000; ☺ 9am-midnight), which serves up *kalguksu* (thick, handmade noodles in broth), a *pajeon* (green-onion pancake) as big as a pizza and *sanchae bibimbap*.

Walk north along the inside of the fortress wall, which soon offers extensive views as well as big butterflies and golden dragonflies in summer. After 15 minutes is **Cheongnyangdae 4**, the shrine to Yi Hoe who was executed after false accusations were made that he had embezzled funds meant for the fortress's construction. His wife and concubine both committed suicide when they heard of his execution.

Ten minutes further on is **Seomun 5** (West Gate) near another panoramic viewpoint, and further on is **Bungmun 6** (North Gate). From here you can carry on round the wall for another 4km to fully appreciate the colossal effort that went into building this huge but hard-to-defend fortress. Otherwise take a five-minute stroll down to **Jungro 7**, a village of restaurants that offers culinary adventures involving chicken, duck, wild pig, pheasant, goat, rabbit and dog meals. At **Jangseong (8;** ☎ 031-743 6600; meals for 2-3 W40,000; ☺ noon-11pm), which has funky little private rooms for diners, the *tokkitang* (a large rabbit stew with potatoes and green vegetables in a red but not too hot sauce) is recommended. It comes with interesting side dishes and is served in a big ceramic bowl that is kept warm on a table stove, with *sikhye* (rice punch) to finish.

From the bus stop near the roundabout bus No 9 (W800, 10 minutes, every 15 minutes) can drop you near Namhansanseong subway station.

Eating

Eating

Eating out every night is a common habit for Seoulites, so with thousands of restaurants scattered throughout every neighbourhood, there is no problem finding somewhere to eat. Small unpretentious Korean restaurants serve up local food at reasonable prices, and restaurants serving Italian and Japanese food are numerous. Western-style fast-food outlets are everywhere.

Most Korean-style restaurants offer a table and chairs option; but in some traditional restaurants customers must sit on floor cushions at low tables. Few restaurant staff speak any English, but most restaurants have some English on the menu or else pictures or plastic replicas of the meals they offer. Menus are often spelled inconsistently – consonants such as 'ch' and 'j', 'p' and 'b', 'l' and 'r' and 'k' and 'g' are often mixed up; so you might find 'bibimbap' spelled 'pipimpab'.

Italian food is super popular in Seoul – not just pizza chains but numerous small pasta restaurants, which serve reasonably authentic meals although often with a touch of fusion somewhere. These days pasta and pizza are more common than *bulgogi* (barbecued beef slices and lettuce wrap) and *bibimbap* (rice, egg, meat and vegies with chilli sauce).

Lotteria is the local version of Western-style fast food, and offers *bulgogi, bulgalbi* and *kimchi* burgers. Many Japanese-style restaurants serve sushi or inexpensive cutlet, salad and soup sets. Budget Chinese restaurants cook up fried rice and *jajangmyeon* (noodles in a black bean sauce), a Chinese dish never seen outside Korea. Luxury hotels have upmarket and more genuine Chinese food.

Thai, Indian, Middle Eastern and other authentic ethnic restaurants are clustered in Itaewon, although a brave few are scattered elsewhere. Fusion restaurants usually provide an American/Italian menu with an Asian twist, such as spaghetti with red chilli sauce and octopus. The possibilities are endless – anyone for *beondegi* (silk worm larvae) pizza or *kimchi* Caesar salad? Drop into any department store or high-rise shopping mall to find a floor of inexpensive restaurants as well as a reasonably priced food court. For dessert, pick one of the countless ice-cream or yogurt parlours.

In Seoul, eating out (like everything else) is a group activity and you don't see many people dining alone. Some Korean meals, such as *bulgogi, galbi* (beef ribs), *jjimdak* (spicy chicken pieces with noodles) or *Hanjeongsik* (a banquet) are not usually available for just one person.

Fill children up with *jajangmyeon, donkkaseu* (pork cutlet with rice and salad), *juk* (rice porridge), barbecue chicken, sandwiches, bakery items, *hotteok* (a kind a pita bread with cinnamon and honey filling) and ice creams.

Some food fads fade fast – a few years ago bubble tea was all the rage, but now it's almost disappeared, and the 'wellbeing' wave has swept in with restaurants proclaiming the health benefits of real fruit juice, yogurt and ginseng rice porridge.

Opening Hours
Like the shops, most restaurants open every day, usually from late morning until 9pm or 10pm, but since times do vary opening times are given for every restaurant. Night owls can always find food as some eateries open 24 hours a day, 365 days a year.

How Much?
Cheap Eats in the following listings cover restaurants where meals are W6000 or less. Royal court cuisine usually starts at W30,000, while *Hanjeongsik* banquets vary in price depending on what is included and

UNBEATABLE BUFFETS
- Eunhasu Buffet – Sejong Hotel (p92)
- Familia Buffet – Imperial Palace Hotel (p97)
- Plaza Fountain Buffet – 63 Building (p97)

SAMPLE KOREAN CUISINE

Department stores usually have a supermarket in the basement where staff offer, and even cook, free samples of food for customers to try. You can taste tofu, umpteen types of *kimchi* and greens, *pajeon* (green-onion pancake), sesame soup, shellfish, rice porridge, ginseng soup, dumplings, grilled eel, acorn jelly, gingko nuts as well as unusual drinks such as aloe and cactus flower. Just pop into a Hyundai department store at COEX (Map pp214–15), Sinchon (Map p210) or Apgujeong (Map p211) to enjoy a feast of flavoursome Korean nibbles offered with a smile.

range from W12,000 to W50,000 or more. Typical mains at Western restaurants cost W20,000 but expect to pay W30,000 at top hotels. *Bulgogi* and *galbi* are both beef and at W15,000 to W20,000 per person cost more than *samgyeopsal* (barbecued bacon-type pork), *jjimdak* and *samgyetang* (ginseng chicken soup), which are pork or chicken dishes that usually cost around W10,000 per person, although plain barbecued or fried chicken is around W5000.

Bibimbap, *naengmyeon* (chewy buckwheat noodles in an icy, sweetish broth, with vegies and hard-boiled egg on top), tofu, *sujebi* (dough flakes in shellfish broth), *bindaetteok* (mung bean pancake) and soups are usually around W5000 as are most food-court meals. *Mandu* (filled dumplings), *ramyeon* (instant noodle soup), *tteokbokki* (rice cakes in a sweet and spicy sauce) and *gimbap* (Korean sushi) are the cheapest food at W2000. Convenience store sandwiches are W1400 and *samgak gimbap* (triangular sushi) is W700.

Booking Tables

It is not necessary to book tables unless you want your own private room or are in a large group. Telephone numbers are given but few restaurants can find anyone who speaks English so ask your hotel receptionist to make the booking for you.

Tipping

Tipping is not a Korean custom and is not expected. Restaurants catering to wealthy businessmen and in top-end hotels may add 21% to the bill (10% service charge and 10% VAT).

Self-Catering

Small convenience stores, such as Mini Stop, 7-Eleven, Buy The Way, GS25 and Family Mart, are never more than a few hundred metres apart. They open long hours, usually all day and night. Pop into one whenever you want a drink, a breakfast snack or a quick and easy lunch. Bakeries are almost as ubiquitous. Huckle-berry Farms (p127) in Apgujeong sells organic food and drinks.

Department store basements and the two Lotte Marts (p120 and p128) house supermarkets.

Other supermarkets:

Itaewon Supermarket (Map p209; ☎ 794 5114; below King's Club, Sobangseo-gil; ☺ 9am-midnight; subway Line 6 to Itaewon, Exit 3)

Koryo Supermarket (Map pp202-3; ☎ 737 9994; ☺ 9am-9pm Mon-Sat; subway Line 5 to Gwanghwamun, Exit 7)

Vegetarian feast

GWANGHWAMUN

While Insadong is Seoul's top restaurant patch, other downtown areas have some fine restaurants too.

ANJIP Map pp202-3   Korean
☎ 3672 7070; meals W8000-15,000; ☻ noon-10pm Mon-Sat; subway Line 3 to Anguk, Exit 2
Sit on embroidered cushions in your own traditional-style private room and order *siksa* (budget-priced banquet), which includes 20 dishes at a budget price. The *bulgogi*, spicy cockles and steamed egg are particularly good and fruit and cinnamon tea finish the feast off nicely.

CHILGAPSAN Map pp202-3   Korean
칠갑산; ☎ 730 7754; meals W5000-15,000; ☻ noon-10pm; subway Line 1 to Jonggak, Exit 2
The specialty in this convivial restaurant is the excellent *neobiani* (너비아니), a beef patty the size of a small pizza, which is meant for sharing and comes with a dressed green salad and crunchy side dishes. You could try *pajeon* (green-onion pancake) with it or *doenjang bibimbap* – salad with rice and soybean paste sauce. Even the barley tea is good. The décor is rustic/artistic and you sit on the floor at a log table. It has no English signs – look for a white frontage covered with ivy.

HOEJEONCHOBAP Map pp202-3 Japanese Sushi
☎ 735 1748; saucers W2500; ☻ 11.30am-2pm, 4.30-9pm; subway Line 5 to Gwanghwamun, Exit 8
Squeeze yourself into this tiny conveyor-belt sushi joint to enjoy Japanese-style raw fish items. It's expensive but this is downtown and not a student area.

SAMCHEONG-DONG SUJEBI
Map pp202-3   Korean
☎ 735 2965; meals W5000-10,000; ☻ noon-9pm; subway Line 3 to Anguk, Exit 1
A no-frills, no-nonsense restaurant that is famous for its *sujebi*, big dough flakes in a non-spicy soup of sliced vegetables and shellfish.

SOLMOEMAEUL Map pp202-3   Korean
☎ 720 0995; meals W10,000-22,000; ☻ 11am-9pm; subway Line 3 to Anguk, Exit 1
Sit on the floor or on chairs on the narrow balcony to enjoy an excellent multicourse

TOP FIVE RESTAURANTS

- Nolboojip (p94)
- Sanchon (p90)
- Gogung (opposite)
- Solmoemaeul (left)
- Baekje Samgyetang (p91)

meal for W16,000. Sweet pumpkin gruel, raw tuna, *pajeon*, decent *bulgogi* and a royal cuisine *gujeolpan* with radish pancakes all arrive before the main dish, which is followed by a cup of traditional tea. It's a bit out of the way and not usually crowded.

TONY ROMA'S Map pp202-3   Western Grill
☎ 2122 2650; Hungkuk Bldg; meals W11,000-30,000; ☻ 11.30am-11pm; subway Line 5 to Gwanghwamun, Exit 6
Ribs, grills, burgers, salads and beer are the popular items at this American chain.

YONGSUSAN Map pp202-3   Korean
☎ 771 5553; B1 Seoul Finance Centre; meals W22,000-52,000, set meals from W41,800; ☻ noon-10pm; subway Line 1 or 2 to City Hall, Exit 4
This stylish traditional restaurant is colourfully decorated with mother-of-pearl panels and serving staff wear *hanbok* (traditional Korean clothing). The food contains elements of royal cuisine and varies with the seasons but is always interesting from the dragon firepot to the five-grain rice cooked in bamboo and the always delicious *omijacha* tea.

CHEAP EATS
HUNGKUK FOOD COURT
Map pp202-3   Korean & Global
Hungkuk Bldg; meals W4000-7000; ☻ 11am-8pm; subway Line 5 to Gwanghwamun, Exit 6
Eat Chinese, Korean, Japanese or Western at this smart but inexpensive food court in the basement of the Hungkuk Bldg next to the Hammering Man statue.

HYANGNAMUSEGEURU Map pp202-3 Korean
☎ 720 9524; meals W5000-10,000; ☻ 10am-11pm; subway Line 3 to Anguk, Exit 1
This recently renovated 2nd floor restaurant is surrounded by trees. Ask for *moksal-*

sogeumgui (W6000), which is pork barbecued at your table that you wrap in lettuce
with sauces and side dishes.

JILSIRU TTEOK CAFÉ

Map pp202-3   Korean Rice Cakes

☎ 741 6521; www.kfr.or.kr; rice cakes W1000-3500;
🕑 10am-9pm Mon-Sat, 10am-7pm Sun; subway
Line 1, 3 or 5 to Jongno 3-ga, Exit 6
The gourmet rice cakes are small but lovingly
made – try the apple flower and chocolate
ones. Traditional teas are W5000. Upstairs
from the café is a **museum** (admission W3000;
🕑 10am-5pm Mon-Sat, noon-5pm Sun)
with displays of 50 types of rice cakes with
all their different colours, flavourings, shapes
and sizes and the utensils to make them. See
p164 for rice-cake cooking classes.

JONGNO BINDAETTEOK

Map pp202-3   Korean

☎ 737 1857; meals W6000; 🕑 noon-2am; subway
Line 5 to Gwanghwamun, Exit 8
Don't let the scruffy décor put you off – the
crispy seafood (haemul) and meat (gogi)
bindaetteok are both great, and made from
freshly-ground mung beans.

WITCH'S TABLE Map pp202-3   Deli

☎ 732 2727; drinks & snacks W2500-6500;
🕑 8am-10pm Mon-Fri, 8am-8pm Sat; subway Line
5 to Gwanghwamun, Exit 7
Join the witches opposite the Koryo Supermarket in this narrow sandwich bar with
soft music. It dispenses fine bagels, salads
and toasted sandwiches along with teas,
coffees, wines and beers.

INSADONG

Insadong is home to a host of traditional-
style restaurants that dish up old-fashioned,
hometown Korean food. Hanjeongsik restaurants offer a banquet of items so you
can try many Korean dishes (especially
side dishes) at one sitting. There are also a
number of vegetarian restaurants, including one that serves Buddhist temple food.

DIMIBANG Map p205   Korean Vegetarian

☎ 720 2417; meals W5000-30,000; 🕑 noon-10pm
Mon-Sat; subway Line 3 to Anguk, Exit 6
This sit-on-floor-cushions vegetarian res-
taurant features hamcho (a salty green

herb that grows near the sea) and other
medicinal herbs that are in the food, teas
and alcoholic drinks. Order hamcho sujebi,
hamcho bibimbap or a set meal.

GOGUNG Map p205   Korean

☎ 736 3211; meals W8000-32,000; 🕑 11.30am-
9.30pm; subway Line 3 to Anguk, Exit 6
In the basement of Ssamziegil is this un-
usually smart and stylish restaurant, with
live gayageum (12-stringed zither) and
drum music (no microphones) between
7pm and 8pm on week nights. It specialises
in Jeonju bibimbap, which is fresh and garnished with nuts, but contains raw minced
beef. If that puts you off, choose the dolsot
bibimbap (served in a stone hotpot). Both
come with side dishes including bean-
sprout soup and a sesame and rice-cake
gruel. Another Jeonju speciality is moju, a
sweet and very thick cinnamon alcoholic
drink (W1500 a bowl) – you must try it! Also
on the menu is an 11-dish royal banquet.

INSADONG SUJEBI Map p205   Korean

☎ 735 5481; meals W4000-10,000;
🕑 11am-9.30pm; subway Line 3 to Anguk, Exit 6
Famous for sujebi, big dough flakes in a potato, seaweed and seafood broth, this rustic
barn also serves up naeng-kongguksu, chewy
noodles in cold soya milk, a popular summer
dish, and oyster pajeon. Kimchi lovers can
enjoy helping themselves from a large pot.

JUK 1001 IYAGI Map p205   Korean Rice Porridge

☎ 733 2587; Insadong 6-gil; meals W5000-10,000;
🕑 8am-10pm Mon-Sat, 9am-9pm Sun; subway
Line 3 to Anguk, Exit 6
The plain, unpretentious surroundings
reflect the food. A large bowl of excellent
chicken and ginseng rice porridge is served
with four side dishes and is flavoured with

SIX OF THE BEST

- Best tofu: Dolkemaeul Tofu House (p91)
- Best bindaetteok (mung bean pancake): Jongno
  Bindaetteok (left)
- Best neobiani (large minced patty): Chilgapsan
  (opposite)
- Best sujebi (dough flakes in shellfish broth):
  Samcheong-dong Sujebi (opposite)
- Best juk (rice porridge): Juk 1001 Iyagi (above)
- Best food court: Techno Mart (p98)

plenty of varied ingredients. There are 19 other options packed with healthy, natural ingredients.

MIN'S CLUB Map p205   Western Fusion

☎ 733 2966; off Insadong-gil; meals W20,000-54,000; ☣ noon-2.30pm, 6-11.30pm; subway Line 3 to Anguk, Exit 6

This classy restaurant housed in a beautifully restored 1930s *hanok* (traditional Korean one-storey wooden house with a tiled roof) offers European/Korean fusion food (more European than Korean) and specialises in French wines under the guidance of sommelier Cho Yun-joo. Popular in diplomatic circles, diners leave happy.

SADONG MYEONOK Map p205   Korean

☎ 735 7393; Insadong 5-gil; meals W5000-9000; ☣ 10am-10.30pm; subway Line 3 to Anguk, Exit 6

A busy, no-frills restaurant that serves deservedly popular *manduguk jeongsik,* which consists of four giant homemade dumplings, containing 10 different ingredients, that are served in soup with side dishes. Other options include a sweet *bulgogi jeongsik* (*bulgogi* with side dished) hotpot, *naengmyeon* and oxtail soup. *Soju* (local vodka) and beer are W3000.

SANCHON Map p205   Korean Vegetarian

☎ 735 0312; off Insadong-gil; lunch sets W20,000, dinner sets W35,000; ☣ 11am-10pm; subway Line 3 to Anguk, Exit 6

This very famous and atmospheric restaurant owned by ex-monk Kim Yun-sik offers genuine vegetarian Buddhist temple food. Relax on floor cushions in a soothing ambience of flute music, candlelight and Buddhist art. Lunch and dinner offer the same set meal of 16 small dishes that include seasonal soups, mountain vegetables, *pajeon,* wild sesame porridge and medicinal tea. The marinades, glazes, sauces and seasoning are unique and traditional dancers put on a show at 8.15pm.

SEOJEONG RESTAURANT Map p205   Korean

☎ 735 8811; off Insadong-gil; Hanjeongsik W10,000; ☣ noon-3pm, 7-10pm; subway Line 3 to Anguk, Exit 6

Tucked away off the beaten track, this traditional restaurant serves up a budget-priced banquet of 14 dishes in your own private room, which is decked out with

scrolls, ceramics and paper-screen doors. Sit on legless chairs or cushions and enjoy *japchae* (stir-fried noodles and vegies), *pajeon,* beans, anchovies, chives and pickled walnuts, fish, rice, salad, two soups and all sorts of other vegetables.

SOSIM Map p205   Korean

☎ 734 4388; meals W7000-20,000; ☣ 11.30am-9.30pm Mon-Sat; subway Line 3 to Anguk, Exit 6

A small, rustic, home-cooking basement restaurant serves mainly vegetarian meals, including organic rice, teas that take a year to make, and side dishes such as boiled peanuts. The set meals are best and can include mushroom soup, fish or *pajeon*. The helpful owner speaks some English.

TOP CLOUD RESTAURANT & BAR

Map p205   Western

☎ 2230 3000; www.topcloud.co.kr; Jongno Tower; meals W40,000-70,000; ☣ noon-midnight; subway Line 1 to Jonggak, Exit 3

Up on the top floor of Jongno Tower, this classy French-style restaurant, noted for its steaks, offers knock-out views of the city, especially at night. The black-clad staff are well-trained and speak English. Come here for a special treat. You can just pop in for a drink (beer W9350, cocktails W14,300, coffee W12,100) and enjoy the romantic night view and the live jazz (nightly at 7.30pm and 11.30pm, except Monday).

Sanchon (left), Insadong

WORLD FOOD COURT

Map p205   Korean & Fusion

B1 Jongno Tower; meals W4000-10,000;
🕑 11am-10pm; subway Line 1 to Jonggak, Exit 3
Fusion food is the theme here, mainly big platters of it, and the **Hite draught beer corner** (🕑 2-9.30pm; 300/500mL W1200/1800) serves about the cheapest beer in Seoul.

CHEAP EATS

CROWN BAKERY Map p205   Bakery
Insadonggil; snacks W800-2000; 🕑 7am-11pm;
subway Line 3 to Anguk, Exit 6
This sweet-smelling bakery is busy all day and has a few tables and chairs inside where you can down a coffee (W3000) with your cake of choice.

DOLKEMAEUL TOFU HOUSE

Map p205   Korean Tofu
☎ 722 8586; Insadonggil; meals W6000;
🕑 11am-11pm; subway Line 3 to Anguk, Exit 6
The star of the show is the excellent *sundubu,* uncurdled tofu, which is cooked in a stone pot, and served with hotpot rice, soup and six side dishes including grilled fish. Add the egg to the *sundubu,* spoon the rice into the small ceramic bowls provided, and pour the hot water from the kettle into the rice hotpot to make scorched-rice tea.

HOTTEOK STALLS Map p205   Korean Snacks
Ujeonggungno; snacks W500-700; subway Line 3 to Anguk, Exit 6
Two types of *hotteok* can be found at these stalls – a fat, flat one with a cinnamon and honey paste inside and a ball-shaped one with red-bean paste inside.

JILSIRU TTEOK CAFÉ

Map p205   Korean Rice Cakes
☎ 733 5477; Insadong-gil; rice cakes W1500-3500;
🕑 10am-9pm; subway Line 3 to Anguk, Exit 6
Enjoy small gourmet rice cakes with unusual flavours such as pear blossom or chocolate, rice cakes that look like cheesecakes, and even a rice-cake sandwich. Five bite-sized *tteok* (rice cake) and tea costs W5000.

KKULTARAE STALL Map p205   Korean Snacks
Insadong-gil; 10 pieces W4000; 🕑 10am-10pm;
subway Line 3 to Anguk, Exit 6
Two cheerful lads make this delicious bite-sized snack in front of you from cornflour threads, honey and nuts.

SOMA 1095 Map p205   Korean
☎ 722 7522; Ujeonggungno; meals W5000;
🕑 8am-10pm; subway Line 3 to Anuk, Exit 6
Colour photos of the 40 well-presented meals available here help you to choose what to eat in this clean and busy budget eatery.

TEMPLE COOKING SHOP

Map p205   Korean Vegetarian
☎ 735 0312; Insadong-gil; snacks W3000-5000;
🕑 10.30am-9pm; subway Line 3, Anguk Exit 6
Snack on genuine Buddhist temple food – dried seaweed and lotus root, seed and nut biscuits or potato crisps. It's run by Sanchon restaurant, which is owned by an ex-monk.

TOSOKMAEUL Map pp202-3   Korean
☎ 735 7018; meals W6000; 🕑 24hr; subway Line 1 to Jonggak, Exit 3
Behind Pizza Hut is this wooden hut where cheerful ladies serve up *gamjatang,* a peasant dish of meaty bones in a spicy potato and sesame-leaf soup with side dishes including homemade *sundae* – black noodle-filled sausages. Finish your meal with free coffee.

MYEONG-DONG & NAMSAN

Myeong-dong offers plenty of reasonably priced options, or for somewhere special head to Korea House or Sejong Hotel.

ANDONG JJIMDAK

Map pp206-7   Korean Chicken
☎ 310 9174; meals W9,000; 🕑 11am-midnight;
subway Line 4 to Myeong-dong, Exit 8
The *jjimdak* (minimum two people) is laced with red chilli so it's hotter than August. Chicken without bones is W2000 extra and *Bokbunja* (wildberry wine) costs W15,000.

BAEKJE SAMGYETANG

Map pp206-7   Korean Chicken
☎ 776 3267; meals W9000-18,000; 🕑 9am-10pm;
subway Line 4 to Myeong-dong, Exit 6
Famous for its brusque, brisk service and *samgyetang* (chicken and ginseng soup), which costs W11,000 and includes *insamju* (ginseng liqueur). The adventurous can try the more expensive *ogolgyetang*

(black chicken cooked in ginseng), which also has medicinal qualities, or the un-adventurous can opt for roast chicken (W9000). This large restaurant with black tables and chairs and a tiled floor is on the 2nd floor but has no English or *hangeul* (Korean phonetic alphabet) sign – look for the red Chinese characters.

EUNHASU BUFFET

Map pp206-7   Korean & Global

☎ 7736000; Sejong Hotel; lunch/dinner buffet incl tax & services W34,000/38,000; ☿ noon-2.30pm, 6-9.30pm; subway Line 4 to Myeong-dong, Exit 10

This long-running buffet is the perfect introduction to a wide variety of Korean food including beef ribs, barbecue pork, rice porridge, fish, oxtail soup, *kimchi* pizza, tradi-tional desserts and tea. Some Western items are included and the green-themed classy surroundings add to the sense of occasion.

GOGUNG Map pp206-7   Korean Bibimbap

☎ 776 3211; meals W8000-15,000; ☿ 11am-10pm; subway Line 4 to Myeong-dong, Exit 10

Come here for authentic Jeonju *bibimbap*, which is said to be the best in Seoul. The décor here is gloomier than at its bright new branch in Insadong (p89).

KOREA HOUSE Map pp206-7   Royal Cuisine

☎ 2266 9101; www.koreahouse.or.kr; lunch W13,000-30,000, dinner W34,000-80,000; ☿ noon-2pm, 5.30-8.50pm; subway Line 3 or 4 to Chungmuro, Exit 3

The excellent royal banquet meals or lunch buffet are the best choice at this leading showcase for Korean food and traditional culture. In this grand *hanok,* dinner is served by *hanbok*-clad staff in two sessions, Monday to Saturday from 5.30pm to 7pm and 7.20pm to 8.50pm, but only once on Sunday from 6.30pm to 8pm. The cooks really care about their food and dinner sets. They start with *gujeolpan* followed by a dozen or so well-presented small dishes – jellyfish in a piquant sauce, perfect beef, heavenly eel, succulent oxtail, mini-*pajeon*, soups, *japchae*-type salad, *sinseollo* (meat, fish and vegies in broth cooked at your table), king prawn and abalone. Evening meals are followed by a one-hour perform-ance at the theatre (p101). The **souvenir shop** (☿ 10.30am-10pm) stocks high quality work by leading craftsfolk.

NUTRITION CENTRE

Map pp206-7   Korean Chicken

☎ 776 2015; meals W6500-10,000; ☿ 11am-10.30pm; subway Line 4 to Myeong-dong, Exit 6

A Myeong-dong institution with a fast-food décor that only offers two items – a whole chicken roasted on a spit or *samgyetang* for W10,000. At lunch a cheaper chicken set is available.

SEOCHOGOL Map pp206-7   Korean Galbi

☎ 777 6911; meals W5000-12,000; ☿ 11am-11pm; subway Line 4 to Myeong-dong, Exit 8

Behind Basic House is this unpretentious *galbi* restaurant with an English-speaking owner where the beef ribs are charcoal-grilled at your table, creating a smoky atmosphere. A bottle of *soju* provides the perfect accompaniment.

TOBANG DUCK RESTAURANT

Map pp206-7   Korean Duck

☎ 778 6727; Namdaemun market; ducks W30,000-41,000; ☿ 10am-10pm; subway Line 4 to Myeong-dong, Exit 7

A pile of delicious sliced smoked duck is kept warm over a small cauldron of steam-ing water that cooks the chives and sesame leaves that accompany the meat. Two dipping sauces are provided, one mustard and the other a delicious local concoction. Order noodles afterwards if required.

CHEAP EATS
GIMBAPGWAMANDUSAI

Map pp206-7   Korean

☎ 755 5559; meals W2000-4000; ☿ 7am-midnight; subway Line 1 or 2 to City Hall, Exit 2

This simple and neat budget eatery spe-cialises in *gimbap*, including nude *gimbap*, but also serves up big bowls of *bibimbap* as well as noodles, homemade dumplings and *sujebi*.

SINSUN SEOLNONGTANG

Map pp206-7   Korean

☎ 777 4531; meals W5500; ☿ 24hr; subway Line 4 to Myeongdong, Exit 8

Sinsun has been serving up excellent *seolleongtang* (beef and vegie soup) for 25 years and never closes its doors. It's plonk-it-on-your-table service and no fancy décor, but people come for the food.

ITAEWON

Every week a new ethnic restaurant opens in Itaewon, with new Middle Eastern restaurants leading the charge at the present time.

ALI BABA Map p209 — Middle Eastern
☎ 790 7754; Itaewonno; meals W5000-15,000; ⏰ noon-midnight; subway Line 6 to Itaewon, Exit 2
Authentic Egyptian food, coffee, music and surroundings are up here on the 2nd floor. Portions are small so sharing a number of dishes is the way to go, and the freshly made pitta bread is particularly delicious. The *sheesha* (water pipe) is an expensive puff at W20,000.

GECKO'S GARDEN Map p209 — Western
☎ 790 0540; tapas W5000, meals W8000-13,000, set meals W50,000; ⏰ noon-2am; subway Line 6 to Itaewon, Exit 1
A lovely garden courtyard but this restaurant, which currently offers tapas, specials such as smoked salmon, king prawns and couscous, with a barbecue Friday to Sunday, hasn't yet hit on a winning formula.

ITAEWON GALBI Map p209 — Korean
☎ 795 1474; meals W7000-25,000; ⏰ 10am-11pm; subway Line 6 to Itaewon, Exit 2
Up on the 2nd floor is this long-established and well-known eatery with helpful staff and traditional genre paintings on the wall. Grab a window seat and enjoy *galbi, galbitang* (beef ribs stew), mushroom *bulgogi, bulgogi* on a hotplate or for something more exotic, try cow's tongue.

LA PLANCHA Map p209 — Western
☎ 796 0063; meals W14,000-17,000; ⏰ 6-11pm; subway Line 6 to Itaewon, Exit 1
Order chicken, pork, steak, lamb, and salmon with vegetables and a sauce at this new indoor/outdoor restaurant that serves fresh meat by weight. Clean, tidy and modern, the food is on view and the cooks and serving staff do their jobs well.

LE SAINT-EX Map p209 — French
☎ 795 2465; meals around W25,000; ⏰ 6pm-midnight; subway Line 6 to Itaewon, Exit 1
The menu changes daily with specials like duck confit and roasted scallops but there is usually fish, seafood, lamb and a steak in this authentic bistro that only does dinners. With a homely atmosphere, a French cook and French wines it has quickly garnered a reputation for excellence.

MEMORIES Map p209 — German
☎ 795 3544; Pokwangdong-gil; meals W10,000-25,000; ⏰ noon-11pm; subway Line 6 to Itaewon, Exit 4
This cosy Deutschland oasis has been running for more than 10 years, and Herr Chef serves up authentic fare: solid soups, unfancy schnitzels, steaks and, of course, bratwurst with sauerkraut and roast potatoes, all washed down with German beer.

MOGHUL Map p209 — Indian
☎ 796 5501; meals W14,000-25,000; ⏰ noon-3pm, 6-10pm; subway Line 6 to Itaewon, Exit 1
Sit inside or outside in this well-established restaurant where lamb is popular and buffets appear on weekends.

SALAM Map p209 — Turkish
☎ 793 4323; meals W5000-18,000; ⏰ noon-10pm, closed 1st & 3rd Mon; subway Line 6 to Itaewon, Exit 3
One of the best Middle Eastern restaurants, this authentic Turkish one is hidden away next to the mosque. *Pide* (thin pizza), kebabs, hummus, baklava and lots of other options are freshly made in the open-plan kitchen. The restaurant has neat tables and Turkish décor and music. A try-everything nine-course meal is W18,000 while a puff on the *sheesha* is W10,000.

SANTORINI Map p209 — Greek
☎ 790 3474; meals around W30,000; ⏰ noon-11pm; subway Line 6 to Itaewon, Exit 1
On the 2nd floor is this new Greek taverna with a wide range of food that arrives at

TOP FIVE SNACKS

- Best street-stall sweet snack: *hotteok* (pita bread with a sweet filling)
- Best street-stall savoury snack: *tteokbokki* (rice cakes in a sweet and spicy sauce)
- Best subway station snack: *delimanjoo* (custard-filled mini-cakes)
- Best convenience-store snack: *samgak gimbap* (triangular sushi)
- Healthiest snack: *tteok* (rice cakes)

Eating

ITAEWON

Mediterranean speed. With its friendly service and good food, this place could be a winner. The best bet is the slab of baby ribs, which are adult-sized and cooked to perfection. The moussaka (W18,000) is tasty but a bit small, although it comes with a basic salad starter. The lunch specials are W9900.

SIGOL BAPSANG Map p209 — Korean
시골밥상; ☎ 793 5390; off Itaewonno; meals W7000-12,000; ⏰ 24hr; subway Line 6 to Itaewon, Exit 2

Sit amidst piles of rustic collectables is this restaurant offering countryside food (traditional Korean food from the days when Korea was a rural society). The restaurant occupies two buildings, both serving the same food. Try a W7000 *sigol bapsang* – 20 mainly vegetarian side dishes along with spicy tofu soup and rice. Order a plate of *bulgogi* if you want meat.

THAI ORCHID Map p209 — Thai
☎ 792 8836; Itaewonno; meals W9000-22,000; ⏰ noon-10.30pm; subway Line 6 to Itaewon, Exit 2

It's been around forever but a recent overhaul has modernised the look of this attractive and relaxing restaurant. Up on the 3rd floor, it's still the expat favourite for when nothing but delicious coconut-based Thai food will do.

OUTBACK STEAKHOUSE
Map p209 — Western Grill
☎ 749 5101; Itaewonno; meals W13,500-25,000; ⏰ 11.30am-10.30pm; subway Line 6 to Itaewon, Exit 4

Steaks star in this popular Aussie-themed restaurant with pine décor, music and a bar, which all combine to create a jovial and relaxed atmosphere.

CHEAP EATS

TACO Map p209 — Mexican
☎ 797 7219; snacks W3000-5000; ⏰ 11am-10pm; subway Line 6 to Naksapyeong, Exit 2

This cheap and cheerful little diner offers five types of Mexican munchies and attracts plenty of foreigners. The flavoursome grub is cooked in front of you by the youthful staff. The burritos and fajitas are the best bet.

DAEHANGNO

Diners are spoilt for choice in this youthful entertainment district with lots of outdoor seating in summer.

BONGCHU JJIMDAK
Map p208 — Korean Chicken
☎ 3676 6981; meals W11,000; ⏰ 11am-midnight; subway Line 4 to Hyehwa, Exit 1 or 2

A popular *jjimdak* restaurant with paper lanterns and Zen-style décor that offers large platters of freshly cooked chicken pieces, potatoes, carrots and onions on top of noodles and a sauce with a kick. You need two people for this party food, no *kimchi* side dishes are served, and you have to wait while it's freshly cooked.

KIJOAM Map p208 — Japanese
☎ 766 6100; meals W8000-15,000; ⏰ 11.30am-10pm; subway Line 4 to Hyehwa, Exit 2

Food fashions in Seoul come and go faster than the KTX train but the non-spicy Japanese noodles, cutlets and *tempura* sets at this chain restaurant never lose their appeal.

MAMA FOOD MARKET
Map p208 — Global Fusion
☎ 745 0308; meals W7000-22,000; ⏰ 11.30am-2am; subway Line 4 to Hyehwa, Exit 1 or 2

A lengthy global menu of fresh fusion Marché-style food is served outside under a smart awning or inside in a variety of sitting areas. Every night from 8pm to 10.30pm, solo singers perform on the terrace balcony.

NOLBOOJIP Map p208 — Korean
☎ 3675 9990; Daehangno; set meals W12,000; ⏰ 11.30am-10pm; subway Line 4 to Hyehwa, Exit 1

Down the steps in front of Pizza Hut is this special restaurant that serves a reasonably priced banquet to the sound of live traditional music, played daily from noon to 2pm and from 6.30pm to 8.30pm. Sit on floor cushions in the large eating arena and order *sangcharim* (minimum two people), which includes 20 dishes including steamed egg, fish, chicken, octopus, *japchae*, *galbi*, soup, quail's eggs and burnt-rice tea.

OPSEOYE Map p208 — Korean
☎ 742 4848; meals W6000-23,000; ⏰ 11.30am-10pm; subway Line 4 to Hyehwa, Exit 2

A lovely little garden surrounds this thatched *hanok* restaurant with a rustic interior. It specialises in hearty and traditional beef, mushroom and seafood casseroles plus *dajinjal galbi* – a giant beef patty.

SANNAEDEULLAE Map p208 · Royal Cuisine
☎ 766 7374; meals W8000-22,000, royal court sets W22,000-38,000; ⏰ 11.30am-10pm; subway Line 4 to Hyehwa, Exit 1

Hidden on the 3rd floor (above Pho Hoa), this restaurant serves up royal court cuisine such as *sinseollo* (steam boat) and *gujeolpan* (eight tiny snacks wrapped in minipancakes). Although just a starter, *gujeolpan* (W20,000) comes with sweet pumpkin porridge, soup, a salad bar of healthy greens, rice cakes and tea, and makes a light lunch.

TGI FRIDAY'S Map p208 · Western
☎ 743 1321; Daehangno; meals W13,000-29,000; ⏰ 11am-11pm; subway Line 4 to Hyehwa, Exit 1

Jack Daniel's chicken, steak, ribs and salad lures customers to this ever-popular American restaurant chain with 12 locations across Seoul. The bar adds to the cheerful and relaxed atmosphere. Bottles of wine start at W20,000, while beer starts at W2900.

YETNAL NONGJANG
Map p208 · Korean Barbecue
옛날농장; ☎ 763 9834; meals W5000-15,000; ⏰ 10am-5pm; subway Line 4 to Hyehwa, Exit 3

Come to this barbecue restaurant with wood beams and traditional murals for the W10,000 barbecue beef. The sauces and side dishes are good, the meat chunkier than *bulgogi* and the place generally has a party atmosphere.

Nolboojip (opposite), Daehangno

ZEN ZEN Map p208 · Korean Barbecue
☎ 3675 1150; meals W5500-8000; ⏰ 11am-11pm; subway Line 4 to Hyehwa, Exit 2

Eat inside or outside at this large new establishment that specialises in *samgyeopsal*, which is often eaten with *naengmyeon,* but *dwaejigalbi* (barbecued pork ribs) is another option. It moved here from Sinchon where the special marinades and the choose-your-own-salad-wrappings were a hit.

CHEAP EATS

BEER OAK Map p208 · Korean Chicken
☎ 745 0087; Daehangno; chickens W12,000; ⏰ 4.30pm-1.30am; subway Line 4 to Hyehwa, Exit 3

Always popular and noisy, Beer Oak serves delicious barbecue chicken roasted on a spit over a wood fire along with cheap beer (W2000 for a big glass). Order *sogeumgui* for a whole chicken on its own or *modeumgui* for a whole chicken cut up and served on a platter with pasta, pressed rice cakes, corn and raisins, covered in a sweet chilli sauce.

HONGIK

Hongik is not a gourmet district, but standards are improving.

AGIO Map p213 · Italian
☎ 334 7311; meals W8500-15,000; ⏰ noon-2am; subway Line 2 to Hongik University, Exit 6

Sit outside in the spacious courtyard under shady trees or inside this charming Italian restaurant that serves interesting salads and pastas, but specialises in large, thin-crusted pizzas, freshly made in a wood-fired oven and served on a wooden platter. Drinkable house wine is W5500.

BAENGNYEON SAMGYETANG
Map p213 · Korean Chicken
☎ 325 3399; Yanghwaro; W10,000; ⏰ 9.30am-10pm; subway Line 2 to Hongik University, Exit 6

This well-known rough-and-ready restaurant only serves chicken and ginseng soup and in summer you will probably have to queue because locals think it's the best in the area.

JENNY'S Map p213 · Italian
☎ 3141 7891; Wausan-gil; meals around W8000; ⏰ 11.30am-11pm; subway Line 2 to Hongik University, Exit 6

Verging on the funky, this laid-back café-style eatery plays good music, the bread is homemade and Jenny makes everything fresh to order, so expect to wait. Even the house wine (W4000) is good. Try the mushroom sandwich and salad. Lunch sets include soup and a soft drink.

NANIWA Map p213 — Japanese

나니와; ☎ 333 5337; meals W5000-9000; ⏰ 11am-10pm; subway Line 2 to Hongik University, Exit 6

Seoulites have still not forgotten Japan's cruel colonial rule, but they have forgiven them to the extent that customers pour into Japanese-style restaurants like the reasonably priced Naniwa chain that serves cutlet and *udong* (thick white noodle broth) set meals. The seats are a bit squashed but are made of *tatami* (woven straw), which adds to the Japanese atmosphere.

NOLBOO Map p213 — Korean

☎ 3141 7766; meals W5500-8000; ⏰ 11am-11.30pm; subway Line 2 to Hongik University, Exit 6

Come to this spacious 2nd floor restaurant for *budae jjigae* (or *Johnsontang*), which consists of ham, sausages, tofu, noodles and vegetable scraps that are thrown into a big wok, cooked at your table and served with rice and good side dishes. See p28 for the origins of this meal.

CHEAP EATS

CABIN OAK Map p213 — Barbecue Chicken

☎ 335 6117; chickens W10,000; ⏰ 4pm-3am; subway Line 2 to Hongik University, Exit 5

Most chicken-and-beer places sell fried chicken, but here at this clean and modern *hof* (pub) it is cooked on a spit over a wood fire. Beer costs W2000.

GIO Map p213 — Korean

☎ 323 1093; meals W4500; ⏰ 11-2am; subway Line 2 to Hongik University, Exit 6

The ladies in this shack serve up unique cheap food. There is no need to order as they only do two dishes that are both cooked at your table. First is a bowl of mushrooms and homemade noodles, which are the widest in Seoul. Remove some of the red pepper sauce if you want to make it less fiery and cook for 15 minutes. Next up is the pre-cooked rice, dried seaweed and herbs, which is mixed together in the same pot.

RICHEMONT BAKERY Map p213 — Bakery

☎ 332 7778; snacks W500-5000; ⏰ 7am-11pm; subway Line 2 to Hongik University, Exit 6

An above-average bakery that is always coming up with new creations and offers a good value European breakfast for W3500. It also sells real bread, specialist chocolates and their own ice lollies.

SINCHON & YEOUIDO

Sinchon has plenty of reasonably priced options, but Yeouido is something of a culinary desert.

BSD DUBU HOUSE Map p210 — Korean Tofu

☎ 362 8897; meals & sets W6000-15,000; ⏰ 11am-midnight; subway Line 2 to Sinchon, Exit 3

Fourteen varieties of spicy *sundubu* are on offer in this neat and clean basement restaurant decorated with collectables, but the traditional beef one is hard to beat. Add a raw egg to the *sundubu*, and empty the rice into a bowl, adding boiling water from the kettle to the rice that's left behind to make burnt-rice tea. Side dishes include freshly fried fish and *odeng* (processed seafood cakes in broth).

CHUNCHEONJIP Map p210 — Korean Chicken

☎ 323 5597; meals W5500-8000; ⏰ 24hr; subway Line 2 to Sinchon, Exit 2

This large and cheerful restaurant with music, a tiled floor and paper lanterns never closes. Try their hot and spicy fusion *dakgalbi* (pan-fried chicken) with cheese and sweet potatoes or noodles that are cooked at your table. You serve yourself side dishes from a buffet – a great idea that reduces waste.

NORYANGJIN FISH MARKET RESTAURANTS Map p210 — Korean Fish

☎ 821 3262; meals W10,000-60,000; ⏰ 10am-midnight; subway Line 1 to Noryangjin, Exit 1

Up on the 2nd floor of the fish market are half a dozen traditional-style restaurants selling the freshest fish and seafood. They specialise in raw fish (small platter W60,000), but also serve soups with octopus, blue crab or fish, but they tend to be very chilli hot. Steamed crab (W60,000), grilled prawns or clams (W30,000), or *jeonbokjuk* (abalone rice porridge) may be more appealing. All come with side dishes such as grilled fish, quail eggs, acorn jelly, beans and tofu. Beware of *sannakji*, which is live baby octopus. One restaurant has an English menu. From the subway exit cross the footbridge over the railway tracks and go down the steps into the fish market.

PLAZA FOUNTAIN BUFFET
Map p210   Korean & Global
☎ 789 5731; adult lunch/dinner W40,000/45,000, child 5-13yr lunch/dinner W25,000/28,000; ⏱ noon-3pm, 6-10pm; subway Line 5 to Yeouinaru, Exit 4
The popular and smart buffet restaurant in the 63 Building puts on an impressive spread of Korean, Japanese and Western favourites. In the centre is a dancing fountain under a glass dome.

CHEAP EATS

HAPPY TABLE Map p210   Fusion
☎ 363 9991; meals W5000; ⏱ 10.30am-9pm; subway Line 2 to Sinchon, Exit 3
The tables and chairs are tiny and squashed together, but this small student restaurant serves up lots of small but inexpensive fusion dishes including chicken salad in a yam basket.

HWEDRA RAMYEON
Map p210   Korean Noodles
☎ 337 1506; meals W3000-10,000; ⏱ 24hr; subway Line 2 to Sinchon, Exit 1
This tiny, dark cell of an eatery serves up the hottest *ramyeon* in Seoul and the *ajumma* (a women who runs a hotel, restaurant or other business) in charge adds chillies with a large ladle. Said to cure even the worst hangover, you can take up this fear-factor challenge for just W3000.

GANGNAM

Masses of restaurants crowd around Gangnam subway station although the turn-over rate is high, while Apgujeong is another dining hotspot.

BERRIES CAFÉ Map p211   Organic Western
☎ 514 9567; Apgujeongno; meals W6000-11,000; ⏱ 10am-10pm; subway Line 3 to Apgujeong, Exit 2
A pleasant but quiet 2nd-floor restaurant decorated with bare bricks, plants and lilac tablecloths, it specialises in organic food and drinks. Organic tea, coffee, juices,

wines, ice creams and beers accompany a short menu of Italianish food – salads with apple mayonnaise, fusion *dorias* (rice covered in spaghetti sauce) and pasta. Downstairs is an organic-food shop (see p127).

BONJUK Map p211   Korean Rice Porridge
☎ 514 6233; Apgujeongno; meals W5000-10,000; ⏱ 9am-10pm Mon-Sat; subway Line 3 to Apgujeong, Exit 2
Big bowls of tasty and healthy rice porridge feature in this chain of small restaurants – try ginseng and chicken, mushroom and oyster, seafood, sweet pumpkin, or red bean.

FAMILIA BUFFET Map p211   Korean & Global
☎ 3440 8090; lunch/dinner incl tax & service W49,000/53,000; ⏱ noon-3pm, 6-10pm; subway Line 7 to Hak-dong, Exit 1
This restaurant in the plush and pukka Imperial Palace Hotel provides a superb buffet banquet. Some of the food is freshly cooked by a squad of cooks who work in the dining area and are dressed in ninja outfits.

HANMIRI Map p211   Royal Cuisine
☎ 569 7165; 2nd fl, Human Touchville, Nonhyeonro; set meals W35,000-77,000; ⏱ noon-3pm, 6-10pm; subway Line 2 to Yeoksam, Exit 6
Be treated like royalty by *hanbok*-clad staff in this oasis of old-fashioned service and décor with embroidery on the tables and walls, and indulge in a well-presented royal-cuisine feast fit for a Joseon king.

HARD ROCK CAFÉ Map p211   Western
☎ 547 5671; Dosandaero; meals W8000-22,000; ⏱ 5pm-2am Mon-Thu, noon-3am Fri & Sat, noon-midnight Sun; subway Line 3 to Apgujeong, Exit 2
Dig into ribs, salads, Mexican and Italian food, amid rock music souvenirs, with the added attraction of live music and dancing nightly (except Monday) from 8.30pm to midnight. DJs are also around and take over on Monday. The music gets louder as the evening progresses, and local draught beer is W3500.

MAD FOR GARLIC Map p211   Italian Fusion
☎ 546 8117; Apgujeongno; meals W12,000-17,000; ⏱ 11.30-2am; subway Line 3 to Apgujeong, Exit 2
A striking décor of bare brick walls adorned with strings of garlic and wine glasses and bottles gives a Mediterranean flavour to

this huge cellar of an Italian bistro. Ten chefs in the open-plan kitchen serve up garlic steak (W33,000), thin-crust pizzas and other favourites along with items such as the Dracula Killer starter – slices of bread that you spread with whole cloves of garlic soaked in hot herby olive oil, and cover in grated cheese. Bottles of wine start at W20,000 while a large glass of house red is W5000 and a beer is W3800.

NOODLE X Map p211 Korean Fusion

☎ 592 7401; meals W5000-8000; 🕑 11.30am-10.30pm; subway Line 2 to Gangnam, Exit 5

Despite the name, inventive fusion food of all kinds is served in this dimly-lit modern eatery with red and black décor and music. This is the best place to try *jajangmyeon* and even baked potato (small) is on the menu.

PHO BAY Map p211 Vietnamese Noodles

☎ 7501 9103; meals W8000-13,000; 🕑 10am-3am Mon-Fri; subway Line 2 to Gangnam, Exit 7

A restaurant chain with simple but clean décor that specialises in fresh-tasting Vietnamese rice noodles. The big plus here is that you mix in whatever amount of bean sprouts, chillies, lemon and onion you want. Service can be slow at busy times.

PULHYANGGI Map p211 Korean Vegetarian

☎ 545 0415; Eonjuro; lunch specials W6000-8000, dinner sets W18,000-50,000; 🕑 10am-10pm; subway Line 3 to Apgujeong, Exit 2

Sit on chairs or floor cushions at this long-running, 2nd-storey restaurant where the main attraction is the dozen or more items served up in the dinner sets. The mainly vegetarian sets offer traditional food such as sweet-and-sour mushrooms, sesame soup, acorn jelly, rice cakes and special teas. *Dongdongju* (fermented rice wine) costs W6000.

SINSUN SEOLNONGTANG

Map p211 Korean

☎ 538 5533; Teheranno; meals W5500-11,000; 🕑 24hr; subway Line 2 to Gangnam, Exit 8

This bright and clean restaurant with greenery is one of a chain that is famous for its *seolleongtang* (adult/child W5500/3500). But it also serves *gyeranjjim*, steamed egg with a spring onion and seafood garnish. In the lobby the vending-machine coffee is the cheapest in Seoul at just W100.

SONGTAN BUDAE JJIGAE Map p211 Korean

☎ 501 8280; Bongeunsaro; meals W8000; 🕑 24hr; subway Line 2 to Gangnam, Exit 7

Sit on floor cushions or chairs at this popular no-frills restaurant with dark décor that never closes. The *budae jjigae* (ham and vegetable stew) is cooked at your table. It comes with a potato side dish, but order rice or instant noodles to go with it.

JAMSIL

Besides the restaurants in the COEX Mall, over the river to the north is Seoul's most fun food court.

MARCHÉ Map pp214-15 European

☎ 6002 6890; COEX Mall; meals W5000-25,000; 🕑 11am-11pm; subway Line 2 to Samseong, COEX Exit

A restaurant chain that has fresh food piled up in market stall sections in an open-plan style and specialises in Euro nosh – Swiss *rostis*, homemade pasta, steak, ribs, sausages and salads. Seoulites have taken to it in a big way.

O'KIM'S BRAUHAUS Map pp214-15 European

☎ 6002 7006; meals W7000, platters W20,000-35,000; 🕑 11.30am-midnight; subway Line 2 to Samseong, COEX Exit

More Deutschland than Ireland, this is a huge but convivial place with an Okto-berfest atmosphere and live music at 8pm nightly (except Sunday). It serves up big platters of steak, ribs, sausages and seafood along with their own brewed-on-the-premises light or dark German-style beer (W4800 a glass). It's near the exhibition halls rather than in the mall.

CHEAP EATS

TECHNO MART FOOD COURT

Map pp214-15 Korean & Global

B1, Techno Mart; meals W5000; 🕑 10am-8pm; subway Line 2 to Gangbyeon, Exit 1

Forty stalls with loquacious staff compete with each other to pile up as much fusion food as possible on huge platters that are meant for sharing – a W10,000 platter feeds three hungry people. Browse the plastic replicas of the food and see the world's largest bowls of *bibimbap* and giant ice-cream concoctions on shaved ice or fruit.

Entertainment

Entertainment

Seoulites of all ages love going out and socialising, whether it's with classmates, work colleagues, friends or dates, so entertainment areas are humming every night of the week until late. On Friday and Saturday the revels continue all night. The usual thing is to choose a neighbourhood, eat and drink, then go to a live music show or sing in a *noraebang* (karaoke room), then drink some more, and finally hit a dance club until the subway system starts up again at 5.30am. Student haunts like Hongik, Sinchon and Daehangno are swarming with bars, live music venues, *noraebang*, DVD *bang* (a room where you can watch DVDs) and dance clubs. The expat Itaewon area has a party atmosphere on Friday and Saturday nights.

THEATRE, DANCE & CASINOS

Plenty of theatres present traditional music, dance and drama, while modern local musicals like *Nanta, Tokebi Storm* and *Taekwon* can be enjoyed by foreigners since there are few or no words. Western-style opera, ballet, modern dance and musicals are regularly staged. The Kim Yun-gyu dance company melds traditional and modern styles.

Daehangno (Map p208) is home to a lively drama scene with 60 small theatres. Ticket prices are a reasonable W11,000 to W25,000, but everything is in Korean. The discount theatre ticket booth (Map p208; ⊙ 1pm-7.30pm Tue-Sun), behind the open-air stage in Marronnier Park, sells W12,000 theatre tickets for W7000, but you need ID and you may have to queue.

Top local bands and famous groups from Western countries often perform at **Jamsil Sports Complex** (Map pp214–15). Ticket prices generally range from W40,000 to W70,000.

CHONGDONG THEATRE Map pp206-7
☎ 751 1500; www.chongdong.com; ⊙ 8pm Tue-Sun Apr-Sep, 4pm Tue-Sun Oct-Mar; subway Line 1 or 2 to City Hall, Exit 2
This well-regarded and well-established theatre is centrally located and puts on 1½-hour performances of traditional music, singing and dancing. The shows are targeted at foreign visitors and English subtitles appear on a screen. After the show you can take photographs of the performers in their traditional clothing. The ticket office opens at 7pm. Tickets cost W30,000 to W40,000 with discounts for students.

TOP FIVE BARS
- Top sports bar: Time Out Sports Bar (p104)
- Top bartender: Bar Bliss (p104)
- Top dark-beer bar: Santana (p105)
- Top garden bar: 360@ (p105)
- Top loud rock-music bar: Woodstock (p106)

DONGSOONG ARTS CENTRE Map p208
☎ 7413391; subway Line 4 to Hyehwa, Exit 1
This complex has a theatre that puts on modern drama (all in Korean) and a cinema that shows foreign festival-style movies from all around the world, including ones on North Korea.

HAKCHON GREEN THEATRE Map p208
☎ 763 8233; www.hakchon.co.kr; tickets adult/student W28,000/22,000; subway Line 4 to Hyehwa, Exit 2
The smash-hit rock musical *Line 1* takes a satirical look at Seoul – the 'Ladies of Gangnam' song and dance is a memorable highlight. The nearly three-hour show has English subtitles on a screen on Wednesday, Friday and Sunday.

KAYAGUM THEATRE Map pp198-9
☎ 455 5000; Sheraton Grande Walkerhill Hotel; show/show plus dinner W60,000/99,000; ⊙ 4.30-7pm, 7.30-10pm Thu-Tue; subway Line 5 to Gwangnaru, Exit 2
These entertaining and lavish 1½-hour shows include traditional Korean music and dance followed by a glitzy Western/Asian cabaret revue. The hotel theatre is over 1km from the subway, so take the hotel shuttle bus or a taxi.

KOREA HOUSE Map pp206-7

☎ 2266 9101; www.koreahouse.or.kr; tickets W29,000; subway Line 3 or 4 to Chungmuro, Exit 3

This intimate 150-seat theatre stages one-hour performances after their fine dinners (p92). Put on by a large troupe of top musicians and dancers, the shows have some commentary in English on a screen. Show items include elegant court dances, *pansori* (Korean opera), a crowd-pleasing fan dance, a spiritual shamanist dance, and female drummers standing up and acrobatically banging on three drums each. The finale is *samulori* (traditional farmers' dance), with swirling dancers trying to outdo each other as they dance to fast and furious percussion rhythms.

MARRONNIER PARK Map p208

Subway Line 4 to Hyehwa, Exit 2

This free performance area in Daehangno usually has something happening on warm weekend afternoons. Student artists draw portraits in one corner while high-school rock bands crank it up on the glass-roofed outdoor stage, and a *samulori* troupe bang their drums and gongs while dancing around under the chestnut trees. 'Mr Guitar', a musician and comedian, regularly performs in front of a large and appreciative audience.

MUNYE THEATRE Map p208

Subway Line 4 to Hyehwa, Exit 2

This large red-brick theatre in Daehangno puts on a varied dance-oriented programme of events and shows as well as hosting the annual Modern Dance Festival (p102). Posters around Daehangno advertise what's on.

TOP SPOTS FOR ROMANCE

- Listen to live jazz over cocktails in **Top Cloud Restaurant & Bar** (p90) with a million flickering lights spread out below you.
  Pedal a tandem bicycle along the **Han River** (p115) as the sun sets.
- Sip fruit teas together in the tiny but incredibly atmospheric **Yetchatjip teashop** (p107), with little birds flying around.
- Share a bottle of wine while cosily watching a movie at the exclusive Charlotte Hall in **Lotte Cinema** (p103).
- Dance to irresistible Latin rhythms at **Bahia** (p111) or **Macondo** (p111) in Hongik.

NANTA THEATRE Map pp202-3

☎ 1588 7890; tickets W20,000-60,000; ⚇ shows 4pm & 8pm Mon-Sat, 3pm & 6pm Sun; subway Line 1 or 2 to City Hall, Exit 2

Set in a kitchen, this long-running, high-energy show mixes varied ingredients – magic, circus tricks, drumming with kitchen utensils, comedy, dance, martial arts and audience participation – to produce a clever and enjoyable musical pantomime.

NATIONAL CENTRE FOR KOREAN TRADITIONAL PERFORMING ARTS

Map pp198-9

☎ 580 3300; www.ncktpa.go.kr; subway Line 3 to Nambu Bus Terminal, Exit 5

Next door to the Seoul Arts Centre, the Yeakdang theatre (☎ 580 3300; tickets W8000 and W10,000) puts on a programme by top performers every Saturday from March to December at 5pm. The 1½-hour show is a bargain and usually contains eight items including court dances, folk songs, *pansori* and drumming. A three-day festival is held at the end of October.

Between early May and early December, at the smaller **Umyeondang theatre**, younger performers put on a similar show every Thursday (same ticket prices). Other traditional performances are held here too. Take the shuttle bus (W500) from the subway exit or walk (15 minutes).

NATIONAL THEATRE Map pp206-7

☎ 2274 3507; www.ntok.go.kr; subway Line 3 Dongguk University, Exit 6

On Namsan, this complex is home to the national drama, national *changgeuk* (Korean opera), national orchestra and national dance companies. Venues include the main hall and outdoor stages where free concerts and movies are held in summer. It's a 15-minute walk from the subway exit or take the yellow bus No 2 (W500, every 10 minutes) from the bus stop just behind Exit 6.

SEENSEE MUSICAL THEATRE Map p208

☎ 745 1987; tickets W30,000; subway Line 4 to Hyehwa, Exit 2

This theatre specialises in musicals that can be enjoyable even if you can't understand Korean (or take a Korean-speaking friend along with you). Some shows are adaptations of Western musicals, while others are home-grown.

SEJONG CENTRE FOR THE PERFORMING ARTS Map pp202-3

☎ 399 1111; Sejongno; subway Line 5 to Gwanghwamun, Exit 1

Centrally located, this newly renovated centre is a leading arts complex that puts on major drama, music and art shows, including an annual three-day international drum festival in early October. It has a grand hall, small theatre and three art galleries.

SEOUL ARTS CENTRE Map pp198-9

☎ 580 1300; www.sac.or.kr; subway Line 3 to Nambu Bus Terminal, Exit 5

This sprawling arts complex has a circular opera house, with a roof shaped like a Korean nobleman's hat, which also houses the 700-seat Towol Theatre and the smaller Jayu Theatre. The national ballet and opera companies are based here. Music House consists of a large concert hall and a smaller recital hall and is home to the national choir, the Korea and Seoul symphony orchestras and the Seoul performing arts company.

The arts centre is 600m from the subway exit – walk straight on from the subway exit and turn left at the end of the bus terminal, or take the frequent shuttle bus (W500).

SEOUL NORIMADANG Map pp214-15

☎ 410 3168; admission free; ☾ shows 3pm & 4pm Sat & Sun Apr-Oct; subway Line 2 or 8 to Jamsil, Exit 3

This covered outdoor arena with seats hosts entertaining traditional music and dance performances that are enjoyed by the mainly elderly local audience who may get up and start dancing. If you are in Lotte World walk through Baby World and go up the stairs for a short cut to the lakeside venue.

SHERATON GRANDE WALKERHILL CASINO Map pp198-9

☎ 456 2121; ☾ 24hr; subway Line 5 to Gwangnaru, Exit 2

This casino offers the usual ways of losing money – one-armed bandits, roulette, poker, blackjack, baccarat, big wheel and tai-sa. Snacks are free, and free drinks can be ordered at the gaming tables. Minimum bets are W2500 or W5000. There is no dress code and Korean nationals are not allowed inside.

A second casino is opening in May 2006 at the Millennium Hilton Hotel. Called Seven Luck, it will be open 24 hours.

FESTIVALS

Seoul hosts a festival almost every week (p8). A well-established, two-week international Modern Dance Festival (www.modafe.org) is held every spring. It's based at Munye Theatre in Daehangno (Map p208). The two-week Seoul Fringe Festival takes over the student area in Hongik in late August with art, dance, drama and street performances. The National Theatre (Map pp206–7) hosts a 10-day Traditional Dance Festival in late August, while the three-week Seoul International Dance Festival (www.sidance.org) in October is held mainly at the Seoul Arts Centre.

TOKEBI STORM THEATRE Map pp202-3

☎ 739 8288; tickets W20,000-80,000; ☾ shows 8pm Tue-Sat, 3pm & 6pm Sun; subway Line 1 or 2 to City Hall, Exit 2

Tokebi Storm is an energetic and fun drumming show with a goblin theme (every culture seems to have its goblins), which is all-action and mime with no dialogue, so will appeal to a global audience.

CINEMAS

Luxurious new multiplex cinemas with large screens and the latest sound equipment are opening all round Seoul. Films are usually shown from 11am to 11pm. English-language films are shown in cinemas with their original soundtrack and Korean subtitles. Unfortunately Korean-language movies shown in cinemas don't have English subtitles, but you can see them in a DVD *bang* (see p103) with English subtitles. Cinema and DVD *bang* tickets usually cost W7000.

CINE CUBE Map pp202-3

☎ 2002 7770; tickets W7000; ☾ 10am-11pm; subway Line 5 to Gwanghwamun, Exit 6

This well-respected art cinema near Deoksugung screens international festival films, which are usually shown in their original language with Korean subtitles. Interest in world cinema is growing, especially amongst young Seoulites.

COEX MALL MEGABOX Map pp214-15

☎ 6002 1200; tickets W7000; ☾ 9am-midnight

A mega popular 17-screen multiplex cinema with over 4000 seats that screens some films at midnight, when most other cinemas have closed for the night. Queues can build up at busy times.

KOREA FILM ARCHIVES Map pp198-9

Seoul Arts Centre; ☎ 521 3147; www.koreafilm .or.kr; admission free; subway Line 3 to Nambu Bus Terminal, Exit 5

The archives screens classic Korean films with English subtitles. The seasonal programmes provide a rare opportunity to see films that are not normally shown.

LOTTE CINEMA Map pp214-15

☎ 1544 8855; tickets W7000; ⏰ 11am-11pm; subway Line 2 to Euljiro 1-ga, Exit 8

This new multiplex has five state-of-the-art cinemas plus **Charlotte Hall** (Mon-Fri W25,000, Sat & Sun W30,000), a luxury cinema with 34 reclining plush red armchairs where you can sip beer (W4000), wine (W3000) or a soft drink (free).

MMC CHEONGDAEMUN MULTIPLEX

Map pp200-1

☎ 2628 9111; tickets W7000; ⏰ 24hr

Another mecca for film goers, this one is in Dongdaemun market and shows films 24 hours a day.

DVD BANG

A DVD *bang* is the best place to see Korean movies, as they can be shown with English subtitles. See p23 for reviews of some excellent Korean films. DVD *bang* are all similar: you watch the film sitting on a comfortable sofa in your own private room. The usual cost is around W7000 per person (the same as a cinema ticket) but can be cheaper in student areas. They're popular with dating couples and most are open all night.

CINE CASTLE DVD Map p208

☎ 741 1580; tickets W6000; ⏰ 12.30pm-2am; subway Line 4 to Hyehwa, Exit 2

Watch DVDs on a big screen, sitting on a sofa in your own little room up on the 4th floor. There is no need to book, just turn up.

DVD CINETIQUE Map p211

☎ 5418005; Rodeo St; s/d W8000/13,000; ⏰ 24hr; subway Line 3 to Apgujeong, Exit 6

Up on the 3rd floor is this typical DVD *bang*, which is open all night and is popular with couples.

NORAEBANG

Seoul has thousands of *noraebang*, where friends and work colleagues sing along to well-known songs, including ones in English. Every Seoulite seems to sing well, and many can sing in English better than they speak it. Most *noraebang* open from 2pm to 2am and prices start at around W15,000 an hour, although luxury ones cost more. No alcohol is served, but a few have hostesses to help patrons have a good time by holding their hand and singing a duet with them, and applauding enthusiastically after each song. The best way for a foreign businessman to impress his Korean hosts is to belt out a heartfelt version of Frank Sinatra's 'My Way'.

LUXURY NORAEBANG Map p213

☎ 332 5204; room per hr W10,000-36,000; ⏰ 24hr; subway Line 2 to Hongik University, Exit 6

Sing along with the video songs in a range of mostly palatial rooms in this new breed of *noraebang*, which is open all night and provides a more luxurious setting for acting out those rock star fantasies.

OPERA HOUSE NORAEBANG Map p208

☎ 766 5198; small/big rooms per hr W15,000/30,000; ⏰ 2pm-5am; subway Line 4 to Hyehwa, Exit 2

Sing as loud as you want in these basement karaoke rooms, which feature a bank of four screens, a tambourine, a disco light and hundreds of English songs.

Seoul Arts Centre (opposite)

BARS

Seoul has an unbelievable number of bars so competition is strong. Most of Seoul's expat and gay bars and clubs can be found in Itaewon, which caters to the US troops stationed nearby (although they'll be moving to bases further south by 2008). Most bars have English-speaking staff, and only get busy around 10pm or later, even on Friday and Saturday. It's the only area where you see lots of foreigners and it has a different atmosphere from the rest of Seoul.

Itaewon's hostess bars are concentrated on the hill (known as Hooker Hill), across the main road from the Hamilton Hotel. Step inside one and a drink for yourself may cost only W5000, but a drink for one of the scantily clad girls plastered in make-up could set you back W20,000 or more. These bars have signs outside that read 'Sweetheart Club – Drink Food Woman', 'Woman & Cocktails' or the slightly more subtle 'For Gentlemen'.

GWANGHWAMUN

BUCK MULLIGAN'S Map pp202-3

☎ 3783 0004; B2, Seoul Finance Centre; meals W22,000-30,000; ☺ noon-12.30am Mon-Sat; subway Line 1 or 2 to City Hall, Exit 4

Guinness is W8000 and live pop and rock music can be enjoyed at 7.30pm and 9pm in this Irish-themed bar with a pool table.

TIME OUT SPORTS BAR Map pp202-3

☎ 3783 0233; B1 & 2, Seoul Finance Centre; lunch W9900, dinner W15,000-28,000; ☺ 11.30am-2am Mon-Fri, noon-11pm Sat; subway Line 1 or 2 to City Hall, Exit 4

A monster collection of signed sporting memorabilia adorns the walls of this sports bar with screens and differing zones to relax in. Beers start at a reasonable W2500, and the fusion-style food includes steaks. An organic salad buffet is available at lunch time.

> ## TOP FIVE BARS FOR ATMOSPHERE
>
> - 3 Alley Pub (right)
> - Mu (p106)
> - Gecko's Terrace (right)
> - US 66 Bar (p112)
> - Bier Halle (opposite)

MYEONG-DONG & NAMSAN

O'KIM'S Map pp206-7

☎ 317 0388; Westin Chosun Hotel; meals W18,000-45,000; ☺ 3pm-2am; subway Line 2 to Euljiro 1-ga, Exit 4

Guinness at this green-themed Irish sports bar costs a hefty W18,000, but other beers are W9000. Live music (currently a Bulgarian duo) is on every night at 8.30pm and you can play darts, pool and (wonder of wonders) bar soccer.

ITAEWON

3 ALLEY PUB Map p209

☎ 749 3336; meals W8000-14,000; ☺ 4pm-1am Mon-Fri, noon-1am Sat & Sun; subway Line 6 to Itaewon, Exit 1

Mixing together an English pub atmosphere (darts, pool and a trivia quiz every Thursday night) with top-notch European-style pub grub and seven draught beers is a formula that makes this an expat magnet.

ALWAYS HOMME Map p209

☎ 798 0578; ☺ 8pm-4am; subway Line 6 to Itaewon, Exit 3

Beer is W4000 and cocktails are W5000 at this homely gay bar with a touch or two of style. The music is not so loud that you can't talk and the staff are friendly.

BAR BLISS Map p209

☎ 749 7738; ☺ 6pm-1am; subway Line 6 to Itaewon, Exit 4

English-speaking, motorbike-riding gay gypsy Ted Park welcomes everyone to his smart wine bar. The armchairs, the music, the good house wine and the cheese and crackers are all so tempting you may never want to leave this bar that's hidden behind Reggae Pub.

GECKO'S TERRACE Map p209

☎ 749 9425; cnr Itaewonno & Pokwangdonggil; meals W9000-23,000; ☺ 11am-2am; subway Line 6 to Itaewon, Exit 4

This comfortable and popular 2nd floor bar and restaurant has a global menu, lunch specials, six draught beers and lots of bottled ones plus the obligatory-in-Itaewon darts and pool. It can get like a rugby scrum at peak times.

NASHVILLE SPORTS BAR Map p209

☎ 798 1592; Itaewonno; ⏱ 2pm-1am; subway Line 6 to Itaewon, Exit 4

A scruffy Itaewon institution with a juke-box, pool, darts and a view. Beer costs W2500 and cocktails W5000. In summer the rooftop garden bar opens except when it's raining. In the basement is an American-style diner and above the sports bar is Club Caliente (p110).

OUR PLACE Map p209

☎ 792 7884; Itaewonno; meals W9000-12,000; ⏱ 4pm-3am; subway Line 6 to Itaewon, Exit 3

Spread over the three top floors with a terrace and rooftop section, this engaging wine bar with candles serves fusion food and is run by Seoul's most famous gay icon, TV actor Hong Seok-chun.

QUEEN Map p209

☎ 793 1290; ⏱ 8pm-4am Sun-Thu, 11am-4am Fri & Sat; subway Line 6 to Itaewon, Exit 3

This comfortable bar attracts a mixture of Korean and Westerners, and welcomes visitors of all orientations. It has chan-deliers and bright red chairs, and beer is W4000.

REGGAE PUB Map p209

☎ 749 1533; Itaewonno; ⏱ 3pm-2am Mon-Fri, 1pm-3am Sat & Sun; subway Line 6 to Itaewon, Exit 4

Reggae rhythms on the sound system are the main attraction at this Jamaican out-post, but there is the usual pool and darts. Jah beef *jjigae* (stew) is W8000, Jamaican chicken barbecue is W10,000, a beer is W2500 and a mug of Jamaican punch or *soju* (local vodka) is W6000.

SEOUL PUB Map p209

☎ 793 6666; Itaewonno; meals W4000-13,000; ⏱ 3pm-3am Mon-Thu, noon-4am Fri-Sun; subway Line 6 to Itaewon, Exit 4

A friendly, laid-back pub with W2000 beers, pool, darts, music and occasional pub games.

SOHO Map p209

☎ 797 2280; ⏱ 8pm-4am; subway Line 6 to Itaewon, Exit 3

Another smart and friendly gay bar with some glitter around that holds special events and attracts an older clientele, and lesbians. Beer is W4000 and you can sit at the bar discussing sexual orientations, or relax in armchairs.

DAEHANGNO

BIER HALLE Map p208

☎ 744 9996; meals W9000-13,000; ⏱ 3pm-midnight; subway Line 4 to Hyehwa, Exit 2

This lively and cheerful bare-brick cellar-style bar lures customers with its cheap beer – W2500 a glass or W12,800 for a giant 2.7L pitcher – and its Euro menu of saus-ages and smoked meats.

BOOGIE BOOGIE BAR Map p208

☎ 744 3626; meals W13,000-19,000; ⏱ 3pm-2am; subway Line 4 to Hyehwa, Exit 2

Homesick Americans can be found here in Daehangno surrounded by icons and para-phernalia of the US of A, including part of a Cadillac above the entrance. Beer is W4000 and cocktails W8000.

SANTANA Map p208

☎ 763 9933; meals W9000-14,000; ⏱ 3pm-2am; subway Line 4 to Hyehwa, Exit 2

Dark beers are the big attraction in this bar that has stacks of room and sells draught Guinness, Becks Dark, Heineken Dark and Miller Dark for W14,000 for 2L. A dozen different bottled dark beers cost W9000 to W14,000 each.

HONGIK

360@ Map p213

☎ 323 2360; ⏱ 11am-3am; subway Line 2 to Hongik University, Exit 6

Dip your feet in the pool, sunbathe on a sunlounger, sit in a garden swing seat or relax in a hammock outside or on a bed in-side this bar, which is full of relaxing ideas and has an all-white upstairs floor. Drinks start at W5000.

GOLD 2 BAR Map p213

☎ 333 9129; ⏱ 5pm-6am; subway Line 2 to Hongik University, Exit 6

Up on the 2nd floor, the bar has wood cabin décor, bar food and, best of all, a 500ml beer costs only W1900. No need to say any more.

LABRIS Map p213

☎ 333 5276; ⊙ 3pm-2am Sun-Fri, 1pm-5am Sat; subway Line 2 to Hongik University, Exit 6
Take the elevator up to this comfortable, quiet and relaxed women-only lesbian bar that has sofas, a big screen showing music videos and friendly staff. Beers cost W5000.

QUEEN'S HEAD Map p213

☎ 3143 0757; meals W12,000-20,000; ⊙ 5pm-3am; subway Line 2 to Hongik University, Exit 6
Five European beers (W5000 to W7000) are on tap here in this English-style pub with an outdoor garden bar that draws crowds in the summer.

SINCHON & YEOUIDO

BEATLES Map p210

☎ 323 6385; ⊙ 7pm-3am; subway Line 2 to Sinchon, Exit 2
An enviable record collection of over 10,000 LPs fills a wall in this basement log cabin 'old music bar' where beers cost W3500. The host is laid-back and the atmosphere is quiet and relaxing.

BLUE BIRD Map p210

☎ 332 3831; ⊙ 6.30pm-2am; subway Line 2 to Sinchon, Exit 2
Young couples are attracted to this bar, which has a romantic ambience with comfortable chairs around tables that are adorned with flickering candles, while soft jazz plays moodily in the background.

MU Map p210

☎ 010-9236 9745; ⊙ 4pm-4am; subway Line 2 to Sinchon, Exit 2
Probably the most amazing bar interior in Seoul, it has overhead waterways, and a sinuous white creeper design that creates individual cubicles for patrons. Imagine a Star Wars bar designed by an Inuit. It feels strange even when you're sober.

WALLFLOWERS Map p210

☎ 3142 5234; ⊙ 6pm-3am; subway Line 2 to Sinchon, Exit 2
A classy black-and-chrome interior sets the tone for the generally cool jazz in this 2nd floor bar, where beers are W5000. It's perfect for a quiet chat with a date rather than somewhere for a raucous night out.

WOODSTOCK Map p210

☎ 334 1310; ⊙ 3pm-3am; subway Line 2 to Sinchon, Exit 2
Years of scribbles have built up on the walls, tables and chairs in this bar where the big attraction is the loud rock music selected from their huge collection. Beer is W2000 a glass or W10,000 a pitcher.

GANGNAM

DUBLIN Map p211

☎ 561 3281; meals W13,000; ⊙ 4pm-2am; subway Line 2 to Gangnam, Exit 7
This large 'Irish' pub has indoor and outdoor seating, five draught beers including Guinness, and bottled Newcastle Brown (W12,000).

JUJU TENT BAR Map p211

Dosandaero; meals W12,000-20,000; ⊙ 6pm-6am; subway Line 3 to Apgujeong, Exit 6
Popular in summer, this outdoor bar near Apgujeong has a retractable roof. Beer and *soju* is W4000 but the food, such as chicken gizzards or feet, grilled eel, stews and fish, is relatively expensive.

PLATINUM MICROBREWERY Map p211

☎ 2052 0022; Teheranno; all-you-can-eat-&-drink buffet Sun & Mon W17,500, Tue-Thu W18,500, Fri & Sat W19,500; ⊙ 6pm-8.30pm; subway Line 2 to Gangnam, Exit 8
Feeling in a party mood? Ten metres from the subway exit is this smart good-deal restaurant that offers the chance to eat and drink too much at the same time. The buffet has 17 items such as salads, sushi, shellfish, *bulgogi* (barbecued beef slices and lettuce wrap), spaghetti, soup and fruit. The on-site brewery produces six beers including a brown ale and a stout. The décor is modern with black furniture and fairy lights.

ROCK'N'ROLL BAR Map p211

☎ 545 4163; meals W10,000-30,000; ⊙ 8pm-5am; subway Line 3 to Apgujeong, Exit 6
A small museum of personal mementoes adds atmosphere to this three-storey log-cabin bar in Apgujeong where the cocktails (W9000) are a better deal than the beers (W8000).

TEASHOPS

Teashops cluster mainly in Insadong, but a few are scattered elsewhere. Many owners put a lot of effort into creating a special atmosphere for their customers with traditional décor and music. The medicinal hot and cold teas are made from roots, leaves, herbs or fruit. A cup of tea costs around W6000 (as much as a cheap meal), but it's a quality product and often served with a rice-cake snack.

GWANGHWAMUN

SIPJEON DAEBOTANG Map pp202-3
☎ 734 5302; teas W4000-5000; ⏰ 11am-9pm; subway Line 3 to Anguk, Exit 1

This tiny two-room medicinal teashop northeast of Gyeongbokgung serves wonderful thick *danpatjuk,* red-bean porridge with ginseng, chestnut and peanuts.

INSADONG

BEAUTIFUL TEA MUSEUM Map p205
☎ 735 6678; teas W5000-8000; ⏰ 10am-10pm; subway Line 3 to Anguk, Exit 6

This is not a traditional Korean teashop, but instead offers the chance to sip teas from around the world in the pleasant covered courtyard of a modern *hanok* (traditional Korean one-storey wooden house with a tiled roof), with tea sets on display.

DALSAENEUN DALMAN SAENGGAK HANDA Map p205
Moon Bird Thinks Only of the Moon; ☎ 723 1504; Insadong 4-gil; teas W6000; ⏰ 11am-11pm; subway Line 3 to Anguk, Exit 6

This special, poetically named teashop is packed with plants and rustic artefacts, and bird song, soothing music and trickling water add to the atmosphere. Huddle in a cubicle and savour one of the many teas, which include *gamnipcha* (persimmon-leaf tea). *Saenggangcha* (ginger tea) is peppery but sweet.

JEONTONG DAWON Map p205
☎ 7306305; off Seokjeongol-gil; teas W6000; ⏰ 8.30am-9.20pm; subway Line 3 to Anguk, Exit 6

Sit outside under the shady fruit trees in the very pleasant courtyard hideaway or inside a 19th-century *hanok* decorated with

scribbles on the walls. Small art exhibition spaces surround the courtyard. In summer sip delicious *omijacha hwaechae* fruit punch (*omija* are tiny dried berries said to contain five flavours). The *nokcha* (green tea) is unusual, as it's served with milk.

SINYETCHATJIP Map p205
New Old Teashop; ☎ 732 6678; teas W6000, wines W10,000-15,000; ⏰ 10am-10pm; subway Line 3 to Anguk, Exit 6

The fascinating décor created in this teashop includes a live squirrel, live birds and even live crabs. Thankfully the monkey has departed. The *maesilcha* (plum tea) is deliciously sweet and sour.

YETCHATJIP Map p205
Old Teashop; ☎ 722 5019; teas W6000; ⏰ 10am-10.30pm; subway Line 3 to Anguk, Exit 6

Seoul's most famous teashop features half a dozen little birds flying around freely. More atmosphere is added by haunting music, water features, candles and unique toilets. Antique bric-a-brac so clutters this goblin-sized teashop that it's hard to squeeze past and find somewhere to sit. The nine hot teas and seven cold ones are all special – try the hot *mogwacha* (quince tea) with a subtle fruity flavour or the cold nashi-pear tea drunk by Joseon kings and queens.

MYEONG-DONG & NAMSAN

O'SULLOC TEAHOUSE Map pp206-7
☎ 774 5460; green-tea items around W4000; ⏰ 9am-10.30pm; subway Line 4 to Myeong-dong, Exit 6

Impeccably presented green-tea drinks, cakes and ice creams are created here in this smart modern teahouse, but prices are not cheap. Everything is produced from the green tea picked on the company's tea plantation on Jejudo. Green-tea ice cream is recommended as are the homemade green-tea chocolates (W1000) but the green-tea latte tastes like hot milk.

TODAM TEASHOP Map pp206-7
토담; ☎ 753 5124; teas W4000; ⏰ 10am-10pm; subway Line 1 or 2 to City Hall, Exit 1

This rustic den next to Chongdong Theatre serves up genuine homemade teas including ones made from apricots, pine needles and even deer antler. Try *sipjeon daebotang,* which has 13 ingredients and is sweetened with honey quince syrup and served with Korean green tea, candied ginger and light-weight rice crackers.

HONGIK

CHASARANG Map p213

차사랑; ☎ 3141 8601; teas around W5000; ⏰ 10am-midnight; subway Line 2 to Hongik University, Exit 6

This traditional teashop brings a relax-ing and rustic Insadong atmosphere to Hongik's youthful clubland. Unusual teas include those made from mountain berries, pine needles and even bamboo.

GANGNAM

O'SULLOC TEAHOUSE Map p211

☎ 774 5480; Gangnamdaero; green-tea items around W4000; ⏰ 9am-11pm; subway Line 2 to Gangnam, Exit 5

See p107 for details on this shrine to *nok-cha* (green tea).

TEA MUSEUM Map p211

☎ 515 2350; Apgujeongno; teas around W7000; ⏰ 10.30am-9pm; subway Line 3 to Apgujeong, Exit 6

Sip unusual teas from around the globe in this tiny, antique-filled teashop in Apgujeong with over 50 herb, flower, fruit and leaf teas (and teapots) for sale. South African rooibos teas are popular.

LIVE MUSIC

Classy live jazz venues can be found in every entertainment district, and luxury hotels often have a live band in the bar. Itaewon has a live music scene, some of it provided by expat bands. But Hongik is the place for live indie music played in tiny underground venues by student bands with names like No Brain, Lazy Bone and Vaseline. But so far only Crying Nut has made it to stadium status. Concerts usually run from 7pm to 10.30pm. Admission varies from nothing to W10,000, which may include a drink.

The new Sound Day (www.soundday .co.kr) is held on the second Friday of the month from 8pm to 5am. W15,000 gains entry to around 10 live music venues in Hongik and includes a free drink.

MYEONG-DONG & NAMSAN

FEEL Map pp206-7   Rhythm & Blues

☎ 778 2401; admission incl a drink W5000; ⏰ 8pm-3am; subway Line 4 to Myeong-dong, Exit 10

This live music rumpus room run by totally eccentric Shin Kyung-so is packed with the mementoes of a lifetime that it's hard to squeeze in. But it's worth it when Shin and his musical friends get together to play anything from jazz to folk rock. Where else can you listen to a Simon and Garfunkel song being played on an accordion?

ITAEWON

ALL THAT JAZZ Map p209   Jazz

☎ 795 5701; Itaewonno; admission free Mon-Wed, Thu-Sun W3000; ⏰ 5pm-midnight; subway Line 6 to Itaewon, Exit 1

Local jazz bands have been playing here since 1976 and still play every night at 9pm (from 7pm on Sunday). Beers cost W5000 and meals are W7000 to W15,000.

J BAR Map p209   Jazz, Blues & Rock

☎ 793 9098; admission free; ⏰ 6.30pm-2am; subway Line 6 to Itaewon, Exit 1

This funky subterranean cellar with a youthful vibe and a dance area generally has live music every Friday and Saturday from 10pm to midnight. At other times the bar staff have a choice of 6000 LPs as well as numerous CDs. There is a pool table, an occasional DJ and beers are W4000.

WOODSTOCK Map p209   Rock

☎ 749 6034; Itaewonno; admission free; ⏰ 6pm-2am; subway Line 6 to Itaewon, Exit 2

Up on the 3rd floor expat bands blast out rock music every night from around 10pm, and pool and darts can keep you amused until then. Beers are W4000 but staff are chilly.

DAEHANGNO

LIVE JAZZ CLUB Map p208   Jazz

☎ 743 5555; admission incl a beer W5,000; ⏰ 4.30pm-3am; subway Line 4 to Hyehwa, Exit 2

The Seoul Jazz Academy (Map p208) is just down the road and three different jazz groups play every weekday night from 7pm until well past midnight, and from 8.30pm on Sunday. Special concerts are held every Saturday. All jazz genres are featured. Beer is W5000 while food costs W15,000 to W25,000. Don't miss out on this serious jazz venue.

HONGIK

ALICE LIVE CLUB Map p213   All Genres
☎ 3141 6876; admission incl a drink W5000-10,000; ⏱ 6pm-midnight; subway Line 2 to Hongik University, Exit 6
Anything from acid and rock to lounge jazz and pop is put on at this new venue in the heart of Hongik, usually between 9pm and 11pm. Ask at the door about what's on.

BEBOP JAZZ CLUB Map p213   Jazz
☎ 338 4932; admission free; ⏱ 6pm-3am; subway Line 2 to Hongik University, Exit 6
Up on the 5th floor Bebop caters to an older crowd with its armchairs and cool jazz. A singer or an instrumental band perform from 8pm to 11pm. Beers are W6000 but rise to W9000 during the live music.

BLUE BIRD Map p213   All Genres
☎ 019-388 4234; admission free; ⏱ 6pm-2am; subway Line 2 to Hongik University, Exit 5
The owner is a genuine music lover at this black basement venue where you can relax in armchairs and listen to live music every night from 9pm to late – it could be blues, jazz, folk, rock or pop. Beers cost W4000.

CLUB EVANS Map p213   Jazz
☎ 337 8361; Wausan-gil; admission W5000; ⏱ 6.30pm-2am; subway Line 2 to Hongik University, Exit 6
Relax at tables and chairs and catch all kinds of jazz from 9pm at this long-running 2nd floor lounge venue that caters to a more mature crowd than other live venues in Hongik.

FREE BIRD Map p213   Rock
☎ 333 2701; admission free; ⏱ 6pm-midnight; subway Line 2 to Hongik University, Exit 6
Rock, punk and funk are blasted out every night by young uni bands between 8pm and 11.30pm. Four different bands, with names like Incubator, Scarface and Bum, perform every night generally at a high volume. Beers cost W7000.

MOONGLOW Map p213   Jazz
☎ 324 5105; admission incl 2 drinks W10,000; ⏱ 6pm-1am Mon-Sat; subway Line 2 to Hongik University, Exit 6
This large underground venue with red armchairs and candles on the tables features live jazz from 9pm, with a different style every day.

SKUNK HELL Map p213   Punk
☎ 010-7720 9841; admission W5000; ⏱ 8-11pm Fri & Sat; subway Line 2 to Hongik University, Exit 6
Skunk Hell is punk heaven – a black messy dungeon with peeling posters on the ceiling and live, loud punk rock from house band Couch. Saturday is the night to crawl in, but you may have to provide your own drinks.

SLUG.ER Map p213   Rock
☎ 3142 0643; admission W5000; ⏱ 6-11pm; subway Line 2 to Hongik University, Exit 6
Live indie rock bands like DNA and N.Fly bring in the customers to this dark underground den of a live venue. Beers cost W4000 and admission includes a drink.

WATERCOCK Map p213   Jazz
☎ 324 2422; admission free-W7000; ⏱ 8pm-midnight; subway Line 2 to Hongik University, Exit 6
Located down an alley behind Alice Live, this serious 2nd floor live jazz venue has drinks for W5000. Musicians play from 9pm to 11.30pm. Blue Rain is a tight group consisting of piano, double bass, guitar, piano and a singer.

Musicians at Once in a Blue Moon (p110), Apgujeong

www.lonelyplanet.com

Entertainment

LIVE MUSIC

109

SINCHON & YEOUIDO

ROLLING STONES Map p210   Rock

☎ 332 9439; next to Sandpresso; admission W8000-12,000; ⏰ 7.30-10.30pm Tue-Sun; subway Line 2 to Sinchon, Exit 8

This small underground cellar sells only soft drinks but is dedicated to putting on all kinds of live rock music, and it's often standing room only at the weekend. Listen out for Broken Pearl.

GANGNAM

ONCE IN A BLUE MOON Map p211   Jazz

☎ 549 5490; Seolleungno; admission free; ⏰ 5pm-2am; subway Line 3 to Apgujeong, Exit 6

A classy venue in Apgujeong with two sessions of quality live jazz daily from 7pm until after midnight. Admission is free but drinks costs W12,000 and food costs even more.

CLUBS

The clubs around Seoul open early but most don't start getting busy until 10pm. Friday and Saturday nights have a real party atmosphere. Most clubs have DJs, dress is informal and food is not available (although luxury hotel clubs generally have live bands, food and a dress code).

Entry costs from W5000 to W10,000 and includes a free drink, but a few clubs charge more on Friday and Saturday nights. The famous Hongik Club Day (www.clubculture.or.kr) is held every last Friday of the month from 9pm to 5am. Pay just W15,000 for a free drink and entry to a dozen clubs, which all feature a bunch of DJs. Take some ID. Clubs that currently participate include Joker Red, Sk@, Saab, MI and M2. A map comes with the Club Day ticket. Clubbers are fickle so venues can blow hot and cold, but the Latin American dance clubs always retain their fan base.

ITAEWON

CLUB CALIENTE Map p209

☎ 798 1592; above Nashville Sports Bar, Itaewonno; admission incl a drink W5000; ⏰ 6pm-1am Thu-Sun; subway Line 6 to Itaewon, Exit 4

The salsa Latin beats will get you up and dancing around the unusual circular bar as the Itaewon expats show off their moves. Ask about lessons if you want to become a star dancer.

G-SPOT Map p209

☎ 332 2849; admission incl 2 drinks W10,000; ⏰ midnight-6am; subway Line 6 to Itaewon, Exit 3

This late-night cellar disco opens very late and irregularly. It attracts mainly Korean gays but is an experience for the daring as the steps down to it are like entering a catacomb.

GRAND OLE OPRY Map p209

☎ 795 9155; admission free; ⏰ 6.30pm-1am; subway Line 6 to Itaewon, Exit 3

This grand ole country-and-western bar and dance hall is still going strong with staff who chat and DJs on Friday and Saturday. Beers cost as little as W2000 and strawberry margaritas are W4000.

JJ MAHONEY'S Map p209

☎ 799 8601; Grand Hyatt Hotel; admission free; ⏰ 6pm-2am; subway Line 6 to Itaewon, Exit 2

Up the hill and inside the Grand Hyatt Hotel is this classy nightclub with nine different zones, and a live Canadian rock band from 9.30pm nightly except Sunday. Drinks are hit with a 34% surcharge, which means a beer costs W13,000 and cocktails W20,000, and there's a dress code. Take a taxi to get there.

KING CLUB Map p209

☎ 794 6869; Sobangseo-gil; admission free; ⏰ 6.30pm-4am; subway Line 6 to Itaewon, Exit 3

Beers are W3000 to W6000 and served by young Filipino girls at this venerable, mainly hip-hop, club with DJs and plenty of off-duty grunts getting down and hooking up.

TRANCE Map p209

☎ 797 3410; admission incl a drink Fri & Sat W10,000; ⏰ 9pm-5am; subway Line 6 to Itaewon, Exit 3

Pouting drag princesses Ms Nina and Ms Ari entertain in their own completely unique style at this small club with a DJ and a stage. Shows start around 2am and the big night is Saturday.

WHY NOT Map p209

☎ 795 8193; admission incl drink W5000; ⏰ 8pm-6am; subway Line 6 to Itaewon, Exit 3

This small gay dance arena has been expensively revamped with the very latest lights and lasers. DJs crank it up at this meet market until dawn when the subway trains start running again and the regrets begin.

HONGIK

BAHIA Map p213
☎ 335 1512; admission incl a drink W5000; ☺ 6pm-midnight Tue-Thu, 6pm-2am Fri & Sat; subway Line 2 to Hongik University, Exit 6
A Latin American dance club that is buzzing by 9pm with a friendly atmosphere, great music and W5000 beers. Wednesday is *bachata* (music originating from the Dominican Republic) night.

CLUB FUNKY FUNKY Map p213
☎ 010-6428 0248; admission incl a drink W10,000; ☺ 7pm-5am; subway Line 2 to Hongik University, Exit 6
This small club (sometimes called Club FF) combines a live band with a DJ who plays anything from rock and funk to hip-hop. Beers are W5000.

CLUB OTWO Map p213
☎ 3142 9278; Hogok Bldg; admission incl a drink Sun-Thu W8000, Fri & Sat W10,000; ☺ 8pm-5am; subway Line 2 to Hongik University, Exit 6
A smart new spacious club with stacks of lights and screens, which is down in the basement on the right side of the Hogok building. They call their dance music 'electro-trance techno'.

CLUB SAAB Map p213
☎ 324 6929; Wausan-gil; admission incl a drink W10,000; ☺ 8pm-4am; subway Line 2 to Hongik University, Exit 6
Plenty of hip-hop DJs with a hard attitude play here including the popular Schedule 1, and beers are W6000. It's the nearest thing to gangsta rap in Seoul, but is it for show or for real?

JOKER RED Map p213
☎ 019-345 7122; admission incl a drink W10,000; ☺ 7pm-midnight Wed & Thu, 7pm-4am Fri & Sat; subway Line 2 to Hongik University, Exit 6
All shades of techno are heard in this club, which has some red lighting effects to justify its name. The chill-out room is useful when it all gets a bit too much.

M2 Map p213
☎ 018-285 6972; admission incl a drink W15,000; ☺ 8pm-6.30am; subway Line 2 to Hongik University, Exit 6
Deep underground is one of the largest and best clubs. It has a high ceiling and plenty of lights, and plays mainly progressive house. Telephone to reserve a chill-out zone upstairs. Wednesday is ladies night and free admission is only the start.

MACONDO Map p213
☎ 010-8255 5819; admission incl a drink W5000; ☺ 7-11.30pm Mon-Thu, 7pm-5am Fri & Sat; subway Line 2 to Hongik University, Exit 5
Like Bahia, this fun and frenetic Latin American dance club in Hongik starts buzzing relatively early, and is soon as crowded as a *Where's Wally?* cartoon. Free dancing lessons are available.

MI Map p213
☎ 3141 2046; admission incl a drink Sun-Thu W8000, Fri & Sat W10,000; ☺ 7.30pm-4am Sun-Thu, 7.30pm-6am Fri & Sat; subway Line 2 to Hongik University, Exit 6
A pioneer of electronic music in Hongik this club's DJs still win prizes and the staff are friendly. Nowadays they play techno and progressive house.

SK@ Map p213
☎ 323 8750; admission incl a drink W10,000; ☺ 7pm-5am; subway Line 2 to Hongik University, Exit 6
A scruffy dark den of a club that attracts those who like their sounds mixed and eclectic. It's nothing fancy and the staff are off-hand, but that's how the regulars like it.

GAY & LESBIAN OPTIONS

Itaewon is the only area in Seoul where gay bars and clubs have English-speaking staff who welcome Koreans and foreigners, whether straight or gay. Look through the Itaewon listings for eight of them. Only one bar, Labris (p106) in Hongik, caters specifically to lesbians and is open to women only. Though attitudes in Seoul are changing slowly and becoming more tolerant, TV actor Hong Seok-chun is still the only Seoul celebrity who has come out of the closet.

Entertainment

CLUBS

ST 102 Map p213

☎ 011-9150 0911; admission incl a drink W10,000-15,000; ⏰ 9pm-5am; subway Line 2 to Hongik University, Exit 6

This brand new smart three-level shrine to hip-hop could blow the competition away with its lounges, bright dance areas, screens, neon and general pizzazz.

US 66 BAR Map p213

☎ 324 5388; ⏰ 5pm-2am Sun-Thu, 5pm-5am Fri & Sat; subway Line 2 to Hongik University, Exit 6

This American-style bar is a gathering place for expats prior to launching out into club-land and the staff speak some English. Beers are W5000, while the notorious 'Long Island iced tea' cocktail is W6000.

CAFÉS

DAEHANGNO

JUMANJI GAME CAFÉ Map p208

☎ 741 1040; per hr W2000; ⏰ 24hr; subway Line 4 to Hyehwa, Exit 2

Select a board game such as Monopoly or Risk from their global selection and start playing – all night long if you want. Most have an explanation in English or a staff member can get you started.

MINDEULLEYEONGTO Map p208

Minto; ☎ 745 5234; drinks & meals from W5000; ⏰ 10am-midnight; subway Line 4 to Hyehwa, Exit 2

Pay W5000 to have basic food and drink for up to five hours, or pay more for special fusion-style meals and drinks. Seven large rooms are furnished with flowery sofas and decorated with fantasy themes, and small alcoves, hideaways and balconies are spread around the five floors. It's a seminar centre designed and named (something to do with dandelions) by New Age hobbits. Downstairs are free movies, there's a piano to practice on and two friendly dogs act as unpaid greeters. Mindeulleyeongto 2, just down the road, is similar but only has one canine greeter, so stress levels are higher. Both need new stair carpets.

MOZART Map p208

☎ 744 7651; drinks & snacks W3000-7000; ⏰ 11am-11pm; subway Line 4 to Hyehwa, Exit 2

A European aura and classical music at-tracts customers to this multizoned café.

HONGIK

PRINCESS Map p213

☎ 335 6703; drinks W5000-8000; ⏰ 10am-4am; subway Line 2 to Hongik University, Exit 6

Candles and chandeliers light the steps down to this winter palace of a café with white curtains around some tables to give privacy, but cigarette smoke sometimes lowers the regal tone.

QUEEN LIZ Map p213

☎ 337 3843; drinks W3500; ⏰ 11am-8.30pm Mon-Sat; subway Line 2 to Hongik University, Exit 6

Ladies can buy a drink in this beauty café with violet velour armchairs, and then use all their make-up and cosmetics for free. If it all goes wrong you can pay for a professional make-up by Lee Eunim who was trained in France and speaks English. A finger package – nail care and colouring plus a finger massage – is W12,000. It's on the 4th floor above US 66 bar.

GANGNAM

IGLOO Map p211

☎ 511 0980; drinks around W8000; ⏰ noon-11pm; subway Line 3 to Apgujeong, Exit 1

This extraordinary Apgujeong café is only for dog-lovers – 30 canine breeds roam around freely. Most of them have starred in Korean movies and they relax here in between engagements.

ACTIVITIES

WATCHING SPORT

Baseball

South Korea has had a professional league (www.koreabaseball.or.kr) since 1982, and teams are sponsored by local *jaebeol* (huge family-run corporate conglomerates). The season runs from April to October. The Doosan Bears and the LG Twins play their home matches at Jamsil Baseball Stadium (Map pp214–15).

Basketball

Seoul has two teams, Samsung Thunders and SK Knights, in the 10-team Korean bas-ketball league (www.kbl.or). Matches are played from late October to March at Jamsil

Gymnasium (Map pp214–15). See the website for the schedule of weekday evening matches and weekend afternoon matches. Two foreign players (usually Americans) are allowed in each team.

Horse Racing

SEOUL RACECOURSE Map pp198-9
☎ 509 2309; www.kra.co.kr; admission W800;
⏰ races 11.30am-5pm Sat & Sun Sep-Jun, 1-9pm Sat & Sun Jul & Aug; subway Line 4 to Seoul Racecourse, Exit 2

Every weekend thousands head south to the horse racing. The spectators used to be mainly men, but racing authorities have had some success at promoting racing as a family or couple activity. Huge screens on the track show the odds, and close-ups of the horses. Short 1km to 2km races take place every half-hour with evening racing in July and August. Foreigners can make use of a smart and comfortable suite – just walk left into the new Lucky Ville grandstand, take the elevator to the 4th floor and walk to section S. English-speaking staff are on hand, but betting is easy enough. Despite the big crowds (legal gambling opportunities are still restricted in Seoul) everything is well-organised. The only problem is picking the winners.

The **Equine Museum** (☎ 509 1283; admission free; ⏰ 9am-6pm) houses some modern displays of historical items relating to horses and some are, quite surprisingly, beautiful.

Meals are limited to budget fast-food outlets, and the track is closed on four weekends of the year – New Year, Chuseok and the last weekend in December and July.

Soccer

Soccer was given a huge boost by the heroic efforts of the talented and spirited South Korean team, which reached the semifinals of the 2002 FIFA World Cup, cohosted by South Korea and Japan. But since then results have been disappointing and two coaches have been sacked. The home soccer league has 13 teams and matches are played from April to October at World Cup Stadium (Map pp198–9).

Ssireum

Ssireum is Korean-style wrestling, which is more similar to Mongolian wrestling than Japanese sumo. Tournament winners are given the title of *jangsa* (the strongest man in the world), and they used to be given a live bull as a prize.

Studying the form guide at Seoul racecourse (above)

JANGCHUNG GYMNASIUM Map pp200-1

☎ 2237 6800; subway Line 3 to Dongguk University, Exit 5

A four-day *ssireum* competition (admission free) is held here around the Lunar New Year.

Taekwondo

KUKKIWON Map p211

☎ 567 4988; www.kukkiwon.or.kr; office ⊗ 9am-5pm Mon-Fri; subway Line 2 to Gangnam, Exit 8

The Kukkiwon *dojang* (hall) hosts a regular schedule of taekwondo displays, training courses and tournaments. Expect to see graceful movements, acrobatic high kicking that defies gravity and spectacular pine-board breaking. Saturday and Wednesday mornings are when demonstration teams practice, except during university holidays. The museum (admission free; ⊗ 9am-5pm Mon-Fri) has photos, cups, medals and uniforms relating to the sport.

OUTDOOR & INDOOR ACTIVITIES

Adventure Sports

White-water rafting tours are run by USO (p46). Contact the Adventure Club (www.adventurekorea.com) for information on caving, rock climbing, white-water rafting and other outdoor activities.

Baseball

You can whack some baseballs from a pitching machine at Baseball Hitting Practice (Map p205; Insadong-gil; 10 balls W500; ⊗ 9am-midnight) in Insadong and Baseball Hitting Practice (Map p211; W500; ⊗ 9am-6pm) near Gangnam station.

Golf

Private golf courses are usually for members only, but there are plenty of driving ranges in top-end hotels and elsewhere. A typical one is Hyosung Golf (Map p211; ☎ 543 3046; Dosandaero; 1hr W15,000; ⊗ 5am-10pm; subway Line 3 to Apgujeong, Exit 2).

Ice-Skating

Lotte World ice-skating rink (p59) is open all year. In winter the swimming pools along the Han River freeze over and become skating rinks.

There's a skating rink (adult W1000, free skates) at the City Hall Plaza (Map pp202–3). The Sheraton Grande Walkerhill (Map pp198–9) and the Grand Hyatt (Map p209) also have ice-skating rinks in winter (entry and skates W30,000), but are only reachable by taxi. Ttukseom Seoul Forest and World Cup Park both have a sledding slope (1hr W500; ⊗ 10am-4pm).

Pool & Four Ball

Seoul is full of pool halls – look for the cues-and-coloured-balls signs. The halls usually have both pool tables (pool is called 'pocketball') and tables for four ball. The cost is usually W6000 per hour.

Four ball is played in Belgium and the Netherlands but is most popular in South Korea. There are no pockets and players must hit cannons. Two red balls and two white ones are used. The players (any number) hit the white balls in turn.

Players try to reach a score of zero. It's a handicap system, so beginners start with a score of three points. When you improve you start with five points, then eight, then 10 and so on. When your score reaches zero, to finish you must do a more difficult shot – hit the side-cushion three times while hitting both red balls without hitting the other white ball. A player scores minus one if they're successful and their white ball hits both the red balls without touching the other white ball, and can take another turn. It sounds easy but isn't. Players score nothing for hitting just one red, and plus one for hitting the other white ball or missing everything.

Skiing

The cold winters and mountainous terrain make Korea an ideal country for winter sports. Prices are reasonable and ski resorts offer a range of accommodation from youth hostels and basic *minbak* (private homes with rooms for rent) to condominiums and luxury hotels. The ski season runs from December to February. Ski clothes and equipment and English-speaking instructors can be hired. The dozen or so ski resorts have offices in Seoul and run all-inclusive one-day package tours from W75,000. USO (p46) organises weekend ski trips.

Five ski resorts are shown on the Seoul Vicinity Map (p146), but they can be very crowded, so you may want to go further a field to Korea's best ski resort at Yongpyong (www.yongpyong.co.kr) in Gangwon-do.

RIVERSIDE CYCLING TRIPS

Cycle paths, sports fields and flower gardens line both banks of the Han River and bicycles can be rented in parks along the river. The cycle paths are shared with pedestrians and flocks of flying rollerbladers. Both cycle rides start from Yeouido Park. Take subway Line 5 to Yeouinaru station and leave by Exit 2. Walk to one of the two **bike hire huts** (Map p210; bicycles/tandems per hour W2000/5000; ☺ 9am-7pm). ID is required and padlocks and bicycle helmets are not supplied.

Yeouido to the World Cup Stadium

This route is 7km return and takes 90 minutes, but lasts longer if you explore the stadium and surrounding parks.

From Yeouido cycle west past the green-domed **National Assembly** (p57) and after about 1km you reach Yanghwa gardens. Five minutes beyond is Yanghwa bridge, which you can use to cross the river. Walk up the steps of the bridge pushing your bike up the little bike path on the right of the steps. Stop to have a look round **Seonyudo**, an island in the middle of the river, which is being transformed from a water treatment plant into an eco park.

Wheel your bicycle down the narrow path on the right of the steps on the other side of the bridge, and then turn right along the cycleway on the northern side of the river. After 10 minutes, turn right at the orange Seongsan bridge, ride over a small bridge and then turn right, following the green signs. After another 10 minutes you should arrive in the large Pyeonghwa (Peace) Park, south of the impressive **World Cup Stadium** (p64) and its shopping malls and cinemas.

For a 6km (30-minute) detour, cycle around what is now an attractive green hill but used to be a mountain of garbage. Cross the major road to **Nanjicheon Park** (Map pp198-9; ☺ 6am-7pm) and keep going. Then return to Yeouido retracing the same route.

Yeouido to Olympic Park

This is a long trip, 38km return, and takes four hours cycling, but virtually all of it is on a cycleway and there are no hills.

Along the way are flower gardens, sports fields and lots of bridges. Herons, geese and other birds live near the river. At Banpo and Jamsil, windsurfers (W10,000), water-skis (W15,000) and jet-skis (W100,000) can be rented by the hour in July and August.

Near the 18km distance marker, turn right, ride under a couple of bridges and follow the left side of the usually dry riverbed. At the road, turn left, cross over the minor road, and then cross the major road using the pedestrian crossing. Then turn right, go over the bridge, and **Olympic Park** (p59) is on your left. It takes at least an hour to tour round Seoul's best park with its museums, stadiums and outdoor sculptures.

Swimming

Outdoor swimming pools only open in July and August. Six swimming pools with the same opening hours and prices can be found along the Han River including the **Yeouido Hangang swimming pool** (Map p210; ☎ 785 1093; adult/teenager/child W4000/3000/2000; ☺ 9am-7pm) and **Ttukseom swimming pool** (Map pp214–15).

The Hamilton Hotel (p137) has a popular pool on its roof-top, which is also open to non-guests. The outdoor pools at the **Sheraton Grande Walkerhill Hotel** (Map pp198-9; ☎ 453 0121; adult/child incl buffet lunch W55,000/35,000; ☺ 10am-6pm; subway Line 5 to Gwangnaru, Exit 2) are the best but the hotel is 2km from the subway and lunch is compulsory.

Lotte World (p59) and most top-end hotels have indoor pools. Carribean Bay (p155) is Seoul's best water park. See p151 for Seoul's nearest island beach.

Taekwondo

This traditional Korean martial art developed out of *taekyon*, which can be traced back to ancient tomb murals in the Goryeo dynasty. Taekwondo is now an Olympic sport and is increasingly popular with martial arts fans all over the world. All Korean army personnel receive taekwondo training and five million people worldwide have reached certificate standard. See opposite for Kukkiwon, the HQ of taekwondo.

HOKI TAEKWONDO

☎ 236 3361; www.taekwontour.com; 1½ hr/3hr courses W35,000/70,000

A 1½-hour introductory programme at the War Memorial & Museum gymnasium costs W35,000 and usually starts at 10am. The best thing about the programme is that you have the opportunity to break a 2cm-thick wooden board. Longer courses are also possible. Contact Hoki first before turning up at the gymnasium.

Tenpin Bowling

Tenpin bowling is available all over the city at around W3000 a game plus W1000 shoe hire. Seoulites take the sport seriously.

LCI Bowling (Map pp206-7; ☎ 771 2345; per game W2900, shoe hire W1000; ⊙ 10.30am-1am; subway Line 4 to Myeong-dong, Exit 3)

Lotte World Bowling (Map pp214-15; B3 fl; adult/child W3000/2800, shoe hire W1200; ⊙ 9am-midnight; subway Line 2 or 8 to Jamsil, Exit 3)

HEALTH & FITNESS
Bathhouses & Saunas

Don't leave Seoul without experiencing an *oncheon* (public bath) and a sauna where you can simmer or steam yourself like a *mandu* (dumpling). Spartan saunas cost only W5000, but *jjimjilbang* (upmarket saunas with Internet cafés, and luxury décor and facilities), cost from W7000 to W14,000. Most are open 24 hours, and some offer unusual green-tea baths or mugwort herbal saunas.

Undress in the locker room and then take a shower, as you must clean yourself thoroughly before getting into the public bath. Soap and shampoo are supplied, as well as toothpaste and toothbrushes, and the ladies section usually has hairdryers, foot massagers, lotions and perfumes. You can often have your hair cut as well as your shoes shined.

The water temperature in the big communal baths varies from hot to extremely hot, but there may also be a cold bath (including a 'waterfall' shower). Relaxing and turning pink in a hot bath is good therapy, especially on a cold winter's day. The heat soaks into weary bodies, soothing tired muscles and minds.

Saunas vary but all are as hot as a pizza oven, and to suffer more you can be pummelled by a masseur. Afterwards take a nap

lying on a wooden floor with a block of wood for a pillow. You can even spend the night in the dormitory, sleeping on a *yo* (a padded quilt that serves as a futon or mattress on the floor).

DONGBANG SAUNA Map p213

☎ 332 0481; B1, Seogyo Plaza 서교플라자; day/night W5000/4000; ⊙ 24hr; subway Line 2 to Hongik University, Exit 6

This clean and spacious sauna in Hongik offers separate sections for men and women. Facilities include an exercise centre, two sleeping rooms (one with bunks), a TV room, a green-tea pool, clay and crystal saunas and massages.

ITAEWONLAND SAUNA Map p209

☎ 749 5115; www.itaewonland.co.kr; day/night rate W7000/10,000; ⊙ 24hr; subway Line 6 to Itaewon, Exit 3

This new luxurious *jjimjilbang,* spread over five floors, is the best in Itaewon. With separate sections for men and women, every customer is loaned a towel and T-shirt. A long list of pools, spa baths and massages is available including a green-tea beauty treatment.

SEOUL MUD Map p209

☎ 747 8012; Itaewonno; ⊙ 9am-11pm; subway Line 6 to Itaewon, Exit 3

Foot massages, mugwort steam treatment, special soft mud packs and a ginseng bath cost from W20,000 to W82,000. It's a cheap price to pay for beauty if it works.

THAI SPIRIT Map p211

☎ 515 0973; Dosandaero; massages from W50,000; ⊙ 10am-8pm Mon-Sat; subway Line 3 to Sinsa, Exit 1

Try aromatic Thai-style foot, facial and body massages at this luxury spa. Afterwards sip exotic tea sitting on a swing seat in the stylish upstairs tearoom.

Shopping ■

Shopping

Seoulites love shopping and although the ever-rising won has increased prices for foreigners, there is something for everyone in the traditional markets, electronics emporiums, underground arcades, upmarket department stores and glitzy malls full of fashion boutiques and brand-name goods. Three of the best general malls are at COEX (p128), Central City (p127) and the World Cup Stadium (p64). Lotte, Hyundai, Shinsegae and Galleria are classy department stores but have regular sales when prices are heavily discounted.

For leather jackets, clothing, shoes, accessories, sports equipment or a flea market head to Dongdaemun market; while ginseng, children's clothes, spectacles and contact lenses are available at Namdaemun market. Larger sizes in clothes and shoes, souvenir T-shirts, leather jackets and hip-hop gear together with custom-made tailors can be found in Itaewon, where English is widely understood. For electronic gizmos drop into Yongsan Electronics Market or Techno Mart. For red ginseng, food and Asian medicines go to Gyeongdong market. Antique-lovers can browse Insadong, Itaewon and Janganpyeong markets. For brand-name boutiques head to Myeong-dong or south of the river to upmarket Apgujeong, but Westerners can struggle to find their size and fit.

Colourful macramé and embroidery, boxes made of handmade paper *(hanji)*, wooden masks, fans, lacquerware boxes inlaid with mother-of-pearl or ox horn and painted wooden wedding ducks can be found in the handicraft and souvenir shops of Insadong. More expensive items include pale-green celadon pottery, reproduction Joseon-dynasty furniture and elegant *hanbok* (p16). Shirts or blouses made of lightweight, see-through ramie (cloth made from pounded bark) material make an unusual fashion gift.

Ginseng, the wonder root, turns up in all sorts of products. You can chew it, eat it, drink it, clean yourself with it or bath in it. Ginseng chewing gum, ginseng chocolate, ginseng tea, ginseng wine, ginseng soup, ginseng soap and ginseng bath salts are all ways of benefiting from its world-famous health-giving properties. The many types of tea are another popular buy.

Opening Hours

Most shops open every day from 10am to around 9pm, but an increasing number are closed on Sunday. Opening hours for department stores are from 10am to 7.30pm daily, although some close one day a week or two days a month. Market opening times vary, but even on days when a market is closed, some stalls are normally open. The listings in this chapter give the opening hours.

Bargaining

Before venturing into the markets or buying from street stalls in and around Seoul, get a handle on approximate prices by looking in a department store or regular fixed-price shops. Some market stallholders start off with a very inflated price whereas others may quote only a slightly inflated figure. You can expect a discount of around 30%, but this is an average figure only and varies case by case. Walking away is the best way of achieving a lower price. Bargaining is part of the way of life in Seoul, so even when shopping in boutiques and opticians you can always request a discount if you feel it is justified or if you are buying more than one item.

TOP FIVE FAVOURITE SHOPS

- Arts and crafts: Ssamziegil (p120)
- CDs: Synnara Record (p126 & p127)
- Korean DVDs: Seoul Selection (opposite)
- Organic food: Huckleberry Farms (p127)
- Second-hand CDs: Pan (p125)

GWANGHWAMUN

The Samcheong neighbourhood between the palaces (p77) is fast becoming a new shopping attraction with small clothing and craft shops springing up among the established art galleries and restaurants.

DONGHWA DUTY-FREE SHOP

Map pp202-3   Brand Name Goods

☎ 399 3100; ⏱ 9.30am-8.30pm; subway Line 5 to Gwanghwamun, Exit 6

This extensive shop is packed with brand-name goods at prices that seem pretty steep despite their being 'duty free'.

GYPSY Map pp202-3   Crafts

⏱ flexible hrs; subway Line 3 to Anguk, Exit 1

The handcrafted goods in this tiny shop (stuck in a '60s Woodstock time warp) are all individually made by the owner.

JEWEL BUTTON Map pp202-3   Jewellery

☎ 733 9394; ⏱ 10am-6.30pm; subway Line 3 to Anguk, Exit 1

The award-winning handmade jewellery designs are created by two top Seoul designers.

KYOBO BOOKSHOP

Map pp202-3   Books & Music

☎ 3973 5100; B1, Kyobo Bldg; ⏱ 9am-9pm; subway Line 5 to Gwanghwamun, Exit 4

A wide selection of English-language books are in Section 10 of this large and famous bookstore that sells CDs and has a fast-food area.

SEOUL SELECTION BOOKSHOP

Map pp202-3   Books & DVDs

☎ 734 9565; www.seoulselection.co.kr; ⏱ 9.30am-6.30pm Mon-Sat; subway Line 3 to Anguk, Exit 1

Run by Hank Kim, this is the friendliest place to buy books on Korean culture in English, along with Korean CDs and DVDs. Staff can advise on which DVDs to buy – or you can hire them for W3000. Coffee, second-hand books and free Internet access are available too. Every Saturday at 11am the bookshop screens a Korean DVD with English subtitles (W3000). The website has a weekly newsletter of 'what's on' cultural events.

TOP FIVE SOUVENIRS

- Embroidery: Insadong (Map p205)
- Ginseng: Gyeongdong market (p122) and Namdaemun market (p123)
- *Hanji* (handmade paper) products: Insadong (Map p205)
- Pottery: Insadong (Map p205)
- Traditional teas: Insadong (Map p205)

YOUNGPOONG BOOKSHOP

Map pp202-3   Books

☎ 399 5656; ⏱ 9.30am-10pm; subway Line 1 to Jonggak, Exit 1

Another mega downtown bookstore with English-language books downstairs in sections F1 and H3 and plenty of people-watching possibilities.

INSADONG

Seoul's most fascinating shopping street, Insadong-gil is traffic-free on Saturday from 2pm until 10pm and on Sunday from 10am until 10pm, a scheme that is likely to be extended to other days. It's worth visiting more than once. Over 50 small art galleries display and sell the work of Seoul's top artists, potters and designers among rural-themed restaurants and atmospheric teashops. Stacks of shops sell pottery, antiques, calligraphy brushes, *hanji*, embroidery and souvenir knick-knacks. Look out for special snacks. Buddhist items, such as cassettes of monks chanting, incense sticks, and monk's and nun's clothing can be bought in shops near the Buddhist temple, Jogyesa (p53).

BANDI & LUNI'S Map p205   Books

☎ 2198 3000; B2 Jongno Tower; ⏱ 10am-10pm; subway Line 1 to Jonggak, Exit 3

This new and very large bookshop with seats has one of Seoul's best selections of books in English (section D2). Another branch is in the COEX Mall.

BEAUTIFUL STORE Map p205   Charity Shop

☎ 3676 1004; Byeolgung-gil; ⏱ 10.30am-8pm Mon-Sat; subway Line 3 to Anguk, Exit 1

Bargain hunters love the second-hand clothing (W2000 per item) as well as the household goods, while upstairs are reasonably priced artworks, CDs and a few English-language books. All profits go to charity.

BUG YOUR FRIENDS

Beondegi, a silkworm larvae snack, is sure to delight your friends and can be bought in a tin (W1000) at supermarkets and convenience stores and taken home as a souvenir gift.

KUKJAE EMBROIDERY Map p205 Handicrafts
☎ 732 0830; Hwaenamu-gil; ⏱ 9.30am-8pm; subway Line 3 to Anguk, Exit 6
This shop sells every type of wonderful Korean-style embroidery and all of it is handmade. The staff speak English and are embroidery experts who can answer your questions.

NAKWON MUSICAL INSTRUMENTS ARCADE Map p205 Musical Instruments
☎ 924 0604; ⏱ 9am-8pm Mon-Sat; subway Line 1 & 5 to Jongno 3-ga, Exit 5
On the 2nd floor are 200 small shops that sell all kinds of musical instruments and equipment. Local musicians may put on impromptu shows as they choose their instruments. Be careful about fakes.

SSAMZIEGIL Map p205 Handicraft Complex
Insadong-gil; ⏱ 10am-10pm; subway Line 3 to Anguk, Exit 6
This stylish new three-floor complex is packed with small arty-crafty shops, has a mini vineyard on the roof and a cool restaurant in the basement (p89).

MYEONG-DONG & NAMSAN

The traffic-quiet narrow streets of Myeong-dong are a leading youth-fashion centre. The customers here are becoming younger and younger – some malls and shops now cater specifically for free-spending middle-school students. Every evening mainly female crowds flock here to shop for local and imported clothes, shoes, bags, accessories, cosmetics and CDs. Cafés, restaurants, department stores and high-rise shopping malls with food courts and cinema multiplexes have made this area mega-popular with young people and Japanese visitors. Seoul railway station is also becoming a retail hotspot.

ABC MART Map pp206-7 Shoes
☎ 771 7777; ⏱ 11am-11pm; subway Line 4 to Myeong-dong, Exit 6 or 8
The biggest and best place for shoes with thousands of pairs on a number of floors – enough to make Imelda Marcos swoon. Another branch is at the other end of Myeong-dong.

GALLERIA CONCOS
Map pp206-7 Designer Clothing
☎ 390 4114; ⏱ 11am-8.30pm; subway Line 1 or 4 to Seoul Station, Exit 1
Experience brand-name nirvana next to Seoul train station in this brand new department store where top world designers sell status and style to folk burdened by too much spare cash.

LOTTE DEPARTMENT STORE
Map pp206-7 Department Store
☎ 771 2500; ⏱ 10.30am-8pm; subway Line 2 to Euljiro 1-ga, Exit 8
This is four classy stores that are linked together – the department store, Lotte Young Plaza, Lotte Avenuel and a duty-free shop – and includes a multiplex cinema (p103), food court, hotel and restaurants. It's almost impossible not to get lost inside this busy beehive but it's an experience.

LOTTE MART Map pp206-7 Supermarket
☎ 390 2500; www.lottemart.com; ⏱ 9-1am; subway Line 1 or 4 to Seoul Station, Exit 2
A mega discount supermarket with a household goods section that is spread over two floors next to Seoul train station. Come here for good-deal gifts and souvenirs, particularly food and drinks.

MIGLIORE Map pp206-7 Fashion Mall
☎ 2124 0005; ⏱ 11am-11.30pm Tue-Sun; subway Line 4 to Myeong-dong, Exit 6
Always teeming with teenage-looking trendsetters, this high-rise Myeong-dong mall is packed with fashion shops, has a food court on the 7th floor and an outdoor stage by the entrance.

SOGONG Map pp206-7 Underground Arcade
subway Line 1 or 2 to City Hall, Exit 6
Shops in this upmarket underground arcade sell ginseng, stationery, antiques, handicrafts, clothing and accessories, and it joins up with Myeong-dong underground arcade.

ITAEWON

This 1km shopping street caters to American soldiers stationed at the nearby Yongsan base, so most retailers speak a bit of English. Tailor-made suits and shirts are a speciality as are custom-made shoes in leather or ostrich skin. Shops will embroider any garment with any design for around W3000. Spectacles (W50,000) and contact lenses are good quality and reasonably priced.

Such disparate items as leather jackets, antique furniture (sold in shops that line Bogwangdong-gil), second-hand books, hip-hop clothing and purple amethyst jewellery are on sale along with piles of souvenir T-shirts and handicrafts sold from market stalls. Don't believe what some shopkeepers say – eel-skin handbags can cost around W35,000 not W70,000 and 50 red-ginseng tea bags cost around W9000, not W44,000.

ABBY'S BOOK NOOK

Map p209 · Second-hand Books
☎ 795 4253; ⏰ 10am-10pm; subway Line 6 to Itaewon, Exit 1
Now centrally located, this excellent second-hand, 2nd floor bookshop has helpful staff, stacks of books that sell for half the cover

TAXES & REFUNDS

Global Refund (☎ 776 2170; www.globalrefund .com) and **Korea Refund** (☎ 537 1755) offer a partial refund of the 10% VAT. Spend more than W30,000 or W50,000 in any participating shop and you can later claim a refund. The retailer gives you a special receipt, which you must show to a customs officer at Incheon International Airport. Go to a Customs Declaration Desk (near check-in counters D and J) before checking in your luggage, as the customs officer will want to see the items before stamping your receipt. After you go through immigration, show your stamped receipt at the relevant refund desk, next to the duty-free shops, to receive your won refund in cash or by cheque. But don't get too excited – the refunds range from 5% to 7%.

price, and others that go for W2000 or less. It also has a café.

DYNASTY TAILOR Map p209 · Tailor
☎ 3785 3035; Itaewonno; ⏰ 10am-8pm; subway Line 6 to Itaewon, Exit 4
Dynasty has a good reputation and charges reasonable prices – pure wool custom-made suits start at W250,000 and take about three days to make.

Dynasty Tailor (above), Itaewon

MARKET BUZZ

You could disappear for a week in Seoul's mind-boggling markets and still not see everything. Whether it's fresh fish, antiques, Asian medicines or the latest electronic gadgets, you can find them here in the sprawling markets of Seoul.

Dongdaemun Market

This huge **market** (Map p122; subway Lines 1 or 4 to Dongdaemun, Exit 6 or 7 or subway Line 2, 4 or 5 to Dong-daemun Stadium, Exit 1) is famous for the thousands of small fashion shops packed into four neighbouring high-rise shopping malls: **Doota Mall** (☎ 3398 2386; ⊙ 10.30am-5am, closed 11pm Sun to 7pm Mon) has children's wear on the 6th floor, while the 8th floor has a bright food court (meals W4500 to W7000). **Migliore Mall** (☎ 3393 0001; ⊙ 10.30am-5am Tue-Sun) has an IT floor and a 24-hour massage service to soothe those aching shopping muscles. **Cheongdaemun** (☎ 2248 4800; ⊙ 10.30am-5am Wed-Mon) is being refurbished but will retain the **MMC 10-screen multiplex** (☎ 2268 9111), which screens films all night and day. **Hello apM** (☎ 6388 1114; ⊙ 10.30am-5am Wed-Mon) is targeted at youth.

Inside a stadium is the undercover **Pungmul flea market** (☎ 793 6908; ⊙ 9am-7pm). Hunt for new and used bargains among the piles of car-boot-sale stuff, everything from *dojang* name stamps, handicrafts and army surplus to CDs, musical instruments and collectables. Around both stadiums are shops selling sports clothing and equipment as well as food stalls. Shop 45 on the outside of Pyeonghwa market has second-hand books in English.

Different sections have different closing times but while many close on Sunday, the four big malls stay open.

Gyeongdong Market

Walk straight ahead from the subway exit and you'll soon be struck by the aromatic odours of the traditional Asian herbal remedies that the **Gyeongdong market** (Map pp200-1; ⊙ 8am-6.30pm, partly closed 1st & 3rd Sun each month; subway Line 1 to Jegi-dong, Exit 2) specialises in. The leaves, herbs, roots, flowers and piles up in the shops and stalls are all medicinal. Bark is sold to be made into soup, while *jine* is a long millipede that is boiled to make a soup or eaten dry. It is said to be good for backache and a handful costs W6000.

Cross the road, turn left at Chohung Bank and then first right, and on the left are 2nd-floor arcades piled high with ginseng and honey products. Don't pay more than W9000 for 50 red-ginseng tea bags.

DONGDAEMUN MARKET

SHOPPING 🏠	
Bags & Clothes................... 1 C2	
Cheongdaemun (Blue Gate)	
Mall & Cinemas................ 2 B2	
Doota Mall........................3 B2	
Embroidery & Hats............4 A2	
Fabrics & Bedding.............5 B1	
Fabrics & Towels................6 A2	
Hello apM........................7 B2	

Leather (2nd floor)....................8 C2	
Migliore Mall..............................9 B2	
Pungmul Flea Market................10 C2	
Shoes..11 C1	
Shop 45 (English books)............12 B2	
Sports Clothing & Equipment.....13 B3	
Toys & Stationary......................14 C1	
Underwear & Suits.....................15 C2	
Underwear, Clothes & Bags.......16 C2	

Janganpyeong Antiques Market

Over a hundred small shops are packed into four **arcades** (Map pp198-9; 🕙 10am-6.30pm, some stalls closed Sun; subway Line 5 to Dapsimni, Exit 2). They're so full of old furniture, paintings, pottery and stone statues that customers can hardly squeeze inside. The atmosphere is quiet compared to the other markets but if you love to browse through treasures – from *yangban* (aristocrat) pipes and hats to wooden shoes, fish-shaped locks and Buddhas – the arcades are easy to visit. At the subway exit walk over to the orange-tiled building behind the car park on the right, Samhee 5, and a similar building on the left, Samhee 6. After visiting them, walk back to Exit 2 and carry on left along the main road for 10 minutes to reach a brown-tiled arcade, Janganpyeong. Outside Exit 2 is **Damoa Donkkaseu** (☎ 2244 9256; meals W5000; 🕙 noon-9.30pm Mon-Sat), which serves Japanese-style food.

Namdaemun Market

This huge night-and-day **market** (Map p123; subway Line 4 to Hoehyeon, Exit 5) dates back to the 15th century and has thousands of shops and stalls selling food, ginseng, dried seaweed, clothes, shoes, hiking gear, watches, handicrafts, spectacles and contact lenses. Different sections have different opening hours – wholesalers are open all night and many shops are open on Sunday. **Alpha** (🕙 8am-7pm Mon-Sat, noon-6pm Sun) has two floors of toys and two floors of stationery. Shops in Hoehyeon underground arcade sell stamps, second-hand cameras, LPs, CDs and DVDs.

Shinsegae department store (☎ 310 1234; 🕙 10.30am-7.30pm, closed 1st & 3rd Mon) is spread over two buildings with a supermarket in the basement. **Mesa family fashion mall** (☎ 2128 5000; 🕙 10am-5am, closed 1st & 3rd Mon) has a food court on the 9th floor, opticians on the 6th floor, sports gear on the 4th floor.

Food stalls offer cheap meals for the adventurous, including octopus and *tteokbokki* (pressed rice cakes and vegies in a spicy sauce). Other food choices include a duck restaurant **Tobang** (p92) or Shinsegae department store food court.

Yongsan Electronics Market

If you can plug it in, you can find it here at this **electronics market** (Map pp198-9; ☎ 701 8200; 🕙 9.30am-7.30pm, partly closed 1st & 3rd Sun each month; subway Line 1 Yongsan, Exit 3). Prices are lower than elsewhere but are not generally marked on the products. Leave the station plaza by Exit 3, turn right, then right again and walk through the pedestrian overpass to enter the first building of Yongsan Electronics Town on the 3rd floor. Go down a floor to another pedestrian overpass to the shops that line both sides of the main street. Head to Najin Mall for computer parts.

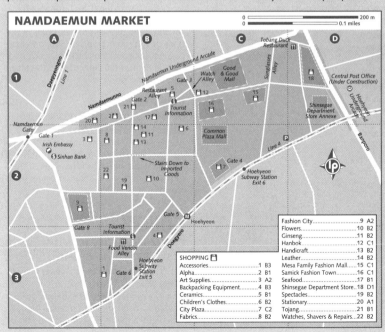

STAR MARKET Map p209 — Fashion Store

☎ 792 7603; Itaewonno; ⏰ 9.30am-9.30pm; subway Line 6 to Itaewon, Exit 4

The sassy style and low prices lure customers inside this new youth-oriented fashion store and café that employs Russian staff who look like they moonlight in hostess bars.

SUPREME OPTICAL Map p209 — Optician

☎ 795 6423; cnr Itaewonno & Banporo; ⏰ 9am-8.30pm; subway Line 6 to Itaewon, Exit 4

Eye checks are free, while spectacles cost from around W50,000 and are ready in an hour. Spectacles and contact lenses can be a good deal in Seoul, especially if you bargain.

WASHINGTON SHIRT Map p209 — Tailor

☎ 792 1650; Itaewonno; ⏰ 11am-9pm; subway Line 6 to Itaewon, Exit 4

Custom-made business shirts cost W28,000 to W55,000. They are on the plain side (wearing an Aloha shirt to work would give your Korean boss a heart attack), but the shop has a range of designs to choose from.

CLOTHING SIZES

Measurements approximate only, try before you buy

Women's Clothing					
Aus/UK	8	10	12	14	16	18
Europe	36	38	40	42	44	46
Japan	5	7	9	11	13	15
USA	6	8	10	12	14	16

Women's Shoes					
Aus/USA	5	6	7	8	9	10
Europe	35	36	37	38	39	40
France only	35	36	38	39	40	42
Japan	22	23	24	25	26	27
UK	3½	4½	5½	6½	7½	8½

Men's Clothing					
Aus	92	96	100	104	108	112
Europe	46	48	50	52	54	56
Japan	S		M	M		L
UK/USA	35	36	37	38	39	40

Men's Shirts (Collar Sizes)					
Aus/Japan	38	39	40	41	42	43
Europe	38	39	40	41	42	43
UK/USA	15	15½	16	16½	17	17½

Men's Shoes					
Aus/UK	7	8	9	10	11	12
Europe	41	42	43	44½	46	47
Japan	26	27	27½	28	29	30
USA	7½	8½	9½	10½	11½	12½

TOP FIVE MARKETS

- Top clothing market: Dongdaemun (p122)
- Top general market: Namdaemun (p123)
- Top food market: Gyeongdong (p122)
- Top antiques market: Janganpyeong (p123)
- Top flea market: Pungmul in Dongdaemun market (p122)

WHAT THE BOOK Map p209 — Second-hand Books

☎ 797 2342; Sobangseo-gil; ⏰ 10am-8pm Mon-Sat, noon-8pm Sun; subway Line 6 to Itaewon, Exit 3

This new bookshop, run by a couple of young and helpful expats, sells mainly second-hand books. They stock thousands of books at reasonable prices, and add a rare touch of culture to the Itaewon scene.

DAEHANGNO

FILIPINO SUNDAY MARKET

Map p208 — Market

Hyehwa Roundabout; ⏰ 9am-5pm Sun; subway Line 4 to Hyehwa, Exit 1

Join the jolly Filipino community in Seoul who gather here in this lively Little Manila every Sunday to meet each other and buy CDs, DVDs, call-back phone cards and second-hand mobile phones. Chefs in the back of vans cook tropical Filipino treats – cassava cakes, *adobo* chicken, *pancit* noodles, *longaniza* sausage, purple rice, stews and banana spring rolls.

IRIVER Map p208 — MP3 Players

☎ 766 7778; Daehangno; ⏰ 10.30am-9pm; subway Line 4 to Hyehwa, Exit 1

All the latest miniature miracle MP3 players and accessories are on display from Korea's top manufacturer, which has 10% of the global market and is adding new features almost every month.

HONGIK

BEAUTIFUL STORE Map p213 — Charity Shop

☎ 332 7778; B1, next to Merae Plaza 미래프라자; ⏰ 10.30am-6pm Mon-Sat; subway Line 2 to Hongik University, Exit 5

One of a pioneering and expanding chain of second-hand shops that raises money for charity and has introduced the joys of op-shopping to Seoul.

HEADRUSH Map p213 — Hairdresser

☎ 338 2773; men/ladies from W15,000/20,000; ◷ 11am-7pm Tue-Sun; subway Line 2 to Hongik University, Exit 6

In this 4th-floor salon above US 66 bar, the English-speaking stylists are not the cheapest but have studied and worked in London. Making an appointment is recommended.

HONGDAE ARTISTS' SATURDAY MARKET Map p213 — Art & Craft Market

☎ 765 0501; ◷ 1pm-6pm Sat in summer; subway Line 2 to Hongik University, Exit 6

With its hair-braiding stalls, tarot-card readers, handmade jewellery, hand-painted hats and T-shirts, appliqué bags, fans with a political message and soap made from rice and honey, this small Saturday market in the park outside Hongik University has a '60s Woodstock feel. Singers and pasty-faced magicians put on shows in the entertainment corner.

KODAK PHOTO SHOP Map p213 Photography

☎ 334 2109; ◷ 9am-9pm; subway Line 2 to Hongik University, Exit 6

This shop can deal with all your photographic needs and keeps up to date on the digital front. Samsung cameras will soon be the size of shirt buttons.

MYTHOS Map p213 — Music

☎ 322 6698; ◷ 5pm-9pm; subway Line 2 to Hongik University, Exit 6

All the Siwan label music can be found here as well as rock, world and progressive music. If the Strawbs are your bag, drop by.

PAN Map p213 — Music

☎ 3142 7584; ◷ noon-midnight; subway Line 2 to Hongik University, Exit 6

Mainly second-hand CDs and LPs are stacked up all over the shop, so who knows what gems you might find if you have the patience to look through them.

PURPLE RECORD Map p213 — Music

☎ 336 3023; Wausan-gil; ◷ 9.30am-midnight; subway Line 2 to Hongik University, Exit 6

All music genres are covered in this established record store that appeals to local art students. It's always worth a browse.

Shopping

HONGIK

Volkswagen (p126), Hongik

RECORD FORUM Map p213 — Music

☎ 323 9565; Wausan-gil; ⏱ noon-10pm; subway Line 2 to Hongik University, Exit 6

This small record store has hardly any room for customers but has a selection guaranteed to interest jazz and blues enthusiasts.

VOLKSWAGEN Map p213 — Fashion Store

☎ 334 8817; ⏱ noon-11pm; subway Line 2 to Hongik University, Exit 6

This middle-of-the-road boutique is bigger than most and has room for all the latest styles as well as half a Volkswagen car inside.

SINCHON & YEOUIDO

Outside the famous Ewha Womans University, a busy but relatively traffic-free neighbourhood of small shops and stalls has been established to sell clothes, bags, shoes, accessories, haircuts and beauty treatments to the fashion-conscious female students. A street of shops near the subway specialises in wedding gear. For something completely different, Seoul's best fish market is south of Yeouido.

AHYEON-DONG WEDDING STREET

Map p210 — Bridal Store

⏱ 10am-8pm Mon-Fri; subway Line 2 to Ewha Womans University, Exit 3

Enjoy a bridal fashion show as you walk past the window displays of the more than 50 wedding shops in this street of romantic dreams. *Hanbok* wedding gowns are on show but Western-style ones are more popular these days.

CROW Map p210 — Body Piercing

☎ 312 8392; ⏱ 11am-10pm; subway Line 2 to Ewha Womans University, Exit 2

Body piercing shops in Seoul are as rare as hen's teeth, but piercing is available in this little hut of a shop that sells studs, henna tattoos and more.

GAJUKGONGYEBANG

Map p210 — Leather Goods

☎ 392 4453; ⏱ noon-9pm; subway Line 2 to Ewha Womans University, Exit 2

Hand-crafted leather goods are made on the spot by an elderly artisan in this tiny shop next door to Crow.

NORYANGJIN FISH MARKET

Map p210 — Fish Market

☎ 814 2211; ⏱ 24hr; subway Line 1 to Noryangjin, Exit 1

All kinds of marine life swim around in tanks and bowls in this covered market – it's an aquarium show that is well worth a visit. Large crabs, rays, tuna and shellfish are on display along with more exotic species such as sea cucumbers and sea squirts – the orange one is called *meongge*. Take-away platters of raw fish sell for W10,000 to W20,000, much cheaper than the restaurants on the 2nd floor (p96). Fresh prawns cost around W12,000kg, while lobsters are around W30,000kg. To make this a popular tourist attraction all that is needed are some stalls that will grill or steam what you buy fresh from the market. To get there, take the exit from the subway station, cross the bridge over the train tracks and go down the stairs into the market.

SYNNARA RECORD Map p210 — Music

☎ 3143 3946; ⏱ 10am-10.30pm; subway Line 2 to Sinchon, Exit 2

There are CDs of all genres and a good selection of DVDs available in this well-stocked chain store. There is also a branch in Gangnam.

GANGNAM

Apgujeong is a haughty *haute couture* shopping area most famous for its designer boutiques, cat-walk clothing and dizzying prices. Here, a second-hand pair of designer shoes can cost W480,000 or, for the same price, you can buy junior a cute-looking BMW pedal car. The most extravagance must be the Rolls Royce Phantom, which will dig a noticeable W650m hole in your credit card account.

In Gangnam, the young women wear Westwood and are as wafer thin as their mobile phones, which they use to ring their cosmetic surgeons while nibbling a tiny slice of green-tea cheesecake in an all-white well-being café. Tiny dogs are a must-have fashion accessory (preferably with pink ears and a green tail), and have their own doggie shops, beauty parlours, surgeons and, of course, doggie cafés.

Noryangjin fish market (opposite), south of Yeouido

BOON THE SHOP Map p211 Designer Clothing
☎ 317 0397; ⏱ 11am-8pm; subway Line 3 to Apgujeong, Exit 2

This slimmed-down version of Galleria has stairways and balconies around an atrium courtyard, which provides a chic atmosphere as you browse lesser-known but cutting-edge brand-name stores.

CENTRAL CITY MALL Map p211 Mall
☎ 6282 0114; www.centralcityseoul.co.kr; ⏱ 10am-10pm; subway Line 3 or 7, Exit 7

A popular mall next to the express bus terminal that includes **Shinsegae department store** (☎ 3479 1234; ⏱ 10.30am-8pm) and **Youngpoong Bookshop** (☎ 595 4700; ⏱ 9.30am-10pm Mon-Sat, 10am-9pm Sun) where books in English are on the 2nd floor in Sections E1 and E2. A food court and the Central 6 Cinema multiplex are other attractions.

GALLERIA Map p211 Designer Clothing
☎ 344 9414; Apgujeongno; ⏱ 10.30am-8.30pm; subway Line 3 to Apgujeong, Exit 1

This luxury boutique department store packs dozens of world-famous fashion-designer stores into two buildings, one of which is covered in plastic discs that look psychedelic at night. Buy a bikini and a top here and you can kiss goodbye to US$1000. On top of the west wing is an Italian restaurant with a vineyard patio with set meals starting at W27,000.

HUCKLEBERRY FARMS
Map p211 Organic Produce
☎ 514 3800; Apgujeongno; ⏱ 10am-10pm; subway Line 3 to Apgujeong, Exit 2

Organic produce is rare in Seoul but this large health food shop stocks Seoul's widest range of organic food and drinks – including Founders organic beer from New Zealand (W7900).

SYNNARA RECORD Map p211 Music
☎ 501 0777; Gangnamdaero; ⏱ 10.30am-10pm; subway Line 2 to Gangnam, Exit 7

A large selection of CDs and DVDs of all genres is available here, and you can listen to the latest sounds before buying.

TASTE MAXIMUM Map p211 Designer Clothing
☎ 3444 7021; ⏱ 11am-10pm; subway Line 3 to Apgujeong, Exit 2

Up-and-coming Seoul fashion designer Kim Gyu-sik and his associates have a cute boutique here in Apgujeong and in Lotte department store in Myeong-dong.

JAMSIL

COEX MALL Map pp214-15   Mall
☎ 6002 5312; www.coexmall.com; ⏰ 10am-10pm; subway Line 2 to Samseong, COEX Exit
This huge underground mall (p58) contains innumerable shops, including an excellent bookshop, record store and department store, but don't expect many bargains.

KIM YOUNG JOO MILANO

Map pp214-15   Designer Clothing
☎ 545 2514; ⏰ 10am-7pm Mon-Sat; subway Line 7 to Cheongdam, Exit 13
In brand-name street in Apgujeong but on the Jamsil map is the boutique of a well-known local designer who is famous for

adapting traditional *hanbok* elements into a modern style.

TECHNO MART

Map pp214-15   Electronics & General
☎ 3424 3000; ⏰ 10am-8pm, closed 2nd & 4th Tue; subway Line 2 Gangbyeon, Exit 1
Electronic gear takes up seven floors of this high-rise next to Gangbyeon station. It's less overwhelming to find your way around than Yongsan Electronics Market. In the basement is a **food court** (p98), a general shopping **mall** (B1; ⏰ 10am-9pm) and **Lotte Mart** (B2; ⏰ 9am-midnight). On the 9th floor is a relaxing outdoor area with views of the Han River, while on the 10th floor is the CGV Gangbyeon multiplex cinema.

Sleeping

Sleeping

Seoul is bursting with accommodation – backpacker guesthouses, budget motels under W50,000, homestays and a stack of midrange and top-end hotels and serviced apartments. Accommodation is invariably charged per room, with little or no discount for singles, although homestays and guesthouses can be a little more generous. Hotel rooms with Western-style beds are most common, but for the same price you can often opt for a Korean-style room where you sleep on a *yo* (padded quilt) on the *ondol* (heated) floor. Gwanghwamun, Insadong and Myeong-dong are central, but it doesn't matter too much where you stay as long as it is near a subway station as although the palaces are downtown, many other tourist sights are scattered further afield and have to be visited by subway. A handful of top-end hotels are not near a subway station so guests there rely on hotel shuttle buses and the city's reasonably priced taxis.

Accommodation Styles

GUESTHOUSES & YOUTH HOSTELS

Seoul has a handful of small, friendly guesthouses/backpackers that cater specifically for budget-conscious foreigners. Dorms are around W15,000 a night, single rooms around W27,000 and double rooms around W37,000. Rooms tend to be small, but the staff speak English and facilities usually include a TV and video lounge, a kitchen, a free washing machine, a free breakfast and free Internet access. Toilets and showers are usually shared. The two youth hostels, Olympic Parktel and Dreamtel, are far from the city centre.

MOTELS & LOVE MOTELS

Motels *(yeogwan)* are small, family-run budget hotels and there are thousands scattered throughout Seoul. Don't be put off by dimly lit corridors and the proprietor napping in a cubicle at the entrance. The rooms are always a bit small but offer a good deal as they are packed with facilities – en suite toilet and shower, TV, video, telephone, fridge, drinking water, aircon and heating, even toothbrushes, lotions and hairdryers. Nearly all the rooms have beds, but some also offer Korean-style rooms with a *yo* on the floor. The staff rarely speak any English so expect to be greeted with a look of alarm rather than a warm welcome.

The motels have no communal facilities – you just get a room, which is why prices are low. Room prices start at W30,000 for a room and those in the upper range (W45,000) are smarter and merge into the love-motel category. Sometimes looking like fairyland castles, love motels cater for daytime, pay-by-the-hour couples, but also accept conventional overnight guests. They provide a good option, especially if you fancy a round bed, satin sheets and a boudoir décor with stars painted on the ceiling.

HOTELS & SERVICED APARTMENTS

There is no shortage of midrange and luxury hotels, and new serviced apartments are springing up everywhere and providing tough competition, as they provide more home conveniences such as kitchen and laundry facilities. They all add 21% to their rates for service and tax, but the trend is to include this in the quoted prices. Unless tourist numbers zoom upwards, hotel prices will remain soft, so rack rates are normally heavily discounted, particularly at slack periods (eg August). Luxury hotel rooms often go for around W200,000 or up to W250,000 for the best ones. Broadband Internet connection is always available as is air-con. Rooms can lack character, but the gym/sauna/spa

> ## TOP FIVE LUXURY HOTELS
> - Westin Chosun (p136)
> - Grand Hyatt Seoul (p137)
> - Grand Inter-Continental (p142)
> - Hotel Shilla (p135)
> - JW Marriott (p140)

facilities and restaurants are often excellent. Hotels and apartments with character and style are rare but Seoul's top hotels rate with the best anywhere in terms of facilities and services. See p162 for online discount booking services.

HOMESTAYS

Some Korean families in Seoul offer *min-bak* (homestay) to foreign visitors who can experience Korean food, customs and family life at close quarters. The cost for bed and breakfast is W30,000 a night for a single person and W50,000 for a couple. Some offer pick-ups and dinner, and rates are greatly reduced if you stay long-term. Book online at least two weeks before your arrival date.

Korea Homestay (www.koreahomestay.com) Small scale.

Labostay (☎ 736 0521; www.labostay.or.kr) Long-established.

LONG-TERM ACCOMMODATION

Renting an apartment can be tricky because of the traditional payment system. *Jeonse* is when you loan W30 million to W500 million to the landlord and get it all back at the end of the rental period. *Weolse* is when you pay a smaller returnable deposit of W3 million to W10 million (usually referred to as 'key money') plus a monthly rental fee. However, some accommodation in Seoul is available to foreigners on the Western system with a small returnable deposit and a monthly rent. Other options include the increasing numbers of modern serviced-apartments (from W75,000 to W230,000 a day). Browse some real estate websites for what's on offer – try www.nicerent .com and www.ace-realty.co.kr. In Seoul real estate is measured in *pyeong* (1 *pyeong* is 3.3 sq m).

Apartment sharing is another option, although spare rooms can be hard to find – view www.english spectrum.com or click on 'Community' at http://eng lish.seoul.go.kr or try the newspaper websites (p169).

Price Ranges

Top luxury hotels are coy about their discount rates, which often depend on the occupancy rate, but you can generally ignore the rack rates, and discount rates range from under W200,000 to W250,000. Some offer special deals if you book through their website or at slack times. Midrange hotels are often discounted to around W100,000. Plenty of hotels under W100,000 offer a good deal, while the ones over that figure offer more facilities – restaurants, bars, health clubs and the like – rather than better rooms. New serviced apartments range from good-value modern studios that can be discounted to W60,000 a night up to large and luxurious apartments at W200,000. Motels provide excellent-value rooms for

INCHEON INTERNATIONAL AIRPORT ACCOMMODATION

A cluster of new hotels and restaurants has been built in Airport Town Sq, less than 10 minutes by taxi or bus northeast of the airport. A transit hotel is inside the airport terminal.

Air Garden Transit Hotel (Map p150; ☎ 032-743 3000; www.airgardenhotel.com; 6hr s/d incl tax & service from W49,500/61,500; 🖳) On the departure side of immigration, the small but smart modern rooms are perfect for a stopover snooze, although ones with a view are generally snapped up by airlines. A minimum 12-hour stay is required after 6pm and an American breakfast costs W14,000. Up on the 4th floor, the hotel is in two parts at both the east and west ends of the terminal. Rejuvenate after your flight with a **massage** (☎ 032-743 3004; W50,000-W120,000; 🕑 8am-7pm).

Guesthouse Korea (Map p150; ☎ 032-747 1872; www.guesthousekorea.co.kr; Airport Town Square; d & tw W45,000; 🖳) This quite luxurious guesthouse has large, light, modern motel-style rooms with their own fully equipped kitchens. It's on the 10th floor of a high-rise building opposite New Airport Hotel. Free Internet and a free pick-up from the airport are available.

New Airport Hotel (Map p150; ☎ 032-752 2066; www.hotelnewairport.co.kr; Airport Town Sq; r regular/deluxe incl tax & service W90,000/99,000; 🖳) Smart new regular rooms have Internet access while deluxe rooms have a computer, and a discount should be possible as a bunch of similar hotels are nearby. A golf driving range is on the roof. See p151 for accommodation on the beach just a few kilometres from the airport. Take bus No 202 (W900, 20 minutes, half-hourly) or a taxi to Eurwangni Beach.

around W35,000, which lack only space, while guesthouses provide not such good rooms but a priceless friendly ambience with communal facilities and free services at a similar price. Guesthouses also have dorm beds that range from W11,000 to W19,000, while the two youth hostels charge W22,000. For something different, *hanok* (traditional Korean house) guesthouses and homestays are available for W50,000. Half the listings are midrange, 20% are in the top-end bracket and the Cheap Sleeps are all under W50,000.

BUKCHON HANOK EXPERIENCE

Anguk Guesthouse (Map pp202–3; ☎ 736 8304; www.angukhouse.com; off Byeolgunggil; s/d/tw/f W40,000/ 50,000/60,000/70,000; subway Line 3 to Anguk, Exit 1; ▣) Soak up the historical atmosphere in this *hanok* with gorgeous varnished wood that nevertheless has all mod cons – every room has its own toilet and shower as well as a computer. This excellent choice has a young owner who speaks English, and beds rather than *yo* mattresses are supplied. Guests can use the kitchen and washing machine, and the simple self-serve breakfast is free. The owner also has dormitory accommodation (only W11,000) in a modern house nearby.

Bukchon Guesthouse (Map pp202–3; ☎ 743 8530; bukchon72@yahoo.co.kr; s/d W35,000/50,000; subway Line 3 to Anguk, Exit 3; ▣) Experience a vanished age of unostentatious elegance in this fine *hanok* built around a court-yard with wooden ceiling beams and paper windows. The communal bathrooms are modern and tiled, and guests can relax in the TV lounge, log onto the Internet, and use the small kitchen and washing machine.

Guesthouse Woorijip (Map pp202–3; ☎ 744 0536; woorijip@hanmail.net; d incl breakfast W50,000; subway Line 3 to Anguk, Exit 3; ▣) This *hanok* is more like a homestay where you share the ups and downs of family life with the Parks, their two young children and a Jindo dog. Sleep as the *yangban* (aristocrats) did on a *yo* (padded quilt) in *ondol* (underfloor-heated) rooms with sliding paper-screen doors that are furnished with authentic traditional wooden chests and paintings.

Seoul Guesthouse (Map pp202–3; ☎ 745 0057; www.seoul110.com; s/d/f W35,000/50,000/100,000; subway Line 3 to Anguk, Exit 3; ▣) Owner Mrs Lee is very kind, speaks English well and was the first person to open her *hanok* to foreign guests. It's a delightful one down a quiet alley and built around a peaceful garden, with other more mod-ern *hanok*-style buildings dotted around. Guests sleep on a *yo* on an *ondol* floor in a bare room with shared facilities (except in the more expensive rooms), and share a TV lounge, kitchen, free Internet and washing machine.

GWANGHWAMUN

The downtown area has budget motels and guesthouses as well as hotels and *hanok* guesthouses. Other downtown hotels are listed under the Myeong-dong & Namsan section.

HOTEL LEES Map pp202-3   Hotel
☎ 762 4343; www.leeshotel.com; r incl tax & service W85,000; subway Line 1 to Jongno 5-ga, Exit 1; ▣
The smart rooms in this modern and clean hotel usually go for as little as W65,000, which makes them a deal worth grabbing. The immediate area is nothing special, but the subway is just a short stroll away. Rooms are fine except for a chair short-age and the receptionist is welcoming and helpful. The bar/restaurant/coffee shop is subterranean, but stay here if you want something fairly central, better than a motel but budget-priced. Free Internet is available on the 11th floor.

KOREANA HOTEL Map pp202-3   Hotel
☎ 2171 7000; www.koreanahotel.com; r from W215,000; subway Line 1 or 2 to City Hall, Exit 3; ▣
Right in the thick of things, the marble lobby, with its friendly staff and jazzy artworks, is a good start. The recently renovated and well-kept rooms are comfortable enough but nothing special and are usually discounted to W170,000. A handful of restaurants offer global grazing, and male guests can de-stress body and mind in the luxury sauna and exercise room. The main attraction though is location, location, location.

NEW KUKJE HOTEL Map pp202-3   Hotel
☎ 732 0161; fax 732 1774; r incl tax & service W127,000; subway Line 1 or 2 to City Hall, Exit 4; ▣
The size of the rooms is okay although they are beginning to look slightly tired and the business centre is just a cubicle under the stairs. The cheerful restaurant serves appealing buffet spreads (W11,000 to W16,500) and you can relax those sightsee-

ing and shopping muscles in the 24-hour sauna (non-guest W11,000, closed Sunday). The hotel is within shouting distance of City Hall and this is reflected in the price.

NEW SEOUL HOTEL Map pp202-3   Hotel
☎ 735 8800; www.bestwesternnewseoul.com; s & d/tw/ste W140,000/160,000/290,000; subway Line 1 or 2 to City Hall, Exit 4; 🖳

This quality hotel makes more effort on the service front than the others and has a perfect downtown location, a bar, a new Italian restaurant called Room 201, and the 24-hour men's sauna (W11,000 for non-guests) is a Little Tokyo. Rooms have light-coloured décor and aren't large but the absolute downtown location more than makes up for that.

CHEAP SLEEPS
BEEWON GUESTHOUSE
Map p205   Guesthouse
☎ 765 0607; www.beewonguesthouse.com; dm/s/tw & d W17,000/27,000/37,000; subway Line 3 to Anguk, Exit 4; 🖳

This new budget option is located in an orange-tiled building down a street behind the GS gas station, opposite Changdeok palace. It sets new standards combining motel-style rooms with guesthouse-style communal facilities. The owner keeps it clean and works hard to please her guests. Rooms have air-con, satellite TV and video, fridge, hairdryer, towels and toiletries. Breakfast, Internet and the washing machine are free and discounts are given for longer stays. Dorms contain only one double bunk, the kitchen is large and the lobby has greenery and a mini chandelier.

GUESTHOUSE KOREA
Map pp202-3   Guesthouse
☎ 3675 2205; www.guesthouseinkorea.com; dm/s/d & tw W15,000/27,000/37,000; subway Line 3 to Anguk, Exit 4; 🖳

Rooms and windows are small and this centrally located backpackers can be a tad untidy, but Internet, laundry and breakfast are all free. Rooms are air-con and have private bathrooms and non-dorm rooms have a TV and fridge. It spreads over three floors and has a laid-back, homely atmosphere. The kitchen has a one-ring cooker and a microwave. The management is (like their dog Kuma) friendly.

GWANGHWA MOTEL
Map pp202-3   Motel
☎ 738 0751; r W38,000; subway Line 5 to Gwanghwamun, Exit 7

The helpful owner speaks a little English and takes great pride in her motel where rooms and bathrooms are immaculate and larger than most. The 31 rooms all vary so look around a few if you are choosy. A few, such as room 205, have a touch of class with ornate furniture similar to the luxury Lotte Hotel. A bagel breakfast awaits just over the road at Witch's Table and a supermarket is next door.

JONGNOWON MOTEL Map p205   Motel
☎ 763 4249; www.jongnowon.com; s/d W25,000/35,000; subway Line 3 to Anguk, Exit 4; 🖳

Next to Seoul Backpackers, staff at this motel are used to dealing with foreigners, and the price includes free Internet, breakfast and laundry. As well maintained as some, there's a matchbox-sized kitchen and handkerchief-sized garden, but the small rooms are fully equipped.

INSADONG
Insadong is not the place for party animals but is the cultural heart and soul of Seoul and the most pleasant place to stay. The area is overflowing with traditional restaurants, teashops, private galleries and handicraft shops that can be browsed day after day.

FRASER SUITES Map p205   Serviced Apartments
☎ 6262 8888; www.fraserhospitality.com; 1/2-bedroom apt incl tax & service per day W242,000/297,000, per month W5m/6m; subway Line 3 to Anguk, Exit 5; 🖳 📺

The apartments still look new and are modern, light and airy thanks to large windows and the splendid inner atrium. All are fully equipped and feel like a home away from home – heat up food in the space-age microwave, listen to the stereo, throw your dirty clothes in the washer/drier, fill the large fridge with beers, watch TV in the bedroom and work-out in the gym. Priceless babysitters (W10,000 per hour) can liberate your evenings. Monthly prices quoted include discounts, which may not always be available.

HOTEL CROWN Map p205   Hotel
☎ 3676 8000; www.hotelcrown.com; r incl tax & service W80,000; subway Line 3 to Anguk, Exit 4; 🖳
The reasonably priced, pleasant rooms in this slightly plush hotel are light-coloured with ornate mock-Regency furniture being their main feature. The bathrooms may be a tad small and old-fashioned, but there's a two-desk business centre and restaurant/bar/coffeeshop.

HOTEL SUNBEE Map p205   Boutique Hotel
☎ 730 3451; www.hotelsunbee.com; off Hoenamu-gil; r incl tax & service W77,000; subway Line 3 to Anguk, Exit 6; 🖳
Hidden away next to the Korea Exchange Bank is this classy but virtually unknown boutique hotel, which offers a touch of luxury at a reasonable cost. Breakfast is included. You can view the room options on a screen and pick a design but all are large with big windows, huge TVs, DVD players, free computers and even free soft drinks. Toilets are separate from the showers or spa baths. If you're happy with just a good room, head to Hotel Sunbee.

CHEAP SLEEPS

MOTEL RITZ Map p205   Love Motel
☎ 764 6353; r Mon-Fri W40,000, Sat & Sun W50,000; subway Line 1 to Jongno 3-ga, Exit 1; 🖳
Looking for a love nest? If circular beds and starry skies painted on the ceiling turn you on then stay at this love motel, with its space-age exterior. It's near Tapgol Park, set amidst a medley of love motels that have plastic drapes screening their guests' cars and number plates. It has a lift to conserve your energy, and a room with a computer costs no extra.

MOTEL SARANGBANG Map p205   Motel
☎ 733 3033; r W35,000-40,000; subway Line 3 to Anguk, Exit 6; 🖳
Smart, fair-sized, facility-filled rooms can be found in this new motel, a chopstick's

throw from 50 traditional restaurants and a teashop aviary. Some rooms have a table and chairs, while room 201 has a whirlpool bath for an extra W5000.

SAERIM HOTEL Map p205   Motel
☎ 739 3377; Eorumgol-gil; r W40,000; subway Line 3 to Anguk, Exit 6; 🖳
An excellent deal is offered by the Saerim, with spotless, well-equipped and reasonably sized rooms that have fully tiled bathrooms that contain electronic bidet toilets. Some rooms even have a computer at no extra cost. If you want a quiet haven that is value-for-money and no hassle, stay here.

SEOUL BACKPACKERS Map p205   Guesthouse
☎ 3672 1972; www.seoulbackpackers.com; dm/s/d W17,000/27,000/37,000; subway Line 3 to Anguk, Exit 4; 🖳
Every room and dorm in this popular and modern purpose-built backpackers has its own bathroom, air-con and *ondol*. Dorms have two or three double bunks. The price here and in the annexe includes the usual guesthouse communal facilities and freebies and the youthful staff speak English. The **deluxe annexe** next door has motel-style rooms (dm/s/d W19,000/32,000/42,000), which have everything including fridges, videos and hairdryers, and the bathrooms are big and have windows. But the deluxe moniker is misleading as the place needs redecorating.

SINGUNGJANG Map p205   Motel
☎ 733 1355; Insadong 3-gil; r W30,000; subway Line 3 to Anguk, Exit 6
Elderly owner, Mr Ryu, speaks a little English and has a friendly smile as well as the lowest price. His small but well-kept motel rooms are available here in an Insadong alley, and one English teacher stayed for a year, which must mean something.

SIX OF THE BEST

- Best cheap sleep: Beewon Guesthouse (p133)
- Most stylish hotel: W Seoul Walkerhill (p143)
- Best *hanok* (traditional Korean wooden house): Anguk Guesthouse (p132)
- Poshest hotel: Imperial Palace Hotel (p139)
- Best hidden gem: Hotel Sunbee (left)
- Least culture shock: Hamilton Hotel (p137)

MYEONG-DONG & NAMSAN

The traffic-quiet streets of Myeong-dong are thronged with young people every evening, and the place is a shopping mecca for locals and foreigners alike. Close to downtown, the area boasts some top hotels.

ASTORIA HOTEL Map pp206-7   Hotel
☎ 2268 7111; fax 2274 3187; Toegyero; d/tw/ ondol incl tax & service W90,000/100,000/120,000; subway Line 3 or 4 to Chungmuro, Exit 4; 🖳
The Astoria deserves a pat on the back for chucking its rack rates out the window and just quoting a reasonable price that includes one breakfast. White and pine-effect décor make for pleasant, clean rooms (a few have Seoul Tower views) and the hotel has a two-desk business corner, bar, restaurant and coffee shop. Twins are bigger than doubles and are variously shaped, so look at more than one. This friendly hotel is just outside Myeong-dong, but near Korea House and Namsangol Hanok Village where you can see, hear and taste traditional Korean culture.

HOTEL SHILLA Map pp206-7   Hotel
☎ 2233 3131; www.shilla.net; r from W430,000; subway Line 3 to Dongguk University, Exit 5; 🖳 📠
This well-run 500-room hotel on the foot-hills of Namsan and close to the subway is the spacious and luxurious flagship of the mighty *jaebeol* (family-run corporate con-glomerate), Samsung. Everything impresses, from the vast lobby to the free use of a mobile phone (Samsung of course), from the sculpture garden and duty-free shop to the restaurants and the lift with CNN on a small screen. The Shilla retains a Korean flavour with local artworks, blind masseurs and a traditional building in front of the hotel. Staff pride themselves on catering to guests' every whim. Clever technology means that incoming room calls cause the TV volume to decrease and can be trans-ferred to the mobile phone. The discount price hovers around W230,000.

LOTTE HOTEL Map pp206-7   Hotel
☎ 771 1000; www.hotel.lotte.co.kr; old/new wing incl tax & service from W471,000/520,000; subway Line 2 to Euljiro 1-ga, Exit 8; 🖳 📠
Public areas are palatial and live classical music by a waterfall adds melodic tones

to the lobby lounge, where a coffee and sandwich costs a cool W31,200. The floral arrangements are spectacular, and a flower rather than a TV screen can be found inside the lift. The giant hotel has 1318 rooms and as many staff, but new manager Mr Lee is vowing to improve the personal touch as well as keeping all the facilities up to scratch. Rooms in the new wing have a lap-top, mobile phone and walk-in shower and are worth paying more for if you can find a room with a clean carpet. In an enviable location and surrounded by upscale fashion shops, expect 50% discounts and look out for special deals that can start at W190,000.

METRO HOTEL Map pp206-7   Boutique Hotel
☎ 752 1112; www.metrohotel.co.kr; behind the Bridge Bldg; s/d/tw incl tax & service W108,900/ 121,000/145,200; subway Line 2 Euljiro 1-ga, Exit 5; 🖳
A hop and a skip from the subway is this brand new, modernist 75-room hideaway. Splashes of style abound starting with the flashy, metallic-style lobby and its smart laptop computers. Room size and design vary, but ones with large windows and glass walk-in showers are best. Avoid smaller ones with a brick-wall view. Prices cover a buffet breakfast in the soothing

Metro Hotel (above), Myeong-dong

art gallery café and in the evening you can relax in the all-white bar with a view (beers W5500), or let off steam in a karaoke room.

MILLENNIUM SEOUL HILTON

Map pp206-7   Hotel

☎ 753 7788; www.millenniumseoulhilton.co.kr; d/ste from W390,000/510,000; subway Line 1 or 4 to Seoul Station, Exit 10; 🖳 🐆

The Namsan-facing Hilton has all the bells and whistles of a luxury hotel from an eight-desk, three-meeting-room business centre to the flashy Areno's nightclub and a casino (opening in spring 2006). Standard rooms have large windows but a mixed-bag of furnishings and are usually discounted to around W230,000. It's a climb up from the subway station, but nearby Namsan (262m) is perfect for serious joggers, with uphill paths and traffic-free roads around the green hillside.

PACIFIC HOTEL Map pp206-7   Hotel

☎ 777 7811; fax 755 5582; d/tw incl tax & service W131,000/140,000; subway Line 4 to Myeong-dong, Exit 3; 🖳

Following renovations, bathrooms have electronic bidet toilets and the 135 rooms are pleasant, clean and well-lit, with natural wood décor and a simple but modern style – except for those that have old-fashioned blankets on the beds. Ask for a room with views of Namsan. Set back from the main road, the hotel lacks a bar (maybe that's why the atmosphere is subdued) but the greenery, artworks and small circular glass business centre combine to create a stylish ambience.

SEJONG HOTEL Map pp206-7   Hotel

☎ 773 6000; www.sejong.co.kr; Toegyero; s/d/ste W180,000/240,000/420,000; subway Line 4 to Myeong-dong, Exit 10; 🖳

This university-owned luxury hotel near the subway in Myeong-dong boasts 20 types of rooms. Namsan-facing rooms are on the small side but those facing the city are bigger. New room décor is pastel shades, the staff are helpful and the general impression is plush and elegant. The fitness centre and men's sauna are great but closed on Sunday. See p92 for their Eunhasu buffet. Prices are usually discounted to W180,000.

SEOUL PLAZA HOTEL Map pp206-7   Hotel

☎ 771 2200; www.seoulplaza.co.kr; s/d from W340,000/360,000; subway Line 1 or 2 to City Hall, Exit 6; 🖳 🐆

As central as a bullseye, the Plaza matches other top hotels with its facilities and service. The lobby has a chandelier, every room has a laptop and you can munch around the world in its stylish restaurants. Staff make a special effort to greet you and remember your name and a posse of them in the lobby are primed to aid new arrivals. Some rooms are on the small side and not as perfect as they should be. Prices are usually discounted to around W200,000.

WESTIN CHOSUN HOTEL

Map pp206-7   Hotel

☎ 317 0404; www.westin.com; s/d from W440,000/470,000; subway Line 2 to Euljiro 1-ga, Exit 4; 🖳 🐆

Seoul's first hotel (the original building opened in 1914) keeps up with the times and so every guest receives free use of a mobile phone and a few rooms have their own gym equipment. Choose your room style after seeing the options on a screen. It's not the most luxurious hotel in Seoul but it has the best location, good atmosphere and well-trained staff. All this means the discount price might stick higher than elsewhere.

The Compass Rose lounge (beers W10,000) is has live jazz at 8pm every evening except Saturday. It has a quality business centre, laptops in the rooms and a lap pool but no lap dancers. The traditional-style barber is a memorable experience. In the garden outside is a pavilion built for King Gojong when he proclaimed himself an emperor and had an altar built to give thanks to heaven. See p104 for O'Kim's bar.

CHEAP SLEEPS
MYEONG-DONG GUESTHOUSE

Map pp206-7   Guesthouse

☎ 755 5437; bravoinn@yahoo.co.kr; r W30,000-50,000; subway Line 4 to Myeong-dong, Exit 2; 🖳

Retired English-speaking bank manager Mr Park will take care of you in his clean and tidy budget guesthouse that is tucked away on a quiet road. The 19 rooms in this converted motel vary and, though small, have all the usual facilities plus free Internet and laundry. It can fill up with young Asian tourists who love the nearby Myeong-dong shopping.

ITAEWON

Popular with American soldiers and expat English teachers, the mix of stalls, shops, pubs, gay bars, nightclubs and ethnic restaurants gives lively Itaewon a different atmosphere to the rest of the city. Stay here and you can party late without having to get a taxi home. Locals here are more likely to speak English, but a few parts are seedy.

GRAND HYATT SEOUL HOTEL

Map p209   Hotel

☎ 797 1234; www.seoul.grand.hyatt.com; r city/mountain view W240,000/225,000; subway Line 6 to Itaewon, Exit 2; 🖳 🛋

Perched on top of a hill, the Hyatt makes the most of the stunning views – nearly everywhere in the hotel, even the outdoor pool, has a condor's view of Seoul. The duo playing classical music in the lobby add a touch of class. American presidents choose to stay here and it's hard to find fault with the service, the facilities or anything else. Though far from the subway, there are shuttle buses (10am to 9pm).

The new, lighter, green-themed décor has freshened up the rooms, although some bathrooms are on the small side. The deli and the nightclub (p110) are excellent as are the sports facilities – an indoor and outside pool, masses of high-tech exercise equipment, plus squash, tennis, yoga and aerobics classes. In winter you can ice-skate on the pool. Exact prices depend on the occupancy rate.

HAMILTON HOTEL Map p209   Hotel

☎ 794 0171; www.hamilton.co.kr; Itaewonno; s/d, tw & ondol W100,000/135,000; subway Line 6 to Itaewon, Exit 1; 🖳 🛋

Summer discount rates for a double can go down to W90,000 at this 150-room Itaewon landmark with an adjoining shopping centre. The subway and Partytown are on its doorstep. The best features are the refurbished 24-hour sauna and the rooftop outdoor pool (adult/child W10,000/7000; ☼ 10am-6pm mid-June–end Aug), which is free to guests and is surrounded by sunloungers but lacks greenery. Rooms are nothing flash and have a quaint, old-fashioned feel, but stay here to reduce culture shock as the atmosphere is more American than elsewhere.

HOTEL CROWN Map p209   Hotel

☎ 797 4111; www.hotelcrown.com; Banporo; r regular/deluxe incl tax & service W100,000/145,000; subway Line 6 to Itaewon, Exit 4; 🖳

Away from the main Itaewon area, the lobby and well-worn, quiet rooms are decorated in an ornate mock-Regency style. Guests can eat in the restaurant, work in the business centre, improve their golf swing and recuperate in the saunas, which offer both invigorating and soothing treatments. Windows are triple glazed but the hotel lacks finishing touches, and the more expensive rooms are hardly worth the extra cost.

ITAEWON HOTEL Map p209   Hotel

☎ 792 3111; www.itaewonhotel.com; Itaewonno; r incl tax & service W120,000; subway Line 6 to Itaewon, Exit 2; 🖳

Ideally located on the main Itaewon strip, 200m from the subway, rooms here have large windows, modern bathrooms and are decked out in neutral tones. Everything is up to standard, but the hotel atmosphere is underwhelming and rooms are often discounted to under W100,000. Stay here if you want a quiet and comfortable oasis to retreat to after a hectic day.

CHEAP SLEEPS

HILLTOP MOTEL Map p209   Motel

☎ 793 4972; r Sun-Thu W25,000, Fri & Sat W30,000; subway Line 6 to Itaewon, Exit 3

Perched on top of Hooker Hill, the main hostess bar area, and next to Itaewon's most luxurious sauna, is this motel with larger and cleaner rooms than other Itaewon motels (which tend to be seedier). Recently redecorated, it offers a good deal if you want to party in Itaewon without having to take a taxi home.

SEOUL MOTEL Map p209   Motel

☎ 795 2266; fax 797 0300; Itaewonno; d/tw Mon-Thu W40,000/70,000, Fri-Sun W45,000/80,000; subway Line 6 to Itaewon, Exit 4

Twin rooms are overpriced but the modern, fully-equipped rooms are the best budget option in Itaewon. The motel attracts long-term male guests who prowl around the Itaewon nightlife. Located right above McDonald's, you only have to walk downstairs for breakfast, and the receptionist speaks English.

SEOUL TOWER HOSTEL

Map p209   Guesthouse

☎ 745 8202; www.towerhostel.com; dm/s/d W14,000/24,000/34,000; subway Line 6 to Noksapyeong, Exit 2; 🖳

A 12-minute walk from the subway and away from the Itaewon strip is this backpackers. The premises are shared with a rough-and-ready bar and a sandwich and muffin shop, and a Mexican eatery is nearby. Dorms have two or three double bunks, and one double has its own bathroom. Prices include free breakfast. The hostel has communal rooms and a terrace, but all rooms have fans, not air-con.

SINCHON & YEOUIDO

HOTEL BENHUR Map p210   Hotel

☎ 783 2233; r incl tax & service from W80,000; subway Line 5 to Yeouinaru, Exit 1; 🖳

This flashy new business hotel is on soulless Yeouido but near the Han River. It offers a good deal as the 60 neutral-toned rooms have a youthful vibe and are well-stocked with jazzy electronic gear such as widescreen TVs, computers and DVDs, as well as having big beds, whirlpool baths and steam saunas. Ask for a free breakfast.

YOIDO HOTEL Map p210   Hotel

☎ 782 0121; fax 785 2510; standard/deluxe r incl tax & service W140,000/163,000; subway Line 5 to Yeouinaru, Exit 1; 🖳

The recent renovation makes this a reasonable Yeouido option, with a more relaxed and refined air than the brasher and flashier new business hotels nearby. Competition is hot so request a hefty discount. The deluxe rooms are bigger with bigger TVs and bathrooms, while river-view rooms cost no extra. The so-called business centre is an office shared with the hotel staff, and there's a grill restaurant.

CHEAP SLEEPS

GUESTHOUSE KOREA Map p210   Guesthouse

☎ 3142 0683; www.guesthousekorea.com; dm/s/tw W15,000/25,000/35,000; subway Line 2 to Hongik University, Exit 2; 🖳

It's a 15-minute walk from the subway so ring for a pick-up at this small backpackers with laid-back youthful staff and a casual atmosphere that's within walking distance of Hongik's kicking clubbing zone. The two dorms each have two double bunks and the one single and two twin rooms share two bathrooms. The kitchen, dining room and lounge have air-con, although bedrooms only have fans. Internet, breakfast and laundry are free.

KIMS' GUESTHOUSE Map p210   Guesthouse

☎ 337 9894; www.kimsguesthouse.com; Huiujeong 4-gil; dm/s/d W17,000/27,000/37,000; subway Line 2 or 6 Hapjeong, Exit 8; 🖳

Helpful Ms Kim speaks good English and has been running this popular guesthouse, now spread over two modern houses, for some years. Located in a quiet residential area and near the Han River, rooms with shared bathrooms vary in size, but both houses have air-con, a courtyard and balcony, as well as the usual guesthouse facilities and freebies. Ring for a pick-up as it's hard to find.

PRINCE HOTEL Map p210   Motel

☎ 363 4700; r W38,000; subway Line 2 to Sinchon, Exit 3

Amidst a cluster of *yeogwan* (small, family-run hotels) and love motels in student-thronged Sinchon is this plain and simple 48-room hotel-cum-motel with an elevator and prices you can't argue with. Clean rooms are well-maintained, have a table and chairs, and feature all facilities although bathrooms are smallish. Over the road is a stack of restaurants and bars – don't miss the surrealist Mu bar.

GANGNAM

This is the best area for midrange and top-end hotels. The cluster of accommodation on Bongeunsaro is around 800m from a subway station but only a short taxi ride from COEX. South of the river is more of a business than sightseeing area, but the subway can whisk you to all the sights.

BEST WESTERN PREMIER GANGNAM

Map p211   Hotel

☎ 6474 2000; www.bestwesterngangnam.com; Bongeunsaro; s/d/ste W160,000/200,000/320,000; subway Line 2 to Gangnam, Exit 7; 🖳

This new business hotel is a step above most Best Westerns and has straightforward but smart rooms with large windows

Kims' Guesthouse (opposite)

and TVs. Head to the sauna, spa and health club to lose what you gained at the fusion restaurant and bar. Ask for a decent discount or you might as well swan around in the luxurious embrace of the Ritz Carlton across the road.

DORMY IN SEOUL

Map p211   Serviced Apartments

☎ 6474 1515; www.dormy.co.kr; Bongeunsaro; studio incl tax & service W121,000; subway Line 2 to Gangnam, Exit 7; 🖳

Opened in 2003, these well-equipped studio apartments have pleasing light colours and a modern look that feature smallish bathrooms with a walk-in shower. With all the conveniences of home, it's a good choice and week-long stays receive a discount. Ask for a free buffet breakfast.

HOTEL DYNASTY Map p211   Hotel

☎ 540 3041; www.hoteldynasty.co.kr; Bongeunsaro; r incl tax & service W85,200; subway Line 2 to Gangnam, Exit 7; 🖳

The price is the attractive feature given the Gangnam location. Rooms have paper screens as well as curtains but lack character and bathrooms look a bit old-fashioned. You can eat, drink and steam in the hotel facilities. Half a dozen adjacent hotels grapple with each other on this street, so good deals are usually there for the asking.

HUMAN TOUCH VILLE

Map p211   Serviced Apartments

☎ 553 0050; www.humantouch.co.kr; Nonhyeonno; standard/deluxe studios incl tax & service W120,000/150,000; subway Line 2 to Yeoksam, Exit 6; 🖳

The reception staff are friendly and the apartments are fully equipped with novel features such as a balcony and a dishwasher. The only problem is that even the deluxe rooms are surprisingly plain, bordering on basic. A lick of paint would do wonders. Discount prices dip below W100,000 for weekly stays and include breakfast. A royal cuisine restaurant is on the first floor and a convenience store is in the basement.

IMPERIAL PALACE HOTEL Map p211   Hotel

☎ 3440 800; www.imperialpalace.co.kr; Eonjuro; r/ste W350,000/750,000; subway Line 7 to Hak-dong, Exit 1; 🖳 🖭

Aptly named and totally renovated with no expense spared, this is more of a stately home than a hotel, and blends traditional European style with modern high-tech. At quiet times prices drop to W210,000. The luxurious lobby lounge features wood panels, a classical water feature and European-style furnishings, and a pianist plays up in the minstrel's gallery. The superb rooms feature genuine king-sized beds

Imperial Palace Hotel (p139), Gangnam

and walk-in showers. Just push a button to raise or lower the seat or lid on the Dobi-dos toilets. Ask for a river view. From the organic-food café Amiga and the porcelain displays (children could prove expensive here) to the health club everything is almost perfect. The outdoor pool is small but has plenty of foliage and sunloungers. A buffet banquet is served at **Familia** (p97).

JELLY HOTEL Map p211   Love Motel
☎ 553 4737; www.jellyhotel.com; incl tax & service short stay W40,000-100,000, overnight W70,000-150,000; subway Line 2 to Gangnam, Exit 8; 💻
The corridors are as dark as a coalmine (to safeguard the anonymity of guests), but the rooms of this upscale love motel are spacious, exotic and classy, with wide-screen DVDs, laptop computers and spa baths. Jelly is as hip as its name suggests, although the receptionist could be friend-lier. Every room is different – one is Chinese style while another has a pool table, but must be booked well ahead. Love motels only provide a room (no coffee shop, restaurant or bar) but the rooms are often better than you'd expect for the price.

JW MARRIOTT HOTEL Map p211   Hotel
☎ 6282 6262; www.marriott.com; r incl tax & service from W300,000; subway Line 3 or 7 to Express Bus Terminal, Exit 7; 💻 🚇
Opened in 2000, this is one of the most recently built luxury hotels and it shows – rooms, bathrooms and beds are all spacious

and modern, and large windows provide plenty of light. Marble bathrooms have walk-in glass showers and a bath. The rest of the hotel lives up to the standard set by the rooms starting with a four-floor lobby atrium. The smart business centre, state-of-the-art spa, fitness club and pool, and the stylish restaurants all have a feel-good factor. The popular new Central Mall is just a few footsteps from the lobby, but for everything else you'll need to hop on a subway train.

M CHEREVILLE Map p211   Serviced Apartments
☎ 553 9600; www.mchereville.com; studio/1-bedroom apt incl tax & service W132,000/154,000; subway Line 2 to Gangnam, Exit 6; 💻
Opened in 2003, just 100m from the sub-way station and with a lively entertainment district on its doorstep, this is one of the new breed of smart and convenient ser-viced apartments. It offers 23 floors of light apartments decked out in plain colours with all mod cons. You can watch DVDs, listen to CDs, throw washing in the ma-chine, and soothe tired muscles in the steam sauna showers. All that's lacking is artwork on the walls. Free Internet is available and breakfast is included.

NOVOTEL AMBASSADOR Map p211   Hotel
☎ 567 1101; www.ambatel.com; Bongeunsaro; r/business fl/exec fl W310,000/325,000/360,000; subway Line 2 to Gangnam, Exit 7; 💻 🚇
The impressive lobby is open plan and looks out on a waterfall, while the bar has

live music nightly except Monday. The service, food and gym are all impressive, but it's best to avoid the standard rooms (discount price W190,000) unless they've been renovated as the business and executive rooms have warmer colours and are more stylish with pleasant meeting rooms and free soft drinks and cakes.

POPGREEN HOTEL Map p211 Hotel

☎ 544 6623; www.popgreenhotel.com; Apgujeongno; r incl tax & service W157,000; subway Line 3 to Apgujeong, Exit 2; 🖳
Near Apgujeong subway station, 80-room Popgreen has some style and is almost a boutique hotel with artworks, greenery and a metallic décor theme. After a hard day of sightseeing and shopping you can sink into an armchair and relax in your contemporary-style room with white décor, mood lighting and Internet access. More expensive rooms are bigger. Beside the cubicle business centre is Katharsis, a minimalist café-cum-bar (drinks from W7000), designed to appeal to the style-conscious gentry of Apgujeong.

PRINCESS HOTEL Map p211 Love Motel

☎ 544 0366; fax 544 0322; r small/large incl tax & service W80,000/120,000; subway Line 3 to Apgujeong, Exit 2
In the heart of Apgujeong is this upmarket, metal-clad love motel with flesh-coloured corridor lighting and 10 room styles to choose from. What turns you on baby? How about lotus-shaped red beds, black-tiled bathrooms and a steam sauna? Windows are small but the TVs are big. If entertainment rather than sleep is your object, short-term rates start at W35,000.

RITZ CARLTON HOTEL Map p211 Hotel

☎ 3451 8000; www.ritzcarltonseoul.com; Bongeunsaro; r W390,000; subway Line 2 to Gangnam, Exit 7; 🖳 📠
This hotel wraps guests in soothing luxury with high levels of service, every facility and a European atmosphere from the furniture to the food. A pianist provides background music in the cavernous lobby lounge, which has memorable artworks, greenery and a waterfall feature down one wall. Rooms have light-green décor and include a CD player and CDs (ask for more at reception if you don't like the choice). Attention to detail is also shown with a small TV in the bathroom and an umbrella in the closet. Discount prices start at W200,000.

SAMJUNG HOTEL Map p211 Hotel

☎ 557 1221; www.samjunghotel.co.kr; Bongeunsaro; r incl tax & service W127,000; subway Line 2 to Gangnam, Exit 7; 🖳
Quite grand in some respects but old-fashioned and scruffy in places, this Dr Jekyll and Mr Hyde hotel has a choice of three restaurants, but there's nowhere to sit in the lobby. The bar on the 12th floor has a good view and the spa/sauna is open day and night. You may prefer the Korean-style *ondol* rooms, which have more character than the rather plain Western-style rooms. Ask for a discount.

HOTEL SUNSHINE Map p211 Hotel

☎ 541 1818; www.hotelsunshine.co.kr; cnr Dosandaero & Nonhyeonno; r W115,000; subway Line 3 to Hak-dong, Exit 8; 🖳
Rooms, decked out in white and neutral tones, are on the small side but are pleasant enough. This friendly, unpretentious hotel on the fringe of upscale Apgujeong has a relaxing restaurant and coffee shop, and the corridors are light and even smell nice. Ask for a 30% discount.

VILLE Map p211 Long-term Apartments

☎ 549 4999 (no English); Hakdongno; per month W1.7m (minimum 2 months); subway Line 7 to Hak-dong, Exit 6
Stay in these plain but quite large modern studio apartments and save yourself hassles with real estate agents and pain-in-the-butt key money. Rooms have everything including views and are only a hop, skip and a jump from the subway station exit. The only snag is finding someone who speaks English.

YOUNGDONG HOTEL Map p211 Hotel

☎ 542 0112; www.youngdonghotel.co.kr; Dosandaero; d standard/deluxe W115,000/135,000; subway Line 3 to Sinsa, Exit 1; 🖳
This hotel makes an effort. You can borrow a laptop computer free of charge, the staff are friendly and the reception desk displays the weather forecast – and discount prices dip under W100,000. However, corridors are gloomy and there's no bar. Deluxe rooms are bigger and kitted out with walk-in showers, microwave ovens and toasters. Aromatic Thai massages are available in a luxury spa just down the road.

JAMSIL

COEX INTER-CONTINENTAL HOTEL

Map pp214-15   Hotel

☎ 3452 2500; www.seoul-coex.intercontinental
.com; r from W350,000; subway Line 2 to Samseong,
COEX Exit; 🖵 🕼

In an enviable position next to the COEX
Mall and Exhibition Centre, this luxury hotel
has a modernist functional design with
spotless rooms and great service. If you
want a youthful vibe, stay here and if you
want character, stay at the Grand Inter-
Continental, which is also nearer the subway. Rooms offer a choice of five pillows
and are decked out in beige with glass-
cased showers. The restaurants, the chrome
sky-bar, the lobby water feature, and the
exercise room, sauna and pool are all up to
standard. Expect to pay around W260,000
(75% occupancy) or W220,000 (58% occupancy), although book in advance on their
website and prices can drop to W175,000.

GRAND INTER-CONTINENTAL HOTEL

Map pp214-15   Hotel

☎ 555 5656; seoul-grand.intercontinental.com;
r from W370,000; subway Line 2 to Samseong,
COEX Exit

As the name suggests, this has a grander
more luxurious style than its more functional and youthful brother COEX Inter-
Continental, but with the touch of class
comes a touch of snootiness. Book through
their website in advance and the price
can drop to W200,000. With a cool jazz
trio playing in its high-ceilinged atrium
lobby, antique-looking furniture, wood-
panelled lift and seven restaurants, it has a
traditional luxury hotel atmosphere. Lower
rooms are a little bigger than those higher
up, and rooms feature paper screens (as
well as curtains), Korean furniture and a
minibar almost as well-stocked as a convenience store. The Hunter's Bar has a live
Filipina band from 8.30pm.

HOTEL LAKE Map pp214-15   Hotel

☎ 422 1001; www.hotellake.com; r incl tax &
service W95,000; subway Line 2 or 8 to Jamsil,
Exit 4; 🖵

Hotel Lake overlooks cherry trees, Seokchon Lake and the Lotte World thrill rides,
but it's a 15-minute walk from the subway.
Rooms offer big-screen TVs with DVD and

video players and lots of freebie stuff.
The bathrooms are large with a separate
shower and spa bath. It's off the beaten
track with a quiet, relaxed, almost genteel
atmosphere – a bit like staying by Lake
Geneva.

IBIS Map pp214-15   Hotel

☎ 3011 8888; www.ambatel.com; r incl tax &
service W97,000; subway Line 2 & Bundang Line to
Seolleung, Exit 1; 🖵

There's a buzz in the air at this new hotel,
hidden behind the Posco centre, which
is only a 10-minute walk from the COEX
Exhibition Centre and Mall. The restaurant,
bar, sauna and exercise room are nothing
special, but there's nothing wrong with
them either. Rooms are a tad on the small
side, but all have walk-in showers and
everything is smart and brand new. The
lobby has free Internet, a handy luggage-
storage room and a global ATM. The price
is pretty reasonable given its close proxim-
ity to the COEX.

LOTTE WORLD HOTEL Map pp214-15   Hotel

☎ 419 7000; www.hotellotte.co.kr; r W360,000;
subway Line 2 or 8 to Jamsil, Exit 4; 🖵 🕼

Near Seokchon Lake and next to Lotte
World, Lotte department store and Lotte
mart, this luxury hotel, its lobby festooned
with chandeliers and Korean art, is typical
of Lotte's Asian version of 'Euro palatial'.
Natural wood and pastel shades make the
rooms less flamboyant than the public
areas and cheaper rooms have a shower
over the bath. Babysitters are W10,000
an hour, and businessmen can escape
from noisy children on the executive floor.
Expect to pay W200,000 or less, except on
public holidays when discounts may not be
so generous.

TIFFANY HOTEL Map pp214-15   Hotel

☎ 545 0015; www.tiffanyhotel.com;
Yeongdongdaero; r incl tax & service W65,000;
subway Line 7 to Cheongdam, Exit 14

Near the subway and an Incheon airport
bus stop, this simple, no-frills hotel has a
helpful receptionist and a restaurant/bar/
coffee shop. Offering 50 quite large, light
rooms, the shower heads are huge and
it's a definite step-up from a motel. Being
out-of-the-way helps to keep the price
reasonable.

CHEAP SLEEPS

OLYMPIC PARKTEL YOUTH HOSTEL

Map pp214-15   Hostel

☎ 421 2111; www.kyha.co.kr; dm W22,000;
subway Line 8 to Mongchontoseong, Exit 1; 🖳

This unusual hostel is located on the 7th
and 9th floors of a luxury hotel inside
Olympic Park, which is a perfect spot for
evening walks and people watching, but
a long way from downtown. The en suite
dorms have plenty of windows with superb
views, TV, air-con, heating and a fridge.
Each dorm, the size of a hotel room, has
two double bunks and two pull-out beds,
so can become crowded, and the separate
toilet and shower cubicles are tiny and
have only vents. Hostel guests can use the
hotel facilities at reduced rates. A YHA office
(☎ 2202 2585; 2nd fl; ⏰ 9.30am-6pm Mon-
Fri) sells membership (W25,000 a year).

OTHER NEIGHBOURHOODS

The accommodation includes Seoul's most
stylish hotel plus good deals near Itaewon
and Dongdaemun.

EULJIRO CO-OP RESIDENCE

Map pp200-1   Serviced Apartments

☎ 2269 4600; http://rent.co-op.co.kr; studio incl
tax & service W84,700; subway Line 2, 4 or 5 to
Dongdaemun, Exit 12; 🖳

These small but cute ultra-modern studio
apartments have wafer-thin TVs and tiny
shower rooms. All the studios are clean,
bright and stylish – perfect if you don't
need a lot of elbow room, especially when
the price drops to W58,000. You can make
your own breakfast or cook up a meal
in the kitchen. A simple business centre,
exercise room and coin-operated washing

machine are part of the package, and the
staff are friendlier than in some hotels. Near
the subway station, the apartments provide
a chic nest above the hurly-burly 24-hour
shopping at Dongdaemun.

HOTEL AIRPORT Map pp198-9   Hotel

☎ 2662 1113; www.hotelairport.co.kr; d incl tax
& service W90,000; subway Line 5 to Songjeong,
Exit 2; 🖳

The attraction of this hotel is the free shuttle bus to the close-by Gimpo international
airport, which operates mainly domestic
flights. Although a bit old-fashioned with
rather dark rooms, bathrooms are large
and there's free Internet in the lobby. The
restaurant and coffee shop/bar mean you
don't have to wander the streets searching
for fodder and refreshments. Walk straight
on from the subway exit for 200m to reach
the hotel.

HOTEL RAINBOW Map pp200-1   Hotel

☎ 792 9993; fax 792 9997; r incl tax & service
W55,000; subway Line 1 to Namyeong, Exit 1; 🖳

Hidden away in a busy area of eateries and
stores around Namyeong subway station,
just two stops south of City Hall, is this
small and homely hotel with clean, modern
rooms that have all you could expect plus
a computer and a few fancy touches. The
restaurant and lobby aren't up to much but
the rooms are quiet and the price is hard to
beat. From the subway exit turn right and
then first right.

KAYA HOTEL Map pp200-1   Hotel

☎ 798 5101; fax 798 5900; d/tw incl tax & service
W53,000/63,000; subway Line 1 to Namyeong,
Exit 1; 🖳

Near the US army's Yongsan base and
convenient for USO tours (p46), this 50-
room, well-priced hotel, with a business
centre cubicle and a comfortable restaurant (meals W6000 to W25,000), coffee
shop and bar, is used to dealing with
foreigners. Rooms are light and pleasant,
and downtown is only 10 minutes away on
the subway.

W SEOUL WALKERHILL Map pp198-9 Hotel

☎ 465 2222; www.wseoul.com; r from W470,000;
subway Line 5 to Gwangnaru, Exit 2; 🖳 🐾

This brand new 250-room hotel sets a new
standard for radically modernist design

TOP FIVE GOOD DEALS UNDER W100,000

- Ibis (opposite)
- Astoria Hotel (p135)
- Hotel Rainbow (right)
- Euljiro Co-op Residence (above)
- Hotel Lees (p132)

and 'whatever whenever' service. From the eye-catching exterior – a glass box adorned with dots – to the jaw-dropping lobby with its egg-shaped seats, moving artworks, open-plan bar, Motown music and fabulous river views, this stellar hotel makes a dramatic design statement. The lobby toilets have red sliding doors, electronic bidet controls as complex as a jetliner's, a space capsule interior and a TV screen.

Everything has attitude, even the menus. Regular rooms are called 'wonderful' and have DVDs, CDs and round beds. Red bedding adds a splash of colour to the white décor. 'Spa' rooms have big baths with a view, 'media' rooms are ultimate designer cool, while 'scent' rooms come with a scent of your choice. Welcome to a designer hotel with a sense of humour from the lingo to the staff uniforms – bellboys dressed like gangsters. A casino is next door. The only drawback is that it's 2km from the subway, although there is a shuttle bus. Book through their website and the price of special deals can drop to W215,000.

CHEAP SLEEPS

DREAMTEL YOUTH HOSTEL

Map pp198-9   Hostel

☎ 2667 0535; www.idreamtel.co.kr; dm/f W22,000/72,000; subway Line 5 to Banghwa, Exit 4; ☐ ☒

Dorms and family rooms have a TV, fridge, air-con and en suite but are nondescript and need more airing. The large modern hostel has an institutional feel and is 45 minutes from downtown by subway. A YHA card is necessary and free Internet is available. For exercise walk around the green hillside out the back or pop downstairs to the large swimming pool (W4500), gym and sauna. From the subway exit walk straight, turn left at the end of the road, then go left again at the end of that road and it's on your right – 400m from the subway exit.

Excursions

NORTH KOREA

Cheorwon

Sincheorwon

Myeongseongsan
(924m)

0   20 km
0   12 miles

Gyeong-wonseon

DMZ

Imjingang

Kaesong

Panmunjeom

37

Dongducheon

Pocheon

47

To Chunch
(28

Third Tunnel
of Aggression

Munsan

Odusan
Unification
Observatory

Geumchon

1

Bear's Town
Ski Resort

Gyodongdo

Bugeun-ri
Dolmen

Ganghwaeup

Uijeongbu

Suraksan
(638m)

Starhill
Ski Resort

Daesong-ri

Seongmodo

Oepo-ri

Bomunsa

Ganghwado

Bukhansan
National
Park

Manisan
(469m)

Gwangseongbo

Gimpo

Han River (Hangang)

46

Seoul Ski
Resort

Jeondeungsa

Gimpo
Airport

✪ SEOUL

Hanam

To
(113

Sindo

Jagyakdo

2

Yeongjongdo

INCHEON

Incheon
International
Airport

Bucheon

Gwanaksan
(632m)

Seoul
Racecourse

Nambansanseong
Provincial Park

To
Baengnyeongdo
Island (183km)

Eulwangni
Beach

Jamjindo
Pier

Muuido

Seoul
Grand
Park

Seongnam

Gwangju

Icheon
Ceramic
Village

WEST SEA
(Yellow Sea)

Ansan

4

Everland
Amusement
Park

To Y
(32

Icheon Hot Springs

Icheor

Simnipo
Beach

Daebudo

Suwon

Suwon
Fortress

Korean Folk
Village

Yangji Pine
Ski Resort

Yeongheungdo

To Deokjeokdo
(10km)

Jebudo

Seosin-myeon

Jisan Fores
Ski Resort

Osan

45

10

Songtan

1

Anseong

Pyeongtaek

CHUNGCHEONGNAM-DO

Seonghwan

Seonggeo

Jincheon

Sōsan

Cheonan

Onyang

Yesan

Excursions

Don't leave Seoul without taking a tour to the weirdest and scariest place on the planet – the Demilitarized Zone (DMZ) that marks the border between North and South Korea. Two armies, both armed to the teeth, have faced each other along the border for over 50 years, ever since the end of the Korean War in 1953.

Another relic of war is the World Heritage Hwaseong, a reconstructed 17th-century fortress in Suwon, which is the best in Korea. Another way to experience the past is to step inside the Korean Folk Village, just outside Suwon. Traditional houses have been re-erected here to recreate the atmosphere of rural life, when peasants and slaves toiled for their Confucian *yangban* (aristocrat) masters.

Another escape from urban stress is on the West Sea Isles, where you can relax and feast on crabs, prawns, shellfish and other aquatic life forms. These small islands are home to fisher folk and are surprisingly unspoilt and laid-back.

The ideal excursion for children is Everland with its Disneyland-with-a-Korean-twist amusement park and excellent water park. The nearby Hoam Art Hall is a top Korean garden and museum that houses national treasures.

THE DMZ & PANMUNJEOM

Situated just 55km north of Seoul, the truce village of **Panmunjeom**, also called the Joint Security Area (JSA), is the only place inside the **Demilitarized Zone** (DMZ) where visitors are permitted. It was established on the ceasefire line at the end of the Korean War in 1953, and the blue UN buildings are where negotiations between North and South still occasionally take place. Only an armistice was signed at the end of the war, not a full peace treaty. Access to Panmunjeom is permitted only for tour groups and you must carry your passport and follow a strict dress code – no T-shirts, shorts, jeans, sandals or miniskirts.

In the past a gun battle and gruesome axe murders have occurred here, but the last such serious incident was in 1984. These events are described by US and ROK (Republic of Korea) soldiers who are stationed here and accompany all the tour groups. These troops are 'In Front of Them All' and would face the brunt of any surprise attack by the North's large army, said to be a million strong.

The 4km-wide DMZ scars the land from coast to coast and divides the Korean peninsula into two antagonistic countries. It's probably the most heavily fortified border in the world – high fences topped with barbed wire, an antitank wall and obstacles, and landmines line both sides of the DMZ. The Berlin Wall was just a child's toy compared to this sucker. Seeing the military preparedness on both sides, war still seems possible and so a visit here is a sobering experience.

Surprisingly there are two villages inside the DMZ near Panmunjeom. On the southern side is Daeseong, a heavily-subsidised farming village with modern houses and an 11pm curfew. On the northern side is Kijong, where the buildings are empty and always have been. It's a ghost town with a 160m tower from which flies a huge North Korean flag that weighs 300kg. The flag on the South Korean side is smaller. While the North's leaders play games with flags, their people are starving to death.

The tour includes visiting one of the small, blue **UN buildings** that straddle the border and look like temporary classrooms. Inside are simple tables and chairs and you can walk to the far end and step into North Korean territory, a strange feeling. North Korean soldiers used to peer in the

TRANSPORT

Distance from Seoul 55km

Travel time All-day tour

Direction North

Bus Panmunjeom can only be visited on a bus tour.

South Korean ROK soldier, DMZ (below)

DMZ NATIONAL PARK?

The Demilitarized Zone (DMZ) separates North and South Korea like a knife. The 4km-wide and 240km-long buffer zone is surrounded by tank traps, mines and electrical fences, and most of it has been sealed off to all human beings for more than 50 years. Ironically, this has made it something of an eco paradise. No other place in the world with a temperate climate has been so well protected from human interference. It has been a boon to wildlife – for example the DMZ is home to flocks of Manchurian cranes, whooper cranes and white herons, as well as rare plants. Environmentalists hope that when the two Koreas are no longer enemies, the DMZ will be preserved as an official nature reserve.

windows, but recently they have kept watch from a distance. On the South Korean side soldiers in sunglasses strike a taekwondo pose – partly to intimidate the North Koreans and partly to provide a photo opportunity.

The Monastery Visitors Centre sells DMZ baseball caps, T-shirts and other souvenirs. Located nearby is 'the world's most dangerous golf course', which has one 192yd par three hole that is surrounded by barbed wire and overlooked by North Korean guard posts manned by armed soldiers. The bunkers around the hole are concrete not sand.

After lunch the highlight is walking along 265m of the 73m-deep **Third Tunnel of Aggression**. The third such tunnel found under the DMZ, it was dug by the North Koreans so that their army could quickly march through and launch a surprise attack on Seoul. Coal was smeared on the walls and when it was discovered in 1978 the North Korean authorities claimed it was an old coal mine!

Sights

Third Tunnel of Aggression (☎ 031-940 8341; admission free; ⏰ 9am-5pm Tue-Sun)

Eating

Bring along a packed lunch or have *bibimbap* (rice, egg, meat and vegies with a chilli sauce; W5000) or *bulgogi* (barbecued beef slices and lettuce wrap; W10,000) at the restaurant where tour buses stop for lunch.

Inside the United Service Organizations (USO) building is a 100% American red, white and blue **diner** (☎ 795 3028; meals US$2-12;

⏰ 7am-2pm Mon-Fri), which serves up burgers (a bit tasteless but there are lashings of sauces), steaks, salads, breakfast and apple pies just like mom would make if only she had the time.

Tours

USO DMZ Tour (Map pp200–1; ☎ 795 3028; www.uso .org.kr; day tours US$40; ⏰ depart 7.30am return 3.30pm, twice weekly; subway Line 4 & 6 to Samgakji, Exit 11) This is the best tour and fills up quickly, so book ahead.

Other DMZ Tours (half/full day W40,000/70,000) Numerous Korean companies run DMZ tours, but check that it includes Panmunjeom as some don't.

DOWNTOWN INCHEON

The most interesting parts of Incheon city can best be explored on a one-hour walking tour with a stopover in the revitalised Chinatown for a meal. Southwest of Dong-Incheon station modern boutiques sell the latest brand-name fashions, while Sinpo market and the 19th-century buildings are reminders of the past.

Walking Tour

Take the only exit of **Dong-Incheon station 1**. To cross the major road, descend into the rabbit warren maze of the **underground shopping arcade 2**. Find your way to the left side of the road in front of the station to visit the **wedding street 3** and the elegant **Dap-dong Catholic Cathedral 4**, built in 1897 with unusual cupolas on its three towers.

Cross the road by the underpass to **Fashion street 5**, which is marked by a blue, green and orange archway set back from the main road. The street is lined with brand-name fashion boutiques. On the left is **Sinpo market 6**.

Follow the road round to the left and on the left is a **stall 7** that sells *gonggalppang* (Chinese-style, balloon-shaped sweet bread, W800) at the entrance to Sinpo market arcade. Take the second road on the right past **Korea First Bank 8**. Along this road are three 19th-century Japanese bank buildings, all with a Western classical design: the **58th Bank building 9**, 1892, with a clock on the roof; the **18th Bank building 10**, 1890, with a Roman façade; and the **Jeil Bank building 11**, 1899, with a dome and two dormer windows.

Seoul's Chinatown was founded in 1884 but almost disappeared after the Korean War (1950-53) when China sided with the North. Nowadays 700 Chinese live here and the area has come back to life. Over two dozen restaurants and shops sell Chinese clothes, souvenirs, food and liquor and the area is a sea of red. Chinese murals, lampposts and three gaudy entrance gates add to the Chinatown atmosphere. This was where one of Korea's favourite dishes, *jajang-myeon* (noodles in black bean sauce), was invented and just about every restaurant sells it for a modest W3000. **Gonghwachun 12** is one of the best Chinese restaurants, while **Jungguk Jeongtong Sujemandu 13** is mainly a dumpling restaurant.

TRANSPORT

Distance from Seoul 36km

Travel time 75 minutes

Direction West

Subway Take Line 1 to Dong-Incheon station (W1400). Return on Line 1 from Incheon station.

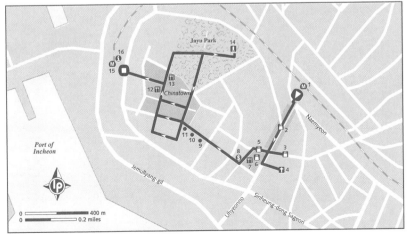

Walk up the steps to visit Jayu (Freedom) Park. The park is famous for its recently controversial **statue of General MacArthur 14**, the American leader of UN forces during the Korean War. General MacArthur changed the course of the country's destiny with his daring and successful landing at Incheon in September 1950. The park has views over Incheon port.

Walk back down to Chinatown and turn right to **Incheon station 15** for the journey back to Seoul, or else carry on to the West Sea Isles (below). The **tourist information centre 16** is next door to the station.

Information

Tourist information centre (☎ 032-1330; outside Incheon station; ⏰ 9am-7pm)

Eating

Both restaurants have a signboard written in Chinese characters only.

Gonghwachun (☎ 032-765 0571; meals W3000-50,000; ⏰ 10am-10pm) On the 2nd and 3rd floor is this clean and immaculate place with a long list of Chinese food to suit all tastes and budgets.

Jungguk Jeongtong Sujemandu (☎ 032-773 7888; meals W3000-10,000; ⏰ 9am-9pm) A basic restaurant that specialises in big Chinese dumplings with mainly vegetable fillings.

THE WEST SEA ISLES

Sandy beaches and mollusc-impregnated mud flats, sea views, rural scenery, vineyards, fresh air and fresh fish and seafood restaurants – the West Sea Isles are a whole different planet to the cars, concrete and neon of Seoul. Accommodation prices double between mid-July and mid-August when the island beaches become crowded, but at other times visitors are few, although this might change with the recent introduction of a five-day working week.

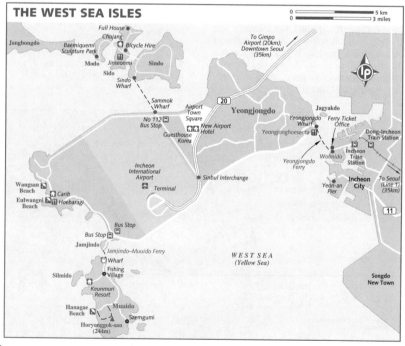

THE WEST SEA ISLES

TRANSPORT

Distance from Seoul 50km

Travel time 2½ hours (Eurwangni Beach)

Direction West

Subway Take the subway Line 1 to Incheon station or Dong-Incheon station (W1400) to get to these get-away-from-it-all islands.

YEONGJONGDO

Despite the nearby Incheon international airport and higgledy-piggledy tourist developments, the island's western beaches and fishing villages still maintain a holiday atmosphere. Beaches have only narrow strips of sand so swimming is only possible at high tide, and (except for high tide) mud flats stretch as far as the eye can see. The upside of the hectares of mud is the harvest of shellfish and crabs that are served up in lines of beachfront restaurants. None have fancy décor or furniture, but customers only have eyes for the seafood. Half a bucket of shellfish, a couple of blue crabs or a raw-fish meal (all meant for sharing) each costs around W30,000, while the other local speciality, *kalguksu* (noodles in broth), is W5000.

Eulwangni Beach is the most popular of the beaches as it has the highest proportion of sand to mud, and most of the accommodation is there along with a string of restaurants and stores.

Information

Tourist information centre (☎ 765 4169; Wolmido Promenade; ☺ 10am-noon & 1-6pm)

Eating

Hoebaragi (회바라기; ☎ 032-746 3611; Eurwangni Beach; meals to share W30,000; ☺ 11am-1am) This large restaurant specialises in do-it-yourself barbecue shellfish, which includes a mini seafood soup, but no rice, just a sweet chilli dip. For the same price, you can substitute prawns for half the shellfish.

Yeongjongdong market & restaurants The small market sells crabs, shellfish, fish and prawns. Buy the produce here and one of the nearby restaurants such as Yeongjonghoesenta will cook it up with side dishes for W5000.

Sleeping

Carib (☎ 751 5455; Eurwangni Beach; r W40,000-80,000) The more expensive rooms are quite luxurious

in this easy-to-spot, ship-shaped motel. Although poorly maintained, it is modern with fully-equipped rooms that have appealing sea and beach views from the circular windows.

TRANSPORT

Subway, taxi, ferry & bus Catch subway Line 1 to Incheon station (W1400, 75 minutes) from Central Seoul. Take a taxi (W1900, five minutes) outside the subway to Wolmido, which has a seafront promenade lined with numerous cafés, bars and seafood restaurants. If you are walking, allow 15 minutes. Then catch the ferry (adult/youth/child W2000/1500/1000, 10 minutes, half-hourly 7am-9pm) to Yeongjongdo wharf. Take bus No 202 (W900, 50 minutes, half-hourly) from the bus stand on the right to Eurwangni Beach via a roundabout route that includes Incheon international airport and Jamjindo.

MUUIDO

Muuido is a hilly green island with little development up to now. The Jamjindo ferry drops you off at Keunmuri wharf on Muuido where you can catch the local bus to **Hanagae beach**, the best on the island. It has plenty of golden sand, a handful of seafood restaurants and a hundred very basic beach huts under the pine trees or on the beach. The chalet-style house on the beach is a film set built for the Korean TV drama *Stairway to Heaven*. Just beyond it is the start of a 2.5km **hike** through dense woods to the top of **Horyonggoksan** (244m).

Another option from Keunmuri wharf is to walk to the fishing village, turn right at the sign and walk on over the hill through the vineyard to **Silmi beach**. The beach is not so good but there is a freshwater swimming pool beside a campsite and basic huts that are shaded by pine trees. At low tide you can walk to **Silmido**, an uninhabited island where the Korean movie of that name was filmed. Hunting for shellfish is a popular activity.

Muuido restaurants specialise in raw fish, crabs (in season), *jogaegui* (barbecue shellfish) and *kalguksu*.

Sights

Hanagae & Silmi beaches (adult Jul & Aug/Sep-Jun W2000/1000) Both have an entry fee.

Eating

Badara Hoejip (바다라회집; ☎ 752 5561; Hanagae Beach; meals W5000-60,000; 🕑 7am-9pm) Order the local speciality, *kalguksu* (W5000), which has lots of clams, diced vegetables and a hint of chilli (minimum two people). Other options are *pajeon* (green onion pancake), crab (in season), octopus and raw fish (*gwangeo* or *ureok*).

Sleeping

Hanagae Beach (☎ 032-751 8833; tents/huts/huts with bathrooms W15,000/30,000/50,000) Huts and facilities are very primitive although the beach huts look picturesque.

TRANSPORT

Bus & ferry From Yeongjongdo wharf local bus No 222 (W900) runs directly to the Jamjindo ferry, while the more frequent **bus** No 202 (W900, 15 minutes, half-hourly) drops you on the main road, a pleasant 1km walk from Jamjindo wharf. You can also pick up bus No 202 at Eurwangni Beach or Incheon international airport. At Jamjindo take the ferry (☎ 032-751 3354; adult/child return W2000/1000; five minutes, half-hourly 7am-8pm) to Keunmuri wharf, Muuido. The Muuido island bus (W1000) runs every 30 minutes from Keunmuri wharf to Hanagae beach, Saemkkumi wharf, Silmi beach and back to Keunmuri wharf.

An alternative is to stay at Eurwangni Beach on Yeongjongdo and visit Muuido on a day trip.

SINDO, SIDO & MODO

These three undeveloped islands, joined by two bridges, are surrounded by mud flats rather than sandy beaches, but you can experience the countryside life that virtually all Koreans are desperate to escape from. Many of the people living on the islands are elderly and the bus driver stops the bus sometimes to have a chat. The greenery is a treat after the greyness of Seoul.

The local bus runs from the wharf on Sindo across to Sido and on to Modo. The best plan is to get off in **Sido village**, which has a few *minbak* (private homes with rooms for rent), an **unusual church** (take a peak inside to see why), a ramshackle shop, restaurant and bicycle stall.

You can easily cycle the 2km to the fake house and **lighthouse** where the TV drama *Full House* was filmed. The beach is only sandy at high tide, but at low tide you can dig for shellfish.

Another easy ride is across the bridge to Modo and the fascinating **Baemiquemi Sculpture Park**, only 2km from Sido village. The Daliesque, erotic sculptures created by Lee Il-ho are outstanding – one is even perched up a tree. This is the best beach and has a café and pension.

A third more challenging cycle ride is around **Sindo**, a hilly green island with a village that overlooks rice fields, vineyards and chilli plants. It's like the Korean Folk Village (p154) but for real. The 10km cycle ride takes 1½ hours.

Sights

Full House (adult/child W3000/2000; Sido; 🕑 10am-5pm)

Eating & Drinking

Baemiquemi Sculpture Park Café (☎ 032-752 7215; Modo; drinks W5000) At this café on the beach, which overlooks the wonderful sculptures, *bibimbap* is W10,000.

Jinseonmi Sikdang (진선미식당; ☎ 032-752 4049; Sido Village; meals W5000; 🕑 noon-2pm, 6-8pm) A bargain restaurant – rice (W4000) consists of *doenjang jjigae* (soybean paste stew), egg, delicious fish, divine eggplant and other side dishes, with fruit to finish.

TRANSPORT

Bus & ferry Take bus No 112 (W3200, 90 minutes, every 15 minutes), which leaves from outside Dong-Incheon train station (one stop before Incheon station) and drops passengers a 10-minute walk from Sammok wharf. If you are already on Yeongjongdo, take bus No 202 (W900, half-hourly) to Sinbul Interchange where you can pick up **bus** No 203 (W900, half-hourly) to Sammok wharf. A ferry (cars/passengers return W30,000/4600, hourly) runs from Sammok wharf to Sindo wharf from 7.10am to 6.10pm. The local island bus (W1000, half-hourly) rattles round all three islands except around noon when the driver has his lunch break. Get off the ferry quickly or the bus may leave without you.

Sleeping

Baemiquemi Sculpture Park Pension (☎ 032-752 7215; Modo; r from W80,000) A special place right on the beach with a fabulous view. As well as a balcony, the comfortable rooms have TV and a kitchen, but it's under the Incheon airport flight path.

Chujang Minbak (☎ 010-7746 7848; Sido Village; r W30,000) Sleep on a *yo* (padded quilt) on the floor in a small bare room with a TV, fridge and fan plus en suite facilities.

HWASEONG (SUWON FORTRESS)

This World Heritage fortress is in Suwon, which is home to a million residents. The majestic fortress wall snakes 5.7km around the city centre and 95% has been faithfully restored. It was originally constructed between 1794 and 1796, during the reign of King Jeongjo, a much-loved monarch due to his filial piety and concern for ordinary people. The fortress wall is made of earth and faced with large stone blocks, while additional features are built of grey bricks. Hiking all the way around the walls takes two hours and includes views of the city, large entrance gates, small secret gates, sentry towers, bastions, command posts, a giant bell, an archery field and a signal beacon platform used for sending messages in an age before mobile phones.

Start at **Paldalmun**, also known as Nammun (South Gate), and walk up the steps to the top of **Paldalsan** (143m), a view point where you might see or hear cuckoos. The ticket office is a little further on. Half way round at **Hwahongmun** (the gate over the stream) you can sample Suwon's famous *galbi* (beef ribs) or *galbitang* (see Eating p86). At the end of the walk explore **Jidong market** (mainly produce) and **Yeongdong market** (mainly clothing).

Before setting off around Hwaseong, visit the recently restored **Haenggung** (temporary palace), built by King Jeongjo who stayed here on his visits to his father's grave, which is nearby. His father (Prince Sado) met a tragic fate – the victim of court intrigues, he was suffocated in a rice chest. Courtyard follows courtyard as you walk around the large walled complex. One hall depicts the 60th birthday party of King Jeongjo's mother, while another hall features Daejanggeum, a female Joseon dynasty cook who rose from humble beginnings to a high position in the royal court. The TV drama about her has been a huge hit throughout Asia and was partly filmed here. Military uniforms and weapons are on display, and you can make a wish and tie it onto the oldest tree in Suwon. Other activities take place, mainly at the weekend.

TRANSPORT

Distance from Seoul 48km

Travel time Two hours

Direction South

Subway, bus or taxi Suwon is easily reached by subway Line 1 (W1100, one hour). Then take bus No 11, 13, 36, 38 or 39 (W850, 10 minutes) from the left side of the train station to Paldalmun (also called Nammun) or nip into a taxi (W3000). Buses back to the station leave from the line of bus stops on the opposite side of Paldalmun.

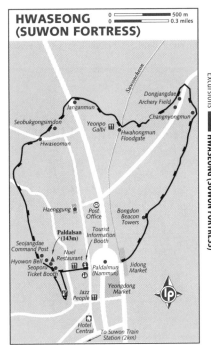

HWASEONG (SUWON FORTRESS)

Sights

Haenggung (☎ 031-228 4407; www.suwonhs.ne.kr; adult/student W1000/500; ✆ 9am-6pm Tue-Sun Mar-Oct, 9am-5pm Tue-Sun Nov-Feb)

Hwaseong (☎ 031-228 4672; adult/youth/child W1000/700/500; ✆ 24hr)

Information

Paldalmun tourist information booth (☎ 031-228 2765; ✆ 9am-6pm)

Tourist information centre (☎ 031-228 4674; outside Suwon train station; ✆ 7am-8pm)

Eating & Drinking

Jazz People (☎ 031-243 8802; meals W8000-22,000; ✆ 10am-2am) This smart bar and fusion restaurant is perched high up on the 8th floor. Meals start at W8000, and the views are great.

Neul (늘; ☎ 031-258 3580; meals W7000-23,000; ✆ 10am-11pm) Fusion food and a wide range of drinks.

Yeonpo Galbi (연포갈비; ☎ 031-255 1337; meals W5000-28,000; ✆ 11.30am-10pm) This famous log cabin restaurant serves up *galbi* including a special Suwon version of *galbitang* – chunks of meat and a big rib in a seasoned broth with noodles and leeks.

Sleeping

Hotel Central (☎ 031-246 0011; www.hotelcentral.co.kr; r incl tax & service W65,000; 💻) Rooms vary (ask for a mountain view) but are generally light and comfortable and the price includes breakfast.

KOREAN FOLK VILLAGE

This very large collection of thatched and tiled Korean traditional houses and buildings takes at least half a day to explore. On view are a Buddhist temple, Confucian shrine, market, magistrate's house with examples of punishments, storehouses, a bullock pulling a cart, household furnishings and agricultural tools. Punishments were cruel and included breaking the offender's legs, branding him and severe floggings – usually 60 to 100 strokes. In a quaint rural atmosphere, artisans in *hanbok* (traditional clothing) create pots, make paper and weave bamboo, while other workers tend vegetable plots and chickens. Snacks, teas and handicrafts are for sale, and traditional musicians, dancers and acrobats put on displays, including tight-rope walking, a wedding ceremony and a farmers' dance, twice daily, starting around 11pm and 3pm.

Dancers at the Korean Folk Village (above)

Sights

Tourist information centre (☎ 031-228 4674; outside Suwon train station; ⊙ 7am-8pm) Has free Internet.

Information

Korean Folk Village (Map p146; ☎ 031-286 0000; www.koreanfolk.co.kr; adult/teenager/child W11,000/8000/7000; ⊙ 9am-6.30pm Apr-Sep, 9am-5.30pm Oct-Mar)

Eating

Traditional Korean meals (W5000 to W9000) such as mushroom stew, barbecues, *bibimbap*, oyster *pajeon*, and ginseng chicken are served in restaurants near the entrance or the folksy food court at the far end of the village.

TRANSPORT

Distance from Seoul 45km

Travel time Three hours return

Direction South

Subway & bus Take subway Line 1 to Suwon station (W1100, one hour). Exit the station and on your left is the large, new tourist information centre. From the tourist centre you can catch the free shuttle bus directly to the Korean Folk Village. The bus takes 30 minutes and leaves at 10.30am, 11.30am, 12.30pm, 1.30pm and 2.30pm and returns to the tourist centre at 2pm, 4pm and 5pm. If these times are inconvenient, take local bus No 37 (W1000).

EVERLAND

This world-class amusement park, less than an hour southeast of Seoul by bus, has four separate parts.

Festival World follows the classic Disneyland formula and encompasses a large area with fantasy buildings, thrill rides, fairground attractions, zoo animals, impressive seasonal gardens, restaurants, live music and shows. A novelty feature is the 15-minute **African Safari bus ride** through wildlife zones, which offers close-up views of tigers, lions, ligers and hyenas in one area; giraffes, zebras and elephants in the next; and bears in another. As it is so popular, you usually have to queue for an hour. The parades and festivals are always something special, and when it's lit up at night, the park takes on a magical atmosphere.

Caribbean Bay is a superb water park, designed so well that a visit here is just like being at the beach. The outdoor section is open from 1 June to mid-September and features a huge wave pool that produces a mini-tsunami every few minutes. Comfortable sunloungers and huts provide places to sunbathe and relax. A body surfing pool, diving pool, speedy tube rides and a super-scary water bobsleigh ride are other features along with swimming pools and a gentle river ride on circular tubes. The indoor section has a small wave pool, a few other pools, a spa and sauna. The place is always packed in summer, despite the high price.

The **Speedway Circuit** is the only one in Seoul and has weekend races. On the right is **X-Park** where you can drive a fun quad bike (ATV) around a twisting course.

The **Hee Won Garden & Hoam Art Museum** is a special place. The wonderful Korean-style gardens act like a Buddhist temple gateway to induce a calm frame of mind so that visitors can fully appreciate the art treasures inside the museum. The emphasis is on spotlighting select historical artworks rather than packing in as many exhibits as possible. Each one of the paintings, screens, celadon and other exhibits reveals stunning skill and craftsmanship. A free shuttle bus runs here on the hour from the main entrance to Festival World.

TRANSPORT

Distance from Seoul 40km

Travel time Two hours return

Direction Southeast

Subway & bus Take subway Line 2 or 3 to Express Bus Terminal station, leave by Exit 7 to Honam terminal and catch the Everland Express (W1600, 50 minutes, every half hour). Otherwise take subway Line 2 to Gangnam station, leave by Exit 6 and take bus No 5002 (W1600, 50 minutes, every 15 minutes).

Sights

Caribbean Bay (adult/child Jul & Aug W60,000/45,000, Jun & Sep W30,000/23,000, Oct-May W25,000/18,000; ⊙ 9am-6pm, 9am-8.30pm summer)

Everland (☎ 031-320 5000; www.everland.com)

Festival World (adult/child under 13 day-pass W30,000/23,000; ⊙ 9.30am-10pm, 9.30am-11pm summer)

Hee Won Garden & Hoam Art Museum (☎ 031-320 1801; www.hoammuseum.org; adult/child W4000/3000; ⊙ 10am-6pm Tue-Sun)

Speedway (admission free; ⊙ 8am-4pm Sat & Sun)

X-Park (per 10-15min W10,000; ⊙ 9.30am-7pm Tue-Sun)

Eating

Festival World and Caribbean Bay both have plenty of budget Korean and fusion options (W7000 to W10,000) as well as fast-food (W5000).

Directory

Directory

TRANSPORT

Flights, tours and rail tickets can be booked online. Visit www.lonelyplanet.com/travel_services.

AIR

South Korea used to have only two domestic carriers – **Korean Air** (☎ 1588 2001; www.koreanair.com) and **Asiana Airlines** (☎ 1588 8000; www.flyasiana.com) – but recently low-cost regional airlines such as Jeju Air have appeared on the scene. Domestic flights are reasonably priced and run to most of the country's major cities as well as Jejudo, Korea's southern holiday and honeymoon island. Fares charged by both major companies are virtually identical on domestic routes. Fares are cheaper from Monday to Thursday when you are also more likely to obtain a seat. Flights on public holidays are more expensive and are often booked out, so avoid travel on these days if possible. There are discounts for students and children. Foreigners should carry their passports for ID purposes on all domestic flights. The longest flight (Seoul to Jejudo) takes just over an hour.

Airlines

The following major airlines have offices in Seoul:

Air Canada (AC; ☎ 3788 0100)

Air China (CA; ☎ 774 6886)

Air France (AF; ☎ 3788 0440)

Asiana Airlines (OZ; ☎ 1588 8000)

British Airways (BA; ☎ 774 5511)

Cathay Pacific Airways (CX; ☎ 311 2800)

Japan Airlines (JL; ☎ 3788 5710)

KLM Royal Dutch Airlines (KL; ☎ 2011 5500)

Korean Air (KE; ☎ 1588 2001)

Lufthansa Airlines (LH; ☎ 3420 0400)

Malaysia Airlines (MH; ☎ 777 7761)

Northwest Airlines (NW; ☎ 732 1700)

Singapore Airlines (SQ; ☎ 755 1226)

United Airlines (UA; ☎ 778 4968)

Airports

Virtually all international passengers arrive at Incheon International Airport, situated on an island in the West Sea that is linked to the mainland by a road bridge. Gimpo International Airport, despite its name, is the domestic airport and only has one international flight destination – to and from Haneda Airport in Tokyo.

GIMPO INTERNATIONAL AIRPORT

The **domestic terminal** (Map pp198–9; ☎ 660 2114; http://gimpo.airport.co.kr; subway Line 5 to Gimpo International Airport, Exit 1) handles all Seoul's domestic flights except for a handful of flights to and from Busan and Jejudo, which arrive and depart from Incheon. The 1st floor is for arrivals and has a **tourist information booth** (☎ 3707 9465; ⏰ 9am-9pm) with free Internet. The 2nd floor is for checking in while the 3rd floor is for departures and has a pharmacy. The 4th floor has restaurants and duty-free shops. Shops, banks, lost luggage, luggage deposit and a medical centre are also available. Just outside the airport is the subway station (W1100 to City Hall) along with limousine buses (W2500 to W6000) and taxis that charge around W18,000 (regular taxi) or W30,000 (deluxe taxi) to City Hall, 18km away.

Gimpo also has a separate **international terminal** (subway Exit 2) but it only handles flights to Haneda (Tokyo) – currently 18 daily, which cost around W350,000 plus tax. Taking this route avoids the hassle of getting out to Incheon and Narita airports, which are a long distance from their respective capital cities. Inside the international terminal are banks and the **Sky City Mall** (☎ 6343 4000; ⏰ 10am-9pm) where clothing, electronics goods and mobile phones all have a floor to themselves. Nearby is **CGVA cinema multiplex** (☎ 1544 1122; ⏰ 11am-2am) and a food court.

INCHEON INTERNATIONAL AIRPORT

This spacious and splendid airport (Map p150; ☎ 032-1577 2600; www.airport.co.kr), 52km west of Seoul, opened in March 2001, and relegated Gimpo International Airport to handling mainly domestic flights.

Built on reclaimed land between two islands in the West Sea off Incheon city, at present no trains run to the airport, although that should change in 2007. Instead, fleets of buses and taxis go back and forth to all parts of Seoul and to other cities. Special airport buses run every 10 to 30 minutes from around 5.30am to 10pm and the trip to downtown Seoul takes around 90 minutes depending on traffic conditions. City limousine buses cost W7000 and run along a dozen routes, while KAL deluxe limousine 25-seat buses cost W12,000 and drop passengers off at 20 major hotels around Seoul. Buses also run every 10 minutes to Gimpo airport along a special airport road, which takes about 30 minutes and costs W4500 on the City limousine buses or W6000 on the KAL ones. If no airport bus travels to where you want to go, you can take a bus to a subway station and transfer. One option is to transfer to the subway at Gimpo airport but it requires a bit of a walk with your bags.

For up-to-date information on airport buses see www.airport.or.kr. When catching a bus back to the airport, remember that the airport buses have their own special, signed stops and don't stop at ordinary bus stops. See p151 for buses around the airport island and to nearby beaches.

Regular taxis charge around W38,000 to downtown Seoul while a deluxe or jumbo taxi costs around W63,000, but the price can be more if traffic is jammed as meters run on a time basis when the taxis are not moving. A road toll (W6400) is added to the meter price. From midnight to 4am regular taxis charge 20% extra.

On the 1st floor (arrivals):

Foreign currency exchanges (☯ 6am-10pm)

Global ATMs There are around a dozen.

Hotel Information Centre (☎ 032-743 2570; h-reservation@hanmail.net; ☯ 9am-10pm) A private company that offers discounts on the rack rates at some midrange and top-end hotels.

Incheon Tourist Information Centre (☎ 032-743 0011; ☯ 7am-10pm)

KTO Tourist Information Centre (☎ 1330; ☯ 7am-10pm)

On the 2nd floor:

Gate A Has a handful of daily domestic flights to and from Busan and Jejudo.

Internet Café Lounge (☎ 032-743 7427; 1hr W3000; ☯ 8am-7.30pm)

Korean Air Lost & Found Office (☎ 032-742 5193; Room 2145; ☯ 6.30am-9.30pm)

KT Plaza (☎ 032-752 1441; ☯ 7am-8pm) Offers 30 minutes free Internet access.

KTF (☎ 032-743 4072) Mobile phone.

LG Telecom (☎ 032-743 4019) Rent a mobile phone.

Luggage Storage (☎ 032-743 5804; Gate B; per item per day W3000-6000; ☯ 6am-10pm)

Post Office (☎ 032-740 2900; ☯ 9am-6pm Mon-Fri)

SK (☎ 032-743 4042) Mobile phone rental.

Transit Tours (☎ 032-741 3139; 2nd fl; 1st fl, Exit 2 & 12) Runs trips for transit passengers to a luxurious seawater spa, around the airport island Yeongjongdo, and further afield around Seoul and Incheon. Tours cost US$30 to US$50 and last two to five hours.

The 3rd floor is for departures and offers retail therapy in the many duty-free shops. Restaurants, fast-food outlets, cafés and bars charge reasonable prices. Banks in the shopping area beyond immigration control enable you to exchange any won before leaving the country. To obtain a tax refund on goods you bought at a shop that participates in one of the tax refund schemes (p121), you must show the goods and receipts to one of the customs officers behind the check-in counters. Also on this floor:

Left-Luggage Storeroom (large item per day W3000; ☯ 7am-9.30pm)

Lost & Found Office (☎ 741 3114; find119@airport.or.kr; ☯ 7am-10.30pm)

On the hard-to-find 4th floor:

Café Royal (American breakfast W12,000, continental breakfast W9300)

Panorama (meals W6000-18,000; ☯ 7am-9pm) Serves up breakfasts, *bulgogi* (barbecued beef slices and lettuce wrap) sets, fancy desserts and a view of the planes.

Snack bar (pumpkin porridge & ginseng tea W5000)

Down in the basement:

Airport Sauna (☎ 032-743 74000; W10,000-15,000; ☯ 24hr) This sauna has the usual hot and cold tubs, steam and sauna rooms along with showers, massages (W30,000-80,000), male hairdresser (W15,000), shoe shine (W3000) and a dormitory with *yo* (padded quilt that serves as a mattress on the floor). The women's sauna has just a sauna and a dormitory. Staying all night costs W15,000.

Carib (☎ 032-743 2550; meals around W8000; ☯ 6am-9.30pm) A quiet and relaxing food court option.

Medical Centre (☎ 032-743 3115, emergency ☎ 743 3119; ☽ 24hr) Run by Inha University, the centre has English-speaking staff who treat up to 200 people a day. A **dental clinic** (☽ 9am-5pm Mon-Fri) is part of the centre.

Pool Hall (☎ 032-743 74000; 10min W2500; ☽ 24hr) Pay at the sauna.

Samil Pharmacy (☎ 032-743 3399; ☽ 7.30am-8.30pm)

Tous Les Jours (☎ 032-743 7007; ☽ 6am-9pm) Has freshly baked items and ice creams.

Vita Via (☎ 032-743 7009; meals W4000-10,000; ☽ 7am-9pm) A clean and buzzing food court that includes conveyor belt sushi.

See p131 for details of accommodation inside and near the airport.

KOREA CITY AIR TERMINAL

If you're booked on a Korean Air or Asiana flight, you can check-in your luggage at the **Korea City Air Terminal** (KCAT; Map pp214–15; ☎ 551 0077; www.kcat.co.kr; ☽ 7am-6.30pm; subway Line 2 to Samseong, COEX Exit) and catch a non-stop limousine bus (W12,000, 1½ hours, every 15 minutes) to Incheon International Airport or Gimpo airport (W6000). Asiana passengers can also use the KCAT at **Central City** (Map p211; ☎ 1544 5551; www.centralcityseoul.co.kr; subway Line 3 or 7 to Express Bus Terminal, Exit 7) where a similar system operates.

BICYCLE

The only safe and enjoyable cycling is in Ttukseom Seoul Forest (p63), around the West Sea islands (p150), and along the cycleways along the Han River (p115). Bicycles cost W2000 an hour. ID is required, and padlocks or helmets are not supplied.

BOAT

Regular ferries connect Incheon City, west of Seoul, with around a dozen port cities in China two or three times a week. Journey times vary from 12 to 24 hours. One-way fares start at W115,000 to most destinations but prices double for the more private and comfortable cabins. A through-ticket from Seoul to Beijing or Shanghai is available, which includes a ferry trip and train journeys in Korea and China – see www .korail.go.kr for details. To reach Incheon port (ferries leave from Yeonan Pier or International Terminal 2), take subway Line 1 to Incheon station (the end of the line) and then take a taxi (W4000).

Ferries to six Japanese cities leave from the southern city of Busan (one-way tickets cost W55,000 to W110,000). See www .korail.go.kr for a Seoul to Tokyo rail-and-ferry through ticket.

BUS
Local

It is easier and usually quicker to travel around Seoul by subway, but the city has a comprehensive and reasonably priced bus system (☎ 414 5005; www.bus.go.kr) that operates from 5.30am to midnight, although buses run on a few routes until 2am. Some bus stops have some bus route maps in English. Most buses have their major destinations written in English on the outside and they usually have a taped announcement of the names of each stop in English, but hardly any bus drivers understand English. What were they all doing during their English lessons at school?

Long-distance express red buses to the outer suburbs cost W1400, while green buses that link subways within a district and blue buses to outer suburbs cost W800, and yellow short-haul buses that circle small districts are W500. The bus number indicates which district or districts the bus travels around or between – thus blue bus No 261 starts in zone 2, and goes to zone 6 via Line 1. Pay with a T-money prepaid card (the card costs W1500 and can be bought, charged and recharged at any subway station ticket office) and tickets cost W100 less and transfers are free, or at least cheaper. Put your card to the screen as you exit as well as when you get on a bus.

Long Distance

Reasonably priced long-distance buses speed to just about every small town in South Korea. Most major roads have a special bus lane that reduces delays due to heavy traffic. Buses are so frequent that it's not necessary to buy a ticket in advance, except perhaps on holidays and weekends. Superior-class buses have more leg room but cost 50% more than ordinary buses. Night-time buses that travel after 10pm have a 10% surcharge and are generally superior class. Buses go to far more places than the trains, but are not as comfortable or safe, so trains are the better option for travelling long distances to major cities.

The **Seoul Express Bus Terminal** (Map p211; www.kobus.co.kr; subway Line 3 or 7 to Express Bus Terminal, Exit 1 or 7) is in two separate buildings:

Gyeongbu-Gumi-Yeongdong Terminal (☎ 535 4151; subway Exit 1) Serves mainly the eastern region and has a tourist information centre (☎ 535 4151; ☺ 9am-5pm), a pharmacy, a post office and lots of shops and restaurants. Downstairs are bars, more restaurants and a sauna. On the nine floors above are countless stalls selling fabrics, bedding and clothes as well as flowers (3rd floor; ☺ 1am-1pm). Sample express/deluxe bus fares include Busan (W19,300/28,800), Gyeongju (W16,300/24,200), Sokcho (W13,900/20,500), Daegu (W13,600/20,100), Daejeon (W7600/11,200) and Gongju (W5800/6300).

Honam Terminal (☎ 6282 0600; subway Exit 7) This smart and new terminal serves the southwestern region. Sample express/deluxe fares include Mokpo (W16,400/24,400), Gwangju (W14,100/20,900) and Jeonju (W10,200/15,000). This terminal is linked to the popular Central City Mall (p127).

Other bus terminals:

Dong Seoul Bus Terminal (Map pp214–15; ☎ 455 3161; subway Line 2 to Gangbyeon, Exit 3) Serves the eastern part of the country and big cities elsewhere. Sample fares include Everland (W2200), Icheon (W3500), Chuncheon (W7000), Daejeon (W8300), Danyang (W11,700), Daegu (W13,700), Gyeongju (W19,000) and Busan (W19,400).

Nambu Bus Terminal (Map p211; ☎ 521 8550; subway Line 3 to Nambu Bus Terminal, Exit 5) Has services south of Seoul such as Daecheon Beach (W8700).

Sinchon Bus Terminal (Map p210; ☎ 324 0611; subway Line 2 to Sinchon, Exit 7) Has services to Ganghwado, a historical island northwest of Seoul.

CAR & MOTORCYCLE

First-timers in Seoul should avoid driving in Seoul due to the traffic jams, the impatience and recklessness of other drivers and the lack of street names, directional signs and parking. Public transport is cheap and convenient so few tourists get behind a steering wheel.

Driving

Driving in Seoul is on the right, but is not recommended. If you do start driving, after one year you must apply for a Korean licence, which means taking an eye test, but otherwise it is a relatively straightforward process as long as you have a driving licence from your home country. However, if you are not from a country such as the USA, Canada, UK, France or Germany, you will need a certificate from your embassy stating that you are licensed to drive in your home country.

Hire

You must be over 21 years of age and have an International Driving Permit (not available in Korea) in order to rent a car. Prices start at W70,000 a day. A safer option is to rent both a car and a driver (3hr/10hr W75,000/142,000) – your hotel reception desk should be able to help and some top hotels have their own limousine service. The best place to hire a car is Incheon International Airport; see what Kumho-Hertz (www.kumhorent.com) or Avis (www.avis.co.kr) has to offer.

SUBWAY

Seoul's subway system (www.subwayworld.co.kr, www.smrt.co.kr) is modern, comprehensive, fast, frequent, clean, safe and cheap, but try to avoid rush hours. The minimum fare is W900 (W800 with a T-money card), less than one American dollar, and that takes you up to 12km. The one-hour trip to Suwon city costs only W1100 while the 75-minute ride to Incheon city costs just W1400. Trains run every few minutes from 5.30am to around midnight. Subway stations connect everywhere with everything. In central Seoul the average time between stations is just over two minutes, so it takes around 25 minutes to go 10 stops.

The T-money card costs W1500 and can be bought from subway station ticket offices and kiosks, and convenience stores that display the T-money logo. Each person needs their own card and the cards can be charged anywhere that sells them. Using a card saves you W100 per trip and saves queuing for tickets. Just touch the card to the sensor when you enter and leave the subway system or bus. When you leave the city, money on the card up to W20,000 can be refunded at any subway ticket office.

Many subway stations have lifts or stair lifts for wheelchairs. Neighbourhood maps inside the stations help you to decide which of the many subway exits to take, although north can be in any position, which makes the maps confusing. The stations all have clean modern toilets, but you need to carry around your own toilet paper. Every station is well signed in English and the whole system is very user-friendly. Most subway stations have storage lockers, although most of them are too small to take a full-size backpack. The lockers cost W1000 a day and are easy to use. Smoking is not permitted on trains or platforms.

Hawkers walk up and down the carriages selling W1000 mobile-phone holders, vegetable slicers, W3000 umbrellas and other bargains. The occasional handicapped or blind beggar shuffles down the aisle with a begging bowl and a cassette playing hymns.

If you leave something on a subway train, contact the relevant **Lost & Found Office** (○ 9am-5pm Mon-Fri, 9am-1pm Sat):

Lines 1 & 2 City Hall station (☎ 753 2408); **Guro station** (☎ 869 0089); **Seoul station** (☎ 755 7108)

Lines 3 & 4 Chungmuro station (☎ 2271 1170)

Lines 5 & 8 Wangsimni station (☎ 2298 6767)

Lines 6 & 7 Taereung station (☎ 949 6767)

Bundang Line Suseo station (☎ 2226 6881)

Incheon Line Bupyeong Samgeori station (☎ 032-451 3650)

TAXI

Regular taxis are a good deal and are cheaper than the bus or subway for three people making a short trip. Regular taxis *(ilban)* cost W1900 for the first 2km and then W100 for every 144m or 41 seconds afterwards. A 20% surcharge is payable between midnight and 4am. Deluxe taxis *(mobeom)* are black with a yellow stripe and cost W4500 for the first 3km and then W200 for every 205m or 50 seconds, and don't have a late-night surcharge. There are plans to drop these fixed prices in 2006 and if this happens taxis will charge varying prices.

Few drivers can speak English, but some taxis have a free interpretation service – you speak on the phone in English to an interpreter who then talks to the taxi driver in Korean. Writing your destination down can help as most Koreans are better at understanding written rather than spoken English. Writing your destination in *hangeul* (Korean phonetic alphabet) would be even better (to help you every map key item in this guidebook has a *hangeul* translation). All taxis have meters, but on the Incheon airport route passengers must pay the road toll on top of the meter charge. Tipping is not a Korean custom and is not necessary.

TRAIN

Seoul is the hub of an extensive domestic rail network operated by **Korean National Railroad** (☎ 1544 7788; www.korail.go.kr). The railway ticketing system is computerised and tickets can be bought up to one month in advance at many travel agents as well as at train stations. Booking ahead is advised. Foreigners can buy a 'KR pass' – see the website for details.

KTX (Korea Train Express) is a new bullet train service that at present extends from Seoul to Daegu but should reach Busan by 2008, which will reduce the journey time between Seoul and Busan from two hours 40 minutes to one hour 50 minutes. The next fastest and most luxurious type of train are *saemaeul* services, which also only stop in major towns. *Mugunghwa* trains are also comfortable and fast, but stop more often, while *tongil* trains are cheap, stop at every station and are an endangered species.

There are on-going talks about the reopening of rail links between North and South Korea, but this depends on the agreement of the unpredictable North Korean government.

PRACTICALITIES

ACCOMMODATION

The Sleeping chapter listings (p130) are 50% midrange, with 20% top-end mixed in, and are followed by Cheap Sleeps, which are Seoul's best budget options and cost less than W50,000. Organised into neighbourhood sections, accommodation is listed in alphabetical order. Seoul has no special peak seasons, but bigger discounts are more likely during mid-summer and mid-winter.

Booking Services

Always check if discounted prices include the 21% service and tax. Some hotels claim that the best rates are obtainable from their own websites, but other websites that offer discounted prices and special deals include these three:

www.khrc.com Check out the special deals.

www.koreahotels.net Has the widest range of hotels.

www.townmax.com Always worth checking.

BUSINESS HOURS

For most government and private offices, business hours are from 9am to 6pm Monday to Friday. Government offices usually close an hour earlier from November to February.

Banking hours are from 9.30am to 4pm Monday to Friday.

Post offices are open from 9am to 6pm Monday to Friday from March to October, and 9am to 5pm November to February.

Department stores traditionally open from 10.30am to 7.30pm daily with one day off a week. Nowadays some open every day and a few open until late evening. New high-rise shopping malls tend to stay open until 10pm and a few, for example in Dongdaemun (p122), are open all night.

Small shops open from 10am to around 9pm but some stay open until midnight, and many convenience stores are open 24 hours.

Restaurants usually open from 11am or noon until 9pm or 10pm seven days a week.

Cinemas are traditionally open from 11am with the last show ending at 11pm, but nowadays some continue later and even all night, like at COEX (p102).

As business hours vary, they are listed in every review in this guide.

Seoul offers plenty for night owls as some saunas, markets, malls, convenience stores, cinemas, Internet cafés and restaurants open all night, while many bars and nightclubs stay open until dawn, particularly on Friday or Saturday night. Clubbing, watching movies, napping in a sauna or shopping until 5.30am means you can catch an early subway train home and save on the taxi fare.

CHILDREN

See p45 for ways of keeping children happy. If you're in Seoul with the darlings on 5 May, Children's Day, take advantage of the many special events for children. The National Museum of Korea (p62) and the National Folk Museum (p50) have fun, hands-on children's sections, and the War Memorial & Museum (p63) has outdoor warplanes and tanks that make for a popular playground.

Children are welcome in restaurants but families usually eat out in their own neighbourhood rather than in central Seoul. High chairs are not common. Koreans are family-oriented but in the past family outings together have not been common, although this is changing with the younger generation of parents and the introduction of a five-day week.

For general advice about taking children abroad, check out a copy of Lonely Planet's *Travel with Children*.

Babysitting

A few top hotels and residences, such as Fraser Suites and Lotte World Hotel, provide babysitting services, but that's about it. See the classifieds in *K Scene* magazine for Filipinas who offer babysitting, nannying and housekeeping services. Otherwise try **H&S** (☎ 720 0870; www.hnskorea.com) who can supply babysitters (W10,000 an hour).

CLIMATE

Seoul has four very distinct seasons – and people never tire of telling you. Weatherwise, the best time of year to visit is autumn, from September to November, when the weather is usually sunny, and in October Seoul's surrounding hillsides are ablaze with autumn colours. Spring, from April to early June, is another beautiful season, with warm temperatures and cherry blossoms in late April.

Winter is dry but often bitterly cold, with average temperatures in Seoul hovering around zero from December to February, when you appreciate the *ondol* (underfloor heating). But white snow on the temple roofs is very picturesque and it's a good time to visit if you enjoy skiing, skateboarding or ice-skating. Try to avoid summer as late June to late July is the wet season when Seoul receives 60% of its annual rainfall. Some weeks in August are unpleasantly hot and humid although most places have aircon these days, which makes it more bearable. See p8 for the best time to visit Seoul in terms of festivals and events.

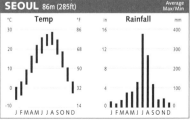

SEOUL 86m (285ft)   Average Max/Min

COURSES

Buddhist Temple Stays

Some Korean temples, usually located in remote and picturesque mountain areas, offer visitors the chance to participate in a number of activities with the monks. A typical overnight temple stay includes sharing a four-bowl meal of rice, soup, vegetables and water with the monks. No talk is allowed and not even a scrap of food should be wasted – Buddhist monks and nuns still follow strict rules. A guided tour of the temple buildings is followed by half an hour of *Seon* (Zen) meditation. Everyone sits cross-legged and a monk tells participants to concentrate and use their minds to focus completely on their breathing.

Another experience is the tea ceremony when a monk prepares green tea, which must be served at exactly the right temperature and should be drunk in three sips. Tea calms the mind and body, and if Korean monks have a disagreement they try and settle it over a cup of green tea. Helping to clean the grounds and a hike in the nearby mountains are other likely activities. View www.templestaykorea. net for details of temple stays or visit the information office at Jogyesa (p53).

Cooking

The best way to learn Korean cooking is to do a homestay with someone willing to teach you. Otherwise a few cooking classes are conducted in English.

Food & Culture Academy (Map p210; ☎ 362 6704; www .fnckorea.com; 3rd fl, Hanuisol A Bldg, Seongsanno; 1½hr courses W25,000-80,000; ☼ 9am-6pm Mon-Sat; subway Line 2 to Ewha Womans University, Exit 2) This friendly and relaxed school, a 15-minute walk from the subway, is outside the back gate of Ewha Womans University. Learn how to make *kimchi*, *dasik* (biscuits), *pajeon* (green-onion pancake), *bulgogi*, special *tteokbokki* (rice cakes in a sweet and spicy sauce), *mandu* (filled dumplings) and *gujeolpan* (eight snacks and wraps). You can also try on *hanbok* (traditional Korean clothing). Reservations are necessary.

Han's Institute of Culinary Arts (Map p205; ☎ 742 3567; www.hancooking.co.kr; courses W60,000-150,000; ☼ 9am-6pm Mon-Fri; subway Line 3 to Anguk, Exit 4) Various two-hour classes are offered in English. You get to eat or take away what you cook and the price includes a cookery book.

Institute of Traditional Korean Food (Map pp202–3; ☎ 741 6521; www.kfr.or.kr; above Jilsiru tteok café; 3hr courses W70,000) The Institute's owner, Mrs Yoon, runs courses on making Korean rice cakes.

Korean Language

Plenty of Seoulites will teach you Korean in return for you teaching them English – check the classifieds in *K Scene* magazine, or view www.englishspectrum.com and click on 'language exchanges'. *Survival Korean* by Stephen Revere (W21,000) includes a book and two cassette tapes.

Korean Foundation Cultural Center (Map pp206–7; ☎ 3789 5600; www.kfcenter.or.kr; ☼ 10.30am-6pm Mon-Sat; subway Lines 1 & 2 to City Hall, Exit 9) Click on 'Communication' on the website for details of free Korean language classes on three evenings a week. The cultural centre has a library and exhibition spaces.

YBM Sisa (Map p205; ☎ 2278 0509; sisakli@ybmsisa .co.kr; office ☼ 6am-7pm Mon-Sat; subway Line 1 or 5 to Jongno 3-ga, Exit 15) Various classes are available at this large institute overlooking Tapgol Park. A month of weekday lessons (two hours daily) costs W199,000 or a month of three-hour Saturday lessons costs W90,000.

Yonsei University (Map p210; ☎ 2123 3465; www.yskli .com) The university runs highly recommended part- and full-time Korean language and culture classes for serious students. Five-week summer courses cost US$1340.

Meditation

A mind-expanding number of meditation techniques are taught and practised at **Meditation Arui Seon** (Map p205; ☎ 722 6653; off Insadong 3-gil; ☼ 11am-10pm Tue-Sun; subway Line 3 to Anguk, Exit 6), a *hanok* (traditional Korean house) meditation and breathing centre. Meditate walking around the mini stone path in the green courtyard, walking on different energy level stones, listening to music or inspirational words on headphones, looking at a picture in a room hung with crystals, or even inside a plastic container. Drinks are W5000, but *Seon* teas are W10,000. Courses in English cost W20,000 for two hours, but every weekend the centre runs a free two-hour introduction course (phone ahead to make a booking).

Traditional Culture

In the grounds of Gyeongbokgung, the **National Folk Museum** (Map p50; ☎ 734 1341; www.nfm.go.kr) runs practical courses that teach foreigners about the tea ceremony and how to make fans, pottery, paper boxes and, of course, *kimchi*. The courses are free and numbers for each course are limited to 50 participants.

CUSTOMS

Visitors must declare all plants, fresh fruit, vegetables, dairy products and meat that they bring into South Korea. If you have more than US$10,000 in cash and travellers cheques, this should be declared and you will have to fill in a form. Gifts worth more than US$400 should also be declared. Leaving the country, the duty-free allowance is 1L of liquor, 200 cigarettes and 59ml (2 ounces) of perfume. Log on to www.customs.go.kr if you need further information. Antiques of national importance are not allowed to be exported, so if you want to buy a very expensive genuine antique, check first with the **Cultural Properties Appraisal Office** (☎ 662 0106).

DISABLED TRAVELLERS

In the past, Seoul has not been geared up to cater for disabled people, as disabled Koreans tended to stay at home or in their neighbourhood, and there were few disabled foreign tourists. But this is changing slowly, and the subway stations in particular are making an effort to become more disabled-friendly. Many stations now have stair-lifts and elevators, and new toilets for the disabled have been built. Tourist attractions, especially government-run ones, offer generous discounts or even free entry for disabled people and a helper. A useful brochure is the *Accessible Seoul* map, available from tourist information offices. More information is available at www.easyaccess.or.kr.

DISCOUNT CARDS

Government-run tourist attractions generally offer discounts to senior citizens over 65, but you will need a passport or some other ID. Other organisations generally restrict discounts to local residents but it is always worth asking.

ELECTRICITY

South Korea is on the 220V standard at 60Hz and uses two round pins with no earth.

EMBASSIES

Diplomatic Missions in Seoul

Australia (Map pp202–3; ☎ 2003 0100; www.australia.or.kr; 11th fl, Kyobo Bldg, Jongno 1-ga, Jongno-gu)

Canada (Map pp206–7; ☎ 3455 6000; www.korea.gc.ca; 10th fl, Kolon Bldg, 45 Mugyo-dong, Jung-gu)

China (Map pp202–3; ☎ 738 1193; www.chinaemb.or.kr; 9th fl, Kyobo Bldg, Jongno 1-ga, Jongno-gu)

France (Map pp200–1; ☎ 3149 4300; ambassade.france .or.kr; 30 Hap-dong, Seodaemun-gu)

Germany (Map pp198–9; ☎ 748 4114; www.gembassy .or.kr; 308-5 Dongbinggo-dong, Yongsan-gu)

Ireland (Map pp206–7; ☎ 774 6455; www.irelandhouse -korea.com; 15th fl, Daehan Fire & Marine Insurance Bldg, 51-1 Namchang-dong, Jung-gu)

Japan (Map pp202–3; ☎ 2170 5200; www.kr.emb-japan .go.jp; 18-11 Junghak-dong, Jongno-gu)

Netherlands (Map pp202–3; ☎ 737 9514; www.nlem bassy.or.kr; 14th fl, Kyobo Bldg, Jongno 1-ga, Jongno-gu)

New Zealand (Map pp202–3; ☎ 730 7794; www.nz embassy.com; 18th fl, Kyobo Bldg, Jongno 1-ga, Jongno-gu)

Philippines (Map p209; ☎ 577 6147; 34-44 Itaewon 1-dong, Yongsan-gu)

Russia (Map pp206–7; ☎ 752 0630; www.russian -embassy.org; 34-16 Jeong-dong, Jung-gu)

Singapore (Map pp206–7; ☎ 744 2464; www.mfa.gov .sg/seoul; 19th fl, Samsung Taepyeongno Bldg, 310 Taepyeongno 2-ga, Jung-gu)

Taiwan (Map pp202–3; ☎ 399 2767; Visa Office, 6th fl, Gwanghwamun Bldg, Jongno-gu)

UK (Map pp206–7; ☎ 3210 5500; www.britishembassy .or.kr; 4 Jeong-dong, Jung-gu)

USA (Map pp202–3; ☎ 397 4114; http://usembassy.state. gov/seoul; 32 Sejongno, Jongno-gu; ⏱ 9am-11.30pm, 1.30-3.30pm, closed Wed, Sat, Sun, Korean & American holidays)

EMERGENCY

Note that English-speaking staff may not be available. If this is the case ring ☎ 1330 (24 hour information and help line).

Ambulance (☎ 119)

Fire Brigade (☎ 119)

Medical Help Line (☎ 1339; English-speaking))

Police (☎ 112)

GAY & LESBIAN TRAVELLERS

Korea has never passed any laws that overtly discriminate against homosexuals. But this should not be taken as a sign of tolerance or acceptance. Korean law does not mention homosexuality because it is considered so bizarre and unnatural that the topic is taboo. Only one celebrity, TV actor Hong Seok-chun, has admitted to being gay and no-one has followed his example. Some older Koreans insist that there are no gays in Korea. Attitudes are changing, especially among young people, but virtually all Korean gays and lesbians keep their sexual orientation a secret from their family, work colleagues and friends. The few gay and lesbian clubs, bars and saunas (p111) in Seoul keep a low profile but are more open than they used to be. Gay and lesbian travellers who publicise the fact can expect some hostile reactions. View www.utopia-asia.com for up-to-date information on gay and lesbian issues and listings of gay bars and events in Seoul.

HEALTH

South Korea is a relatively well-developed country and the quality of medical care in Seoul is high. It is still, however, worth taking some basic health precautions.

At the time of writing there have been no human cases of 'bird flu' in Korea. In late 2005 there were concerns raised about imported Chinese *kimchi* (pickled vegetables). The nation's food regulator found parasite eggs in some imported *kimchi*, and other samples were found to contain five times as much lead as the Korean product. Earlier in the year it was revealed that some *mandu* (dumplings) manufacturers were using rotten radishes as stuffing for mass-produced *mandu*. The government has since increased penalties for those found to be adulterating foodstuffs, so hopefully this will be a practice of the past.

If you take regular medication make sure it is packed in clearly labelled, original containers. A letter from your physician outlining your medical condition and a list of your medications (using generic names) is useful. In Korea you need a doctor's prescription to buy medication and it may be difficult to find the exact medication you use at home – take extra in case of loss or theft.

No matter how fit and healthy you are it is unwise to travel without health insurance. Ensure you declare any pre-existing conditions. If your insurance company doesn't cover you for medical expenses abroad, look at getting extra cover – check Lonely Planet's subwwway (www.lonelyplanet.com) for more information.

Recommended Vaccinations

Travellers are advised to seek medical advice about vaccinations. Specialised travel-medicine clinics are your best source of information. Most vaccines don't produce immunity until at least two weeks after they're given, so visit a doctor four to eight weeks before departure. Travellers should particularly consider immunisation against hepatitis A.

Diseases
HEPATITIS A

A problem throughout the country, this food- and water-borne virus infects the liver, causing jaundice (yellow skin and eyes), nausea and lethargy. There is no specific treatment for hepatitis A, you just need to allow time for the liver to heal. All travellers to Korea should be vaccinated against hepatitis A.

HEPATITIS B

The only sexually transmitted disease that can be prevented by vaccination, hepatitis B is spread by body fluids, including sexual contact. Up to 10% of the population are carriers of hepatitis B, and usually are unaware of this. The long-term consequences can include liver cancer and cirrhosis.

HIV

HIV is also spread by body fluids. Avoid unsafe sex, sharing needles, invasive cosmetic procedures such as tattooing, and needles that have not been sterilised in a medical setting.

INFLUENZA

Influenza (flu) symptoms include high fever, muscle aches, runny nose, cough and sore throat. It can be very severe in people over the age of 65 or in those with underlying medical conditions such as heart disease or diabetes – vaccination is recommended for these individuals. There is no specific treatment, just rest and paracetamol.

STDS

Sexually transmitted diseases are common throughout the world and the most common include herpes, warts, syphilis, gonorrhoea and chlamydia. People carrying these diseases often have no signs of infection. Condoms will prevent gonorrhoea and chlamydia but not warts or herpes. If after a sexual encounter you develop any rash, lumps, discharge or pain when passing urine seek immediate medical attention. If you have been sexually active during your travels have an STD check on your return home.

TRAVELLER'S DIARRHOEA

Eating in restaurants is the biggest risk for contracting traveller's diarrhoea. Eat only freshly cooked food and avoid shellfish and food that has been sitting around in buffets. Peel all fruit, cook vegetables, and eat in busy restaurants with a high turnover of customers. Avoid tap water – bottled or boiled water is safer to drink.

In most cases, traveller's diarrhoea is caused by a bacteria (there are numerous potential culprits), and therefore responds promptly to treatment with antibiotics.

The treatment consists of staying well-hydrated, using rehydration solutions such as Gastrolyte. Antibiotics such as Norfloxacin, Ciprofloxacin or Azithromycin will kill the bacteria quickly.

Loperamide is just a 'stopper' and doesn't get to the cause of the problem. Don't take it if you have a fever, or blood in your stools. Seek medical attention quickly if you do not respond to an appropriate antibiotic.

Environmental Hazards

AIR POLLUTION

Air pollution, particularly vehicle pollution, is an increasing problem in Seoul. If you have severe respiratory problems speak with your doctor before travelling to any heavily polluted urban centres. This pollution also causes minor respiratory problems such as sinusitis, dry throat and irritated eyes.

PARASITES

The most common parasite in Korea is Clonorchis. Infection occurs after eating infected freshwater fish – these may be raw, pickled, smoked or dried. Fortunately raw freshwater fish are rarely served in Seoul restaurants, so it is easy to avoid.

Light infections usually cause no symptoms, however heavy infections can cause liver problems. In some areas along rivers where raw river fish are commonly eaten, up to 20% of the local population are infected.

Online Resources

There is a wealth of travel health advice on the Internet. For further information, Lonely Planet (www.lonelyplanet.com) is a good place to start. The **World Health Organization** (WHO; www.who.int/ith) publishes a superb book called *International Travel & Health*, which is revised annually and is available online at no cost. The **Centers for Disease Control and Prevention** (CDC; www.cdc.gov) website also has good general information.

HOLIDAYS
Public Holidays

Nine Korean public holidays are set according to the solar calendar and three according to the lunar calendar, meaning that they fall on different days each year. See p8 for Seoul's festivals and annual events. The government is threatening to abolish Arbour Day, Children's Day and Memorial Day as public holidays due to the recent reduction of the working week from six to five days.

New Year's Day 1 January

Lunar New Year 17-19 February 2007, 6-8 February 2008, 25-27 January 2009, 13-15 February 2010

Independence Movement Day 1 March

Arbour Day 5 April

Children's Day 5 May

Buddha's Birthday 24 May 2007, 12 May 2008, 2 May 2009, 21 May 2010

Memorial Day 6 June

Constitution Day 17 July

Liberation Day 15 August

National Foundation Day 3 October

Chuseok (Thanksgiving) 5-7 October 2006, 24-26 September 2007, 13-15 September 2008, 2-4 October 2009, 21-23 September 2010

Christmas Day 25 December

INTERNET ACCESS

Internet cafés can be found on every street of Seoul – just look for the 'PC 방' signs. The Internet rooms charge around W1200 per hour and are usually full of teenagers playing Starcraft or some other game. Addiction to these games is a major social problem. The PC rooms all have fast broadband connections and keyboards feature English and *hangeul*. Some are open 24 hours, but they don't usually offer much refreshment beyond instant noodles, biscuits and soft drinks so game addicts have an unhealthy diet. Some are full of cigarette smoke, but these days more and more smokers go outside.

Places that offer free Internet include most post offices, Seoul Help Centre for Foreigners at City Hall, Seoul Selection Bookshop, Incheon International Airport, Megaweb and McDonald's at the COEX Mall, and tourist information bureaux at KTO, Itaewon subway station, Insadong and Gimpo airport. Guesthouses offer free Internet access to their guests, and although budget motels don't usually have Internet access, all the hotels offer Internet-enabled computers or broadband access that you can plug into.

If you are working and living in Seoul, many Internet Service Providers (ISPs) can offer an English-language home page and continuous broadband access for around W35,000 a month.

LEGAL MATTERS

Most legal problems involving foreigners concern visa violations or illegal drugs. In the case of visa transgressions, the penalty is normally a fine and possible expulsion from the country. As for using or selling narcotics, think twice: you could spend years researching the living conditions in a South Korean prison. The age of consent for sex is 18 (unless you're married to each other), anyone under 20 is not allowed to buy alcohol or cigarettes, and to hire a car you must be at least 21 years old.

MAPS

The Korean Tourism Organisation (KTO) and Seoul Metropolitan Government publish numerous free brochures and maps of Seoul. They only show major roads but are fine for most purposes. **Chungang Atlas** (Map p205; ☎ 730 9191; ☷ 9am-6.30pm Mon-Sat, 9am-5.30pm Sun; subway Line 1 to Jonggak, Exit 2) has racks of detailed maps of Seoul in *hangeul*, but nothing very useful in English. There are no detailed, up-to-date and accurate maps in English and probably not in *hangeul* either.

MEDICAL SERVICES

Seoul is a healthy city with standards of sanitation and medical care that are equal to those of other developed countries. Doctors are overworked but surgeons are particularly skilled. There are two health systems – one is Western-style and the other is based on traditional Asian principles and makes use of herbal remedies and acupuncture. Gyeongdong market (p122) is the place to go for traditional remedies.

It is customary for a relative or friend to stay with a patient who is in hospital, staying overnight in the case of a serious illness, to help with the nursing work. Nurses concentrate on the medicine and monitoring aspects, while relatives handle the small talk and wield the bedpans. Doctors have a heavier caseload than in the US and are not used to offering patients options or giving long explanations (even if their English is up to it). Hospitals normally require cash upfront and then you have to claim the money back from your insurance company.

Daewon Dental Clinic (Map p209; Itaewonno; ☎ 794 0551; fax 794 0512; ☷ 10am-6.30pm Mon-Fri, 10am-2pm Sat; subway Line 6 to Itaewon, Exit 4) Kind and gentle Dr Park can take care of your dental problems – a check-up is W15,000, while a crown or front tooth root canal are both around W350,000.

International Clinic (Severance Hospital; Map p210; ☎ 2228 5800, 24hr emergency only 012-263 6556; www.severance .or.kr; Seongsanno; consultation W55,000; ☷ 8.30am-12.30pm & 1.30-5.30pm Mon-Fri, 8.30am-12.30pm Sat; subway Line 2 to Sinchon, Exit 3) A 700m walk from the subway, the impressive clinic has five English-speaking doctors led by jovial and experienced Dr Linton who speaks English and Korean. The hospital is ultra modern, a cross between a luxury hotel and a department store with water features, artworks, an impressive lobby, a food court and shops.

International Clinic (Map p209; ☎ 790 0857; www .internationalclinic.co.kr; Hannam Bldg, Itaewonno; ☷ 9am-noon & 2-6pm Mon-Fri, 9am-noon & 2-3pm Sat; subway Line 6 to Itaewon, Exit 2) Consultations cost W30,000 to W50,000, but a house call costs a whole lot more. Psychiatric services are also available.

MONEY

The South Korean unit of currency is the won (W), with W10, W50, W100 and W500 coins. Notes come in denominations of W1000, W5000 and W10,000. The highest value note is worth only US$10 at the current exchange rate, so you will probably have to carry around a thick wad of notes.

The Bank of Korea wants to introduce a W100,000 note, but so far the government has vetoed it. Recently the won has been strengthening against the US dollar and most other currencies, and this trend is expected to continue, given South Korea's balance of payments surplus. See the Quick Reference guide inside the front cover for the exchange rate at the time of printing or view www.keb.co.kr for the up-to-date exchange rate. See p18 to get an idea of costs in Seoul. It is easy enough for foreign residents in Seoul to open a bank account at one of the big banks – just find a clerk who can speak some English and have your passport and alien registration card with you.

ATMs

Automated teller machines (ATMs) in Seoul are a little strange but more and more accept foreign cards. If you have a foreign credit card, you need to find an ATM with a 'Global' sign or the logo of your credit card company. A few Global ATMs have all their instructions in Korean, so you may need help the first time you use one, but most have some English instructions. ATMs can be found outside banks and post offices, and inside deluxe hotels, subway stations, airports, convenience stores and department stores.

ATMs often operate from 9am to 11pm, but some are 24 hours. Restrictions on the amount you can withdraw vary. It can be as low as W100,000 or W300,000 per day, but most have a W700,000 limit. Outside banking hours you may be charged a higher commission. Convenient Global ATMs in Itaewon include:

Itaewon subway station (Map p209; subway Line 6 to Itaewon) Inside the subway station.

Korea Exchange Bank (KEB; Map p209; Itaewonno; subway Line 6 to Itaewon, Exit 1)

Changing Money

You can use US dollars on American military bases, including the United Service Organizations (USO), at Panmunjeom on the Demilitarized Zone (DMZ) tour, at duty-free shops, and in some tourist shops in Itaewon, but otherwise you will need Korean won. Duty-free shops also accept Japanese yen and some other foreign currencies.

Many banks in Seoul offer a foreign-exchange service and there are licensed moneychangers, particularly in Itaewon,

that keep longer hours than the banks and provide a faster service but may only exchange cash. As with any shops and hotels that offer to exchange money, compare their rates and commissions with the banks first.

US dollars are easiest to exchange but banks accept any major currency. If you have trouble exchanging a particular currency, try the Korea Exchange Bank (KEB). Traveller's cheques usually have a slightly better exchange rate than cash. Don't forget to reconvert any surplus won into another currency before you leave the country, as exchanging won outside Korea can be a problem. If you need to reconvert more than US$2000 of won at Incheon airport, you must show receipts for the money.

Citibank (Map p205; ☎ 731 8100; Hwaenamu-gil; ⊙ 9.30am-4.30pm Mon-Fri; subway Line 1 to Jonggak, Exit 3) Has a global ATM and exchanges foreign currency.

Hana Bank (Map p213; ☎ 3143 1111; Yanghwaro; ⊙ 9.30am-4.30pm Mon-Fri; subway Line 2 to Hongik University, Exit 5) Exchanges foreign currency.

Korea Exchange Bank (KEB; Map p209; ☎ 792 3911; Itaewonno; ⊙ 9.30am-4.30pm Mon-Fri; subway Line 6 to Itaewon, Exit 1) Has a global ATM and exchanges foreign currency.

Shinhan Bank (Map pp202–3; ☎ 774 5800; ⊙ 9.30am-4.30pm Mon-Fri; subway Line 1 to Jonggak, Exit 5) Has a Global ATM, can exchange money and is next door to the KTO tourist information centre.

Credit Cards

More and more upmarket hotels, shops and restaurants accept foreign credit cards, but plenty of places including budget accommodation, market stalls and restaurants require hard cash. Cash payment is still surprisingly common in Seoul so always have a stash of W10,000 notes handy as it will almost certainly be needed.

NEWSPAPERS & MAGAZINES

Korea has two locally published English-language newspapers: the *Korea Times* (W700; http://times.hankooki.com) and *Korea Herald* (W700; www.koreaherald.co.kr). Both are published Monday to Saturday, and like Tweedledum and Tweedledee, it's difficult to tell them apart as both fill most of their pages with news agency reports and local business and political news. But the Friday *Korea Times* and the Saturday *Korea Herald* have a weekender section with 'What's On' listings and articles on Seoul restaurants, shows and movies. The websites are useful – the *Times* has a 'jobs for foreigners' section with new postings every day, while the *Herald* website has accommodation classifieds.

Chosun Ilbo (http://english.chosun.com) and **Donga Ilbo** (http://english.donga.com) are for news junkies with web access. Neither has printed editions in English but maintain websites in English.

JoongAng Daily (http://joongangdaily.joins.com) is an eight-page insert in the *International Herald Tribune* (W1300). The website has useful 'event calendar' and 'J-style and weekend' sections.

K Scene is a free biweekly magazine for expats with a youthful vibe, lots of classifieds plus reviews and a calendar of events that is plugged into Seoul's clubbing scene.

Korea Now is published biweekly by the Korean Information Service and covers current affairs and the arts. Read the current issue online at http://kn.koreaherald.co.kr.

Koreana (www.koreana.or.kr) is a quarterly scholarly magazine on all things Korean that can be read online.

Seoul is a free monthly magazine that is always worth reading and has what's-on information, interviews, reviews and articles on cultural topics.

Seoul Scope is a free monthly arts, events and entertainment magazine in English and *hangeul*.

PHARMACIES

Seoul has two medical systems – Western and Asian, but virtually all pharmacies stock at least some Western medicines. Pharmacists sometimes know some English but it may help them if you write down your symptoms or the medicine you want on a piece of paper as they can usually understand English better if it enters through the eyes rather than the ears. If you have a language problem and a mobile phone dial ☎ 02 1330, explain what you want in English, and ask the interpreter to explain in Korean to the pharmacist.

Pharmacists in Itaewon can communicate in English, and a doctor's clinic for foreigners is situated on the main street (Map p209). Some brand-name medications, special sunscreens, deodorants, dental floss and specialised health products may be difficult to obtain in Seoul, so stock up on them before you arrive. Condoms can be bought in any convenience store.

MediPharm (Map p210; ☎ 336 0011; ⊕ 9am-11pm; subway Line 2 to Sinchon, Exit 8)

Sudo Pharmacy (Map p205; ☎ 732 3336; Insadong-gil; ⊕ 8.30am-9.20pm Mon-Sat, noon-7pm Sun; subway Line 3 to Anguk, Exit 6)

POST

Post offices (www.koreapost.go.kr) have a red/orange sign. Most offer free Internet. Domestic postal rates start at W190 for a regular-sized letter, W270 for express. Postcards (W350) and aerograms (W400) cost the same to any country, but international letter and parcel rates vary according to the destination. Airmail letters (10g) cost W580 for Zone 3, which includes North America, Europe, Australia and New Zealand. Also for Zone 3 a 2kg parcel costs W28,000 by airmail or W12,000 by surface mail. The heaviest parcel you can post (20kg) costs W94,000 by airmail, W48,000 by surface mail.

Anguk Post Office (Map p205; ☎ 735 2005; ⊕ 9am-6pm Mon-Fri; subway Line 3 to Anguk, Exit 1) Has free Internet.

Central Post Office (Map p206–7) Is being rebuilt but should reopen in 2007.

Gwanghwamun Post Office (Map pp202–3; ☎ 3703 9011; ⊕ 9am-8pm Mon-Fri, 9am-6pm Sat & Sun; subway Line 5 to Gwanghwamun, Exit 5) This downtown post office has extended hours compared to regular post offices as well as free Internet and even a free blood pressure test machine.

RADIO

Radio Gugak is a digital, government-funded station that broadcasts to the Seoul area for 22 hours a day (off-air from 3am to 5am). It broadcasts traditional Korean music on 99.1FM. You can also listen by accessing www.gugakfm.co.kr and clicking on 'Replay Broadcasting' and then 'Gugak Player'. AFN provides radio broadcasts for American troops on 1530AM (country music, news and sport) and 102.7FM (rock music and news).

SAFETY

Seoul is a relatively safe city, except when it comes to traffic. Drivers tend to be impatient with *kimchi*-hot tempers, and most of them, including bus drivers, routinely go through red lights, so don't be the first or last person to cross over any pedestrian crossing. Vehicles never stop at pedestrian crossings that are not protected by traffic lights so it's better not to use them. Crossing any road except at traffic lights is not a sensible idea, and jaywalking is illegal. Also keep two eyes out for motorcyclists who routinely speed along pavements and across pedestrian crossings. A high proportion of road deaths (38%) are pedestrians, so take extra care when walking round Seoul.

Drunks in Seoul are better behaved than elsewhere so walking around at 3am shouldn't pose a problem. The swaying packs of late-night revellers usually pose more of a threat to themselves than to other people. Of course there is always an exception, so arguing with a drunk should be avoided.

Visitors are often surprised to see police in full riot gear, carrying large shields and long batons, streaming out of blue police buses that have their windows covered in protective wire. Student, trade-union, anti-American, environmental and other protests do still occasionally turn violent, although this is much less common than it used to be. Needless to say, it is wise to keep well out of the way of any confrontations that may occur.

TELEPHONE

Despite the popularity of mobile phones, there are still plenty of public telephones in Seoul, especially at subway stations. Some public phones accept only W10, W50 and W100 coins and are used for local calls. Other phones accept phone cards and can be used for local or long-distance calls. Phones that can make international calls have a sign to that effect. The cost of a local call is W70 for three minutes, while calls to mobile phones cost W300 a minute.

When using local-call phones, you may find that the phone has been left off the hook. The reason is that the phones do not give change for partially used coins and the local custom is to let someone else use your unused credit. There is a 30% discount on long-distance local and international calls made between 9pm and 8am Monday to Saturday, and all day on Sunday and public holidays.

Gyeonggi-do code (☎ 031) This province surrounds Seoul.

Incheon city and airport code (☎ 032)

International access codes KT (☎ 001), Dacom (☎ 002) and Onse (☎ 008).

Seoul code (☎ 02) Do not dial the zero if calling from outside Korea.

South Korea country code (☎ 82)

Toll-Free code (☎ 080)

Fax

To send a fax, ask at your hotel or guesthouse. If they can't help, try the nearest Internet room, photocopy shop or hotel with a business centre. **Insadong Tourist Information**

Centre (Map p205; ☎ 734 0222; Insadonggil; 🕙 10am-10pm; subway Line 3 to Anguk, Exit 6) has a fax (W1000 per sheet) and copier (W100 per sheet).

Mobile Phones

The bad news is that Korea uses the CDMA network system, which few other countries use, so you may need to hire a mobile phone while you're in Seoul unless someone comes up with a clever chip that allows your phone to use the CDMA network. Mobile phone hire is available from three companies, **KTF** (☎ 032-743 4072), **SK** (☎ 032-743 4042) and **LG Telecom** (☎ 032-743 4019). They compete with each other and so may offer different services or prices.

The best place to rent a mobile phone is at Incheon International Airport as soon as you arrive. Currently the rental fee is W3000 a day, incoming calls are free and outgoing domestic calls cost around W600 a minute, while calls to the US, for example, cost around W900 a minute. Check if the price includes 10% VAT. A few luxury hotels provide their guests with a mobile phone in which case you won't need to hire one.

Phonecards

Telephone cards usually give you a 10% bonus and can be bought at convenience stores and many small shops. There are two types of cards so if your card does not fit in one type of phone, try a different-looking one. A few phones accept credit cards.

But for phoning abroad a much better deal is offered by the dozens of call-back cards that can be bought in Itaewon, the Filipino Sunday market (p124) or outside the main Immigration office (Map pp198–9). The cards that give the best deal are always changing and some are sold at a discount on their face value. At present W10,000 buys four or five hours of talk to the US or the UK.

TELEVISION

There are five Korean-language TV networks: KBS1, KBS2, MBC, SBS and EBS. They often show American films that are dubbed into Korean, but many TVs have a button you can press to hear the original English version. EBS is an education channel.

AFN Korea (www.afnkorea.net) is an English-language TV station run by the US military, which broadcasts American shows, sport and action films.

Arirang (www.arirangtv.com) is a government-funded TV station that broadcasts documentary, interview and educational programmes in both Korean and English, and sometimes runs BBC World News. It is only available on cable and satellite channels.

Seoul has over 50 cable channels, which include CNN, film, documentary, home shopping, golf, music video, cartoon, *baduk* (go) and Buddhist programmes. Satellite TV is also available. Most accommodation offers cable or satellite channels.

TIME

South Korea has one time zone, Greenwich Mean Time (GMT) plus nine hours. When it's noon in Seoul it is 7pm the previous day in San Francisco, 10pm the previous day in New York, 3am in London and 1pm in Sydney. Korea does not have daylight saving.

TIPPING

Tipping is not necessary in Seoul, although a compulsory 10% service charge is added to the bill at some midrange and all top-end hotels and restaurants. Taxi drivers may surprise visitors by insisting on giving change.

TOILETS

A big effort has gone into improving standards so that Seoul now has plenty of clean, modern and well-signed public toilets. Virtually all toilets are free of charge, some are decorated with flowers and artwork, and the cleaning staff generally do an excellent job. Toilet paper is usually outside the cubicles by the washbasins, so don't forget to grab some before entering the cubicle. As always, it's wise to carry a stash of toilet tissue around with you in case a toilet has run out.

Restaurants, cafés and bars all have toilets, and many buildings have toilets off the stairways that are available. All major tourist attractions, parks, subway, train and bus stations have public toilet facilities. The small district of Insadong has no less than eight public toilets dotted around the area. Even when you go hiking in the mountains you will find plenty of toilets although they are rudimentary. Asian-style squat toilets are losing their battle with European-style sit-down ones, but there are still some around. Face the hooded end when you squat down.

Toilets in Korea always use international symbols rather than *hangeul*.

TOURIST INFORMATION

KTO Tourist Information Centre is the best one with knowledgeable staff, free Internet and the best range of brochures and maps.

City Hall Tourist Information Centre (Map pp206–7; ☎ 731 6671; ☽ 9am-6pm; subway Line 1 or 2 to City Hall, Exit 4) One hour free Internet access plus free booklets (including one on Seoul bus routes) are available here.

Deoksugung Tourist Information Booth (Map pp206–7; ☎ 753 5505; ☽ 9am-6pm; subway Line 1 or 2 to City Hall, Exit 2)

Dongdaemun Market Tourist Information Centre (Map p122; ☎ 2236 9135; ☽ 10am-6pm; subway Line 2, 4 or 5 to Dongdaemun Stadium, Exit 1)

Goodwill Guides (www.goodwillguide.com) This organisation provides volunteer guides for foreign tourists. You only pay for their expenses such as transportation, admission tickets and food. Apply at least two weeks in advance.

Gyeongbokgung Tourist Information Centre (Map pp202–3; ☎ 720 7465; ☽ 9am-6pm; subway Line 3 to Gyeongbokgung, Exit 5)

Insadong Tourist Information Centre & Souvenir Shop (Map p205; ☎ 734 0222; Insadonggil; ☽ 10am-10pm; subway Line 3 to Anguk, Exit 6) A useful centre manned by volunteers that has free Internet, a global ATM, and a fax (W1000 per sheet) and copier (W100 per sheet).

Itaewon Subway Tourist Information Centre (Map p209; ☎ 3785 2514; ☽ 9am-10pm) Has free Internet, but may close earlier in winter.

KTO Tourist Complaints Centre (☎ 735 0101; fax 777 0102; tourcom@mail.KTO.or.kr; PO Box 1879, Seoul 110-618) If you have problems with a particular hotel, guesthouse, restaurant, shop or taxi, contact this centre.

KTO Tourist Information Centre (Map pp202–3; ☎ 729 9497; http://english.tour2korea.com; ☽ 9am-8pm; subway Line 1 to Jonggak, Exit 5) The best source of tourist information and advice in Seoul is here along with free Internet and superior handicraft souvenirs. For the addresses of KTO's overseas offices in 12 countries log onto their website.

Lotte World Tourist Information Centre (Map pp214–15; ☎ 2143 7005; ☽ 9.30am-10pm; subway Line 2 or 8 to Jamsil, Exit 3) On the arrival concourse.

Myeong-dong Tourist Information Centre (Map pp206–7; ☎ 757 0088; ☽ 9am-6pm; subway Line 2 to Euljiro 1-ga, Exit 8)

Namdaemun Market Tourist Information Centre (Map p123; ☎ 752 1913; ☽ 9am-6pm; Subway line 4 to Hoehyeon, Exit 5)

North Insadong Tourist Information Centre (Map p205; ☎ 731 1621; cnr Insadong-gil & Yulgongno; ☽ 10am-6pm; subway Line 3 to Anguk, Exit 6)

Seoul Help Centre for Foreigners (Map pp206–7; ☎ 731 6800; http://shc.seoul.go.kr; 2nd flr, City Hall; ☽ 9am-6pm

Mon-Fri, 9am-1pm Sat; subway Line 1 or 2 to City Hall, Exit 4) Offers free Internet and a reference library of current newspapers, magazines and a few books. Information and help for foreigners in Seoul can be accessed here – everything from starting a business to medical advice and job vacancies.

Seoul Tourist Information Centre (Map pp202–3; ☎ 735 8688; Sejongno; ☯ 9am-10pm; subway Line 1 or 2 to City Hall, Exit 3)

Seoul Train Station Tourist Information Centre (Map pp206–7; ☎ 2392 1324; ☯ 9am-9pm; subway Line 1 or 4 to Seoul Station, Exit 1)

TRAVEL AGENCIES

Apple Tours (Map pp200–1; ☎ 793 3478; fax 798 0698; USO Bldg; ☯ 10am-6pm Mon-Fri, 10am-2pm Sat; subway Line 4 & 6 to Samgakji, Exit 11). This travel agency has English-speaking staff and specialises in short package tours to Thailand, Indo-China, China, Malaysia and Australia.

KISES (Map p205; ☎ 733 9494; fax 732 9568; 5th fl, YMCA Bldg, Jongno; ☯ 9am-6pm Mon-Fri, 9am-3pm Sat; subway Line 1 to Jonggak, Exit 8) The STA Travel agent in Seoul, it is next door to Top Travel and convenient for comparing prices.

Shoestring Travel (Map p213; ☎ 333 4151; off Wausan-gil; ☯ 9am-6pm Mon-Fri, 9am-2.30pm Sat; subway Line 2 to Hongik University, Exit 6) This youth-oriented travel agent in Hongik has snazzy new offices, English-speaking staff and an awesome collection of Lonely Planet guidebooks for sale.

Top Travel Service (Map p205; ☎ 720 8056; fax 722 0329; 5th fl, YMCA Bldg, Jongno; ☯ 8am-7pm Mon-Fri; subway Line 1 to Jonggak, Exit 8) Usually has the cheapest flights but it can be difficult to find a competent English speaker.

VISAS

With a confirmed onward ticket, visitors from nearly all West European countries, New Zealand, Australia and around 30 other countries receive 90-day permits on arrival. Visitors from the USA and a handful of countries receive 30-day permits, while 60-day permits are granted to citizens of Italy and Portugal, and lucky Canadians receive a six-month permit.

About 30 countries – including the Russian Federation, China, India and Nigeria – do not qualify for visa exemptions. Citizens from these countries must apply for a tourist visa, which allows a stay of 90 days.

You can't extend your stay beyond 90 days except in cases such as a medical emergency; if you overstay the fine starts at W100,000. View www.mofat.go.kr to find out more.

The conveniently located **Seoul Immigration Office** (Map pp206–7; ☎ 2171 2248; City Hall Bldg; ☯ 9am-6pm Mon-Fri; subway Line 1 or 2 to City Hall, Exit 5) can deal with re-entry permits and investment visas, but other matters have to be dealt with at the **Seoul Immigration Head Office** (Map pp198–9; ☎ 2650 6212; ☯ 9am-6pm Mon-Fri; subway Line 5 to Omokgyo, Exit 7) way out in Mok-dong. This office is always busy so take some reading matter. To reach it, carry straight on from the subway exit and walk along the road until it ends, where you'll see a white-tiled building on your left with a big blue sign in English. It's a 10 minute walk (700m).

One problem is that applicants must leave the country to pick up their work visa. Most applicants fly to Fukuoka in Japan where you can usually pick up the visa the day after you submit it. Check that you have all the paperwork and take enough funds for your stay. You can also apply for a one-year work visa before entering Korea but it can take a few weeks to process. Note that the visa authorities will want to see originals or notarised copies (not simply photocopies) of your educational qualifications, as some applicants have tried to use fake degree certificates.

You don't need to leave Korea to renew a work visa as long as you carry on working for the same employer. But the catch is that if you change employers you must apply for a new visa and pick it up from outside Korea.

If you don't want to forfeit your work or study visa, you must apply at your local immigration office for a re-entry permit before making any trips outside South Korea. The fee is W30,000 for a single re-entry or W50,000 for a multiple re-entry permit.

If you are working or studying in Korea on a long-term visa, it is necessary to apply for an alien registration card within 90 days of arrival. This costs W10,000 and is done at your local immigration office.

For up-to-date visa information, visit the Lonely Planet website (www.lonelyplanet.com) and follow the links.

WOMEN TRAVELLERS

Seoul is a relatively safe city for women (as well as men), but the usual precautions should be taken. Many women walk alone late at night but it's probably not a sensible idea in any big city.

Confucianism ruled Korea for six centuries and still lingers into the 21st century despite all the modernisation and Westernisation that has occurred over the past hundred years. In the Joseon era, Korea was a male-dominated society and women were expected to obey first their father, then their husband, and if widowed, their eldest son. Upon marriage, daughters left their birth family, and most if not all of the parents' wealth was inherited by the eldest son. Women visitors should therefore expect some interesting discussions with older people who may still have a somewhat Confucian view of a woman's role.

Tampons and condoms are readily available but it would be best to bring other forms of contraception with you.

For expat women the **Seoul International Women's Association** (www.siwapage.com) is a very active group that has been running for 50 years and organises coffee mornings, weekly outings and even a choir. Membership is W50,000 a year.

WORK

Seoul is a popular place for English teachers to work, and since Koreans have an insatiable appetite for studying English finding a teaching job shouldn't be too hard. A university degree in any subject is sufficient as long as English is your native language. However it's a good idea to obtain some kind of English teaching certificate before you arrive as this increases your options if not your salary. Some foreigners who go to Seoul to teach bitch about everything and probably should have stayed at home. Take an honest look at yourself before cutting loose and don't go if you struggle to maintain a positive attitude or are unwilling to adapt to a different culture.

Teachers can expect to teach 30 hours per week and earn around W1.9 million a month (income tax is around 5%), with a furnished apartment, medical insurance, return flights, paid holiday (10 days) and completion bonus all part of a one-year package.

Most English teachers work in a *hagwon* (private language school) but others work in government schools or universities. Private tutoring, company classes and even teaching via the telephone are also possible. Teaching in a *hagwon* usually involves evening and weekend work.

Some *hagwon* owners don't keep the promises made in the employment contract, so check out your embassy in Seoul's website and the websites below before committing yourself. Ask for the email address of a teacher who works for your prospective employer if you have any concerns. Remember

that if you change employers, you will need to go through the hassle of obtaining a new work visa, which requires you to leave the country. Most make the visa run to Fukuoka or Osaka in Japan, but take sufficient funds as Japan is mega expensive and you cannot always rely on picking up a visa the next day.

The *Korea Times* website (times.hankooki .com) has job vacancies, but most English teaching jobs are on specialist websites:

www.englishspectrum.com Stacks of stuff for expats in Seoul including job vacancies, classifieds, discussion forums and links to blogs.

www.eslcafé.com A wonderful site run by the one and only Dave Sperling has new English teaching vacancies posted daily, lively discussion forums about life in Seoul and masses of help to make you a better teacher.

www.eslhub.com This Seoul site has job and accommodation classifieds and great links.

www.koreajoblink.com Registration is necessary but it's free.

www.kotesol.org Run by a group of English teachers who organise conferences, it has useful links for teachers.

www.worknplay.co.kr Jobs and other stuff.

Doing Business

Seoul Help Centre for Foreigners (Map pp206–7; ☎ 731 6800; http://shc.seoul.go.kr; City Hall; ☑ 9am-6pm Mon-Fri, 9am-1pm Sat; subway Line 1 or 2 to City Hall, Exit 4) has brochures and advice about doing business in Seoul and a reference library of newspapers, magazines and books. Across the corridor is an immigration office (p173) that can help with business visas. Information and links are also available at www.investkorea.org. Some countries have their own chambers of commerce in Seoul that can provide invaluable contacts and networking opportunities.

Volunteering

Seoul Orphanages (www.yheesun.com) Seoul families are reluctant to adopt children, so volunteer English teachers are always needed to teach and have some fun with the many children who live in orphanages.

Willing Workers on Organic Farms (WWOOF; ☎ 723 4458; www.wwoofkorea.com; KPO Box 1516, Seoul 110-601) A good way to experience rural life outside Seoul, the programme involves 40 farms and market gardens where volunteers work for four to five hours per day in return for board and food. Most hosts speak some English. The minimum stay is a few days and the maximum is by mutual agreement between volunteers and their hosts. Joining costs W15,000 and you receive a list of participating farms.

Language

Language

It's true – anyone can speak another language. Don't worry if you haven't studied languages before or that you studied a language at school for years and can't remember any of it. It doesn't even matter if you failed English grammar. After all, that's never affected your ability to speak English! And this is the key to picking up a language in another country. You just need to start speaking.

Learn a few key phrases before you go. Write them on pieces of paper and stick them on the fridge, by the bed or even on the computer – anywhere that you'll see them often.

You'll find that locals appreciate travellers trying their language, no matter how muddled you may think you sound. So don't just stand there, say something! If you want to learn more Korean than we've included here, pick up a copy of Lonely Planet's comprehensive but user-friendly *Korean Phrasebook.*

Writing System

Chinese characters *(hanja)* are usually restricted to use in maps and occasionally in newspapers and written names. For the most part Korean is written in *hangeul,* the alphabet developed under King Sejong's reign in the 15th century. Many users of the Korean language argue that the Korean script is one of the most scientific and consistent alphabets used today.

Hangeul consists of only 24 characters and isn't that difficult to learn. However, the formation of words using *hangeul* is very different from the way that Western alphabets are used to form words. The emphasis is on the formation of a syllable so that it resembles a Chinese character. Thus the first syllable of the word 'hangeul' (한) is formed by an 'h' (ㅎ) in the top left corner, an 'a' (ㅏ) in the top right corner and an 'n' (ㄴ) at the bottom, with this whole syllabic grouping forming a syllabic 'box'. These syllabic 'boxes' are strung together to form words.

Romanisation

In July 2000, the Korean government adopted a new method of Romanising the Korean language (known as NAKL). The new system has been energetically promoted throughout the government and tourist bureaus, but it will take a long time for everyone to fall into line. Local governments were given until 2005 to change all the road signs around the country, and the central government has actively encouraged the adoption of the new system overseas.

SOCIAL
Polite Korean

Korea's pervasive social hierarchy means that varying degrees of politeness are codified into the grammar. Young Koreans tend to use the very polite forms a lot less than the older generation, but it's always best to use the polite form if you're unsure. The phrases included in this section employ polite forms.

Meeting People

Hello.
annyeong hasimnikka (polite)
안녕 하십니까
annyeong haseyo (informal)
안녕 하세요
Goodbye.
annyeong·hi gyeseyo (to person staying)
안녕히 계세요
annyeong·hi gaseyo (to person leaving)
안녕히 가세요
May I ask your name?
ireumeul yeojjwo bwado doelkkayo?
이름을 여쭤봐도 될까요?
My name is ...
je ireumeun ... imnida
제 이름은…입니다
Where are you from?
eodiseo oseosseoyo?
어디서 오셨어요?

I'm from ...
jeoneun ... eseo wasseumnida
저는...에서 왔습니다
I'd like to introduce you to ...
(ibuneun) ... imnida
(이분은)...입니다

Yes.
ye/ne   예/네
No.
aniyo   아니요
Please.
juseyo   주세요
Thank you.
gamsa hamnida   감사 합니다
That's fine/You're welcome.
gwaenchan seumnida   괜찮습니다
Excuse me.
sillye hamnida   실례 합니다
Sorry (forgive me).
mian hamnida   미안 합니다
How are you?
annyeong haseyo?   안녕 하세요?
I'm fine, thanks.
ne, jo·ayo   네 좋아요

Going Out

Is anything interesting on ...?
... jaemi itneun·geo isseoyo?
...재미 있는 거 있어요?
  locally
  i-jiyeoge   이 지역에
  this weekend
  ibon jumare   이번 주말에
  today
  oneul   오늘
  tonight
  oneul bame   오늘 밤에

Where are the ...?
... eodi isseoyo?
...어디 있어요?
  clubs
  keulleop   클럽
  places to eat
  eumsik jeom   음식점
  pubs
  hopeu jip   호프집

Is there a local entertainment guide in
  English?
yeong·eoro doen jiyeok yeohaeng gaideu
  isseoyo?
영어로 된 지역 여행 가이드 있어요?

PRACTICAL
Accommodation
I'm looking for a ...
... reul/eul chatgo isseoyo
...를/을 찾고 있어요
  guesthouse
  yeogwan/minbak jip   여관/민박집
  hotel
  hotel   호텔
  youth hostel
  yuseu hoseutel   유스호스텔

Do you have any rooms available?
bang isseoyo?   방 있어요?

I'd like (a) ...
... ro/euro juseyo
...로/으로 주세요
  bed
  chimdae   침대
  single bed
  singgeul chimdae   싱글 침대
  double bed
  deobeul chimdae   더블 침대
  twin beds
  chimdae dugae   침대 두개
  to share a room
  gachi sseuneun bang   같이 쓰는 방
  Western-style room
  chimdae bang   침대 방
  a room with sleeping mats
  ondol bang juseyo   온돌 방 주세요
  room with a bathroom
  yoksil itneun bang   욕실있는 방
   juseyo   주세요

How much is it ...?
... e eolma eyo?
...에 얼마에요?
  per night
  harutbam   하룻밤
  per person
  han saram   한사람

Directions
Where is ...?
... i/ga eodi isseoyo?
...이/가 어디 있어요?
Go straight ahead.
ttokbaro gaseyo
똑바로 가세요
Turn left.
oen·jjogeuro gaseyo
왼쪽으로 가세요

Turn right.
oreun·jjogeuro gaseyo
오른쪽으로 가세요
at the next corner
da·eum motung·i e-seo
다음 모퉁이에서
at the traffic lights
sinhodeung eseo
신호등에서

Language Difficulties

Do you speak English?
yeong·eo haseyo?
영어 하세요?
What does ... mean?
... ga/i museun tteusieyo?
...가/이 무슨뜻 이에요?
I don't understand.
jal moreuget·neun deyo
잘 모르겠는데요
Please write it down.
jeogeo jusillaeyo
적어 주실래요
Can you show me (on the map)?
boyeo jusillaeyo?
보여 주실래요?

Numbers

Korean has two counting systems. One is of Chinese origin, with Korean pronunciation, and the other is a native Korean system – the latter only goes up to 99 and is used for counting objects, expressing your age and for the hours when telling the time. They're always written in *hangeul* or digits (never in Chinese characters). Sino-Korean numbers are used to express minutes when telling the time, as well as dates, months, kilometres, money, floors of buildings. Numbers above 99 may be written in Hangul, in digits or in Chinese characters. Either Chinese or Korean numbers can be used to count days.

	Sino-Korean		Korean	
1	il	일	hana	하나
2	i	이	dul	둘
3	sam	삼	set	셋
4	sa	사	net	넷
5	o	오	daseot	다섯
6	yuk	육	yeoseot	여섯
7	chil	칠	ilgop	일곱
8	pal	팔	yeodeol	여덟
9	gu	구	ahop	아홉
10	sip	십	yeol	열

11	sibil	십일
12	sibi	십이
13	sipsam	십삼
14	sipsa	십사
15	sibo	십오
16	simnyuk	십육
17	sipchil	십칠
18	sippal	십팔
19	sipgu	십구
20	isip	이십
21	isibil	이십일
22	isibi	이십이
30	samsip	삼십
40	sasip	사십
50	osip	오십
60	yuksip	육십
70	chilsip	칠십
80	palsip	팔십
90	gusip	구십
100	baek	백
1000	cheon	천

Question Words

Who? (as subject)
nugu? 누구?
What? (as subject)
mu·eot? 무엇?
When?
eonje? 언제?
Where?
eodi? 어디?
How?
eotteoke? 어떻게?

Banking

I want to change ...
... reul/eul bakku ryeogo haneun deyo
...를/을 바꾸려고 하는데요
　money
　don 돈
　travellers cheques
　yeohaengja supyo 여행자 수표

Where's the nearest ...?
jeil gakkaun ... i/ga eodi isseoyo?
제일 가까운...이/가 어디있어요
　automatic teller machine/ATM
　hyeon·geup jigeupgi
　현금지급기
　foreign exchange office
　oe·hwan georaeso
　외한 거래소

Post

I'm looking for the post office.
uchegug·eul chatgo isseoyo
우체국을 찾고 있어요

I want to send a ...
... bonaego sipeundeyo
...보내고 싶은데요

fax	
paekseu	팩스
parcel	
sopo	소포
postcard	
yeopseo	엽서

I want to buy ...
... sago sipeundeyo
...사고 싶은데요

an aerogram	
hanggongupeon	항공우편
an envelope	
peonji bongtu	편지 봉투
a stamp	
upyo	우표

Phones & Mobiles

I want to buy a phone card.
jeonhwa kadeu·reul sago sipeoyo
전화 카드를 사고 싶어요

I want to make ...
... hago sipeoyo ...
...하고 싶어요

a call (to ...)
jeonhwareul ...
전화를...
reverse-charge/collect call
sushinja budameuro/collectcall eul
수신자 부담으로/콜렉트 콜을

Where can I find a/an ...?
... eodiseo salsu isseoyo
... 어디서 살 수 있어요?
I'd like a/an ...
...juseyo
...주세요

adaptor plug
eodaepteo
어댑터
charger for my phone
haendeupon chungjeon·gi
핸드폰 충전기
mobile (cell) phone for hire
imdae haendeupon
임대핸드폰

prepaid mobile/cell phone
seonbul yogeum haendeupon
선불 요금 핸드폰

Internet

Where's the local Internet café?
cheil gakka·un pissi bang eodi·eyo?
제일 가까운 PC방 어디에요?

I'd like to ...
... haryeogo haneun deyo
...하려고 하는데요

check my email	
imeil hwagin	이 메일 확인
get online	
inteo·neseul	인터넷을

Days

Monday	woryoil	월요일
Tuesday	hwayoil	화요일
Wednesday	suyoil	수요일
Thursday	mogyoil	목요일
Friday	geumyoil	금요일
Saturday	toyoil	토요일
Sunday	iryoil	일요일

Transport

What time does the ... leave/arrive?
... i/ga (eonje tteonayo/eonje dochak-haeyo)?
...이/가 언제 떠나요/언제 도착해요?

airport bus	
gonghang beoseu	공항버스
boat (ferry)	
yeogaek seon	여객선
bus	
beoseu	버스
(city) bus	
(sinae) beoseu	(시내)버스
train	
gicha	기차

I want to go to ...
... e gago sipseumnida
...에 가고 싶습니다

the first	
cheot	첫
the last	
maji mak	마지막
bus station	
beoseu jeongnyu jang	버스정류장
subway station	
jihacheol yeok	지하철역

ticket vending machine
pyo japan·gi | 표 자판기
timetable
sigan pyo | 시간표
train station
gicha yeok | 기차역

FOOD

breakfast
achim | 아침
lunch
jeomsim | 점심
dinner
jeonyeok | 저녁
snack
seunaek | 스낵
eat
meogeoyo | 먹어
drink
masheoyo | 마셔요

Can you recommend a ...
... chucheon hae jusillaeyo?
...추천 해주실래요?
  bar/pub
  hopeu jip | 호프 집
  café
  kkape/keopi·shop | 까페/커피숍
  restaurant
  sikdang | 식당

Will a service charge be added to the bill?
seobiseu ryodo pohami doenayo?
서비스료도 포함이 되나요?

*For more detailed information on food and
dining out, see p27 and p85.*

HEALTH

Where's the nearest ...?
gajang gakka·un ... eodi isseoyo?
가장 가까운...어디있어요?
  chemist
  yakguk | 약국
  night chemist
  seumulle sigan yeong·eop haneun yakguk
  24시간 영업하는 약국
  dentist
  chikwa | 치과

doctor
uisanim | 의사님
hospital
byeong·won | 병원

I'm ill.
jeon apayo
저 아파요
I need a doctor (who speaks English).
(yeong·eo haneun) uisaga piryo haeyo
(영어하는) 의사가 필요해요

I'm allergic to ...
... allereugiga isseoyo
...알레르기가있어요
  antibiotics
  hangsaengje | 항생제
  nuts
  ttang kkong | 땅꽁

Symptoms

I have (a) ...
jeon ...
전...
  diarrhoea
  seolsa·reul haeyo | 설사를 해요
  fever
  yeori nayo | 열이 나요
  headache
  dutong·i isseoyo | 두통이 있어요
  pain
  tongjeung·i isseoyo | 통증이 있어요

EMERGENCIES

Help!
saram sallyeo! | 사람살려!
I'm lost.
gireul ireosseoyo | 길을 잃었어요
Go away!
jeori ga! | 저리가!

Call ...!
... bulleo juseyo!
...불러 주세요!
  a doctor
  uisa | 의사
  the police
  gyeongcha | 경찰
  an ambulance
  gugeupcha | 구급차

GLOSSARY

ajumma – a married or older woman; a term of respect for a woman who runs a hotel, restaurant or other business
anju – snacks eaten when drinking alcohol

bang – room; PC *bang* are Internet rooms and DVD *bang* are rooms where DVDs are shown
bong – peak
buk – north
bukbu – northern area
buncheong – pottery decorated with simple folk designs

changgeuk – Korean opera
Chuseok – thanksgiving

DMZ – the Demilitarized Zone that runs along the 38th parallel of the Korean peninsula, separating North and South
-do – province
do – island
-dong – ward
dong – east
dongbu – eastern area

-eup – town

-ga – section of a long street
gang – river
geobukseon – 'turtle ships'; iron-clad warships
gibun – harmonious feelings; face
gil – small street
-gu – urban district
-gun – county
gung – palace
gugak – traditional Korean music
gut – shamanist ceremony
gwageo – Joseon civil-service examination

hae – sea
haesuyokjang – beach
hagwon – private schools where students study after school or work; foreigners are often employed here to teach English
hallyu – Korean Wave
hanbok – traditional Korean clothing
hangeul – Korean phonetic alphabet
hanja – Chinese-style writing system
hanji – traditional Korean handmade paper
hanok – traditional Korean one-storey wooden house with a tiled roof
ho – lake
hof – bar or pub

insam – ginseng

jaebeol – huge family-run corporate conglomerate
jeon – hall of a temple
jeong – pavilion

KTO – Korea Tourism Organisation
minbak – a private home with rooms for rent
mobeom – deluxe taxi
mudang – shaman, usually female
mugunghwa – limited express train
mun – gate
-myeon – township

nam – south
nambu – southern area
neung – tomb
no – large street, boulevard
noraebang – karaoke room

oncheon – hot-spring bath
ondol – underfloor heating

pansori – traditional Korean opera
pungsu – Korean geomancy
pyeong – a unit of measurement equal to 3.3 sq m

ramie – cloth made from pounded bark
-ri – village
reung – tomb
ro – large street, boulevard
ROK – Republic of Korea (South Korea)
ru – pavilion

sa – temple
saemaeul – luxury express train
samullori – traditional farmer's dance
san – mountain
sandaenori – a type of mask dance
sanjang – mountain hut
sanseong – mountain fortress
seo – west
seobu – western area
Seon – a version of Zen Buddhism native to Korea
seowon – Confucian academies
si – city
sicheong – city hall
sinae – local, as in local bus terminal
ssireum – Korean-style wrestling

taegyeon – the original form of taekwondo
taekwondo – Korean martial arts
tang – a bathhouse that usually includes a sauna
tap – pagoda
tongil – slow local train

USO – United Service Organizations, which provides leisure services for US troops and civilians

yangban – aristocrat
yeogwan – small family-run hotel, usually with a private bathroom
yo – padded quilt that serves as a futon or mattress for sleeping on the floor

Behind the Scenes

THE LONELY PLANET STORY

The story begins with a classic travel adventure: Tony and Maureen Wheeler's 1972 journey across Europe and Asia to Australia. There was no useful information about the overland trail then, so Tony and Maureen published the first Lonely Planet guidebook to meet a growing need.

From a kitchen table, Lonely Planet has grown to become the largest independent travel publisher in the world, with offices in Melbourne (Australia), Oakland (USA) and London (UK). Today Lonely Planet guidebooks cover the globe. There is an ever-growing list of books and information in a variety of media. Some things haven't changed. The main aim is still to make it possible for adventurous travellers to get out there – to explore and better understand the world.

At Lonely Planet we believe travellers can make a positive contribution to the countries they visit – if they respect their host communities and spend their money wisely. Every year 5% of company profit is donated to charities around the world.

THIS BOOK

The 4th and this, the 5th edition, of *Seoul* were written by Martin Robinson. Robert Storey wrote the 3rd edition. For this edition, Donald N Clark wrote the History chapter and Thomas Huhti wrote the City Life chapter. The Health Section was written by Dr Trish Batchelor. This edition was commissioned in Lonely Planet's Melbourne office and produced by:

Commissioning Editor Rebecca Chau

Coordinating Editor Dianne Schallmeiner

Coordinating Cartographers Malisa Plesa, Simon Tillema

Coordinating Layout Designer Laura Jane

Managing Cartographer Corie Waddell

Proofreader Martine Lleonart

Cover Designer Marika Kozak

Project Manager Fabrice Rocher

Language Content Coordinator Quentin Frayne

Thanks to Imogen Bannister, Glenn Beanland, Carolyn Boicos, Sally Darmody, Justin Flynn, Jennifer Garrett, Mark Germanchis, JD 'Nate' Hilts, Jacqueline McLeod, Wayne Murphy, and June Park and her colleagues at the Korea Tourism Organisation (Sydney).

Cover photographs: Members of the Little Angels, a Korean childrens' dance group, APL/Corbis (top); Techno Mart, Seoul (bottom); Guards at Namdaemun, Anthony Plummer/ Lonely Planet Images (back).

Internal photographs by Anthony Plummer/Lonely Planet Images except for the following: p68 (#1) Dennis Johnson; p68 (#3), p73 (#2) Jeff Yates; p69 (#3) Juliet Coombe; p9, p73 (#1), p79 Martin Vincent Robinson; p82 Martin Moos; p154 John Elk III.

All images are the copyright of the photographers unless otherwise indicated. Many of the images in this guide are available for licensing from Lonely Planet Images: www .lonelyplanetimages.com.

THANKS
MARTIN ROBINSON

Thanks to Kang Soondeog, Kwak Sangsub, Moon Young-nam, Jason Jang, Park Woong-soon, Haim Kim, Yongbok Jang, Hae-nam Chee, Bae Jeong-hee, Yu Gwan-chan, Lee Ji-min, Lee Chang-hak, Yi Yuan and Choi Myung-hee. Special thanks to indefatigable Mr Song, and love and more than special thanks to my wife, Marie.

SEND US YOUR FEEDBACK

We love to hear from travellers – your comments keep us on our toes and help make our books better. Our well-travelled team reads every word on what you loved or loathed about this book. Although we cannot reply individually to postal submissions, we always guarantee that your feedback goes straight to the appropriate authors, in time for the next edition. Each person who sends us information is thanked in the next edition – and the most useful submissions are rewarded with a free book.

To send us your updates – and find out about Lonely Planet events, newsletters and travel news – visit our award-winning website: www.lonelyplanet.com /feedback.

Note: We may edit, reproduce and incorporate your comments in Lonely Planet products such as guidebooks, websites and digital products, so let us know if you don't want your comments reproduced or your name acknowledged. For a copy of our privacy policy visit www.lonelyplanet.com/privacy.

OUR READERS

Many thanks to the following travellers who used the last edition and wrote to us with helpful hints, useful advice and interesting anecdotes.

Alaina Barron, David Carroll, Jim Cathcart, Michael Cop, Brian Dennehy, Richard Elberfield, Sung Hui Elberfield, Scott Fallis, Charmaine Gahan, Anthony Gain, Michele Gain, Roger Hodgerson, David Hopper, Amir Hozaien, Larry Jackson, Yeo Junghyun, Ute Keck, Eugene Kim, Ho Kim, Shidon Kim, Julia Loge, Anderson McCammont, David Mccann, Marie-Loe Molenaar, Deirdre Ni Dhea, Henrik Skov Nielsen, Ramon Pacheco Pardo, Hyunah Park, Adrian Reid, Sarah Riches, Jenny Rödseth, Jean Savage, Jana Seaman, Matthias Seidl, Linda Takahashi, Huihong Tang, Hauke Wendt, Jacqui Wendt, Anthony P White, Catherine Wilson, Kim Yangjung, Kim Young-Ah, Jee Young-Yu

LONELY PLANET AUTHORS

Why is our travel information the best in the world? It's simple: our authors are independent, dedicated travellers. They don't research using just the Internet or phone, and they don't take freebies in exchange for positive coverage. They travel widely, to all the popular spots and off the beaten track. They personally visit thousands of hotels, restaurants, cafés, bars, galleries, palaces, museums and more – and they take pride in getting all the details right, and telling it how it is. For more, see the authors section on **www.lonelyplanet.com**.

Notes

Notes

Notes

Notes

Notes

Notes

Index

See also separate indexes for Eating (p194), Entertainment (p194), Shopping (p195) and Sleeping (p195).

Index

000 map pages
000 photographs

Index

Index

195

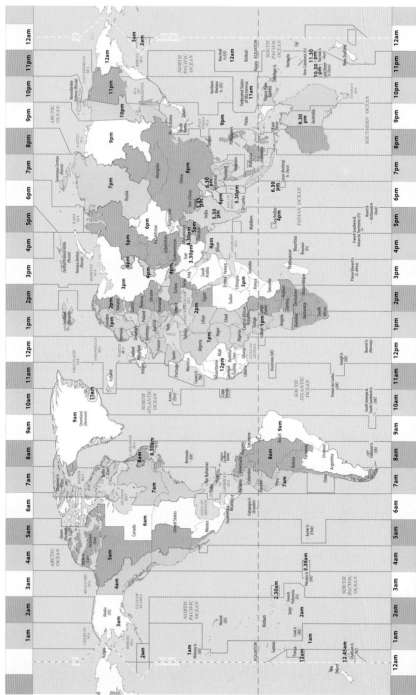

MAP LEGEND

ROUTES

Tollway	One-Way Street
Freeway	Mall/Steps
Primary Road	Tunnel
Secondary Road	Walking Tour
Tertiary Road	Walking Tour Detour
Lane	Walking Trail
Track	Walking Path
Unsealed Road	Pedestrian Overpass

TRANSPORT

Ferry	Rail
Metro	Rail (Underground)

HYDROGRAPHY

River, Creek	Canal
Water	

BOUNDARIES

Ancient Wall	Cliff

AREA FEATURES

Airport	Forest
Area of Interest	Land
Beach, Desert	Mall
Building, Featured	Park
Building, Information	Park (Special)
Building, Other	Sports
Building, Underground	

POPULATION

✪ CAPITAL (NATIONAL)	◉ CAPITAL (STATE)
● Large City	● Medium City
● Small City	● Town, Village

SYMBOLS

Sights/Activities	Eating	Information
Beach	Eating	Bank, ATM
Buddhist	**Drinking**	Embassy/Consulate
Castle, Fortress	Drinking	Hospital, Medical
Christian	Café	Information
Confucian	**Entertainment**	Internet Facilities
Hindu	Entertainment	Police Station
Islamic	**Shopping**	Post Office, GPO
Monument	Shopping	Telephone
Museum, Gallery	**Sleeping**	Toilets
Other Site	Sleeping	**Geographic**
Ruin	**Transport**	Lookout
Shinto	Airport, Airfield	Mountain, Volcano
Swimming Pool	Bus Station	National Park
Taoist	Cycling, Bicycle Path	Picnic Area
Trail Head	General Transport	Pass, Canyon
Winery, Vineyard	Parking Area	River Flow
Zoo, Bird Sanctuary	Taxi Rank	Waterfall

Maps

GREATER SEOUL

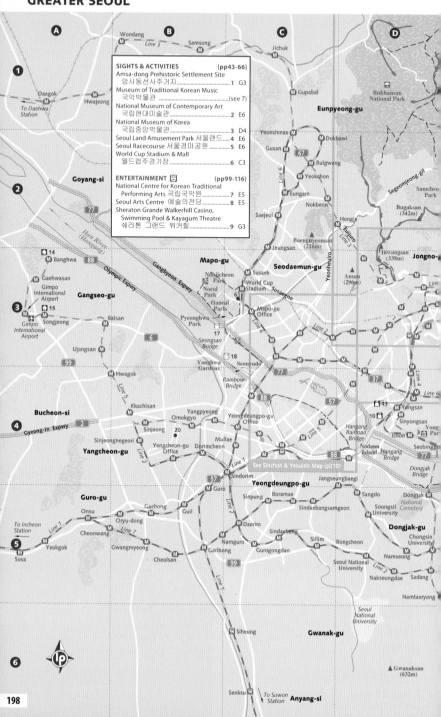

SIGHTS & ACTIVITIES (pp43–66)

Amsa-dong Prehistoric Settlement Site	
암사동선사주거지	1 G3
Museum of Traditional Korean Music	
국악박물관	(see 7)
National Museum of Contemporary Art	
국립현대미술관	2 E6
National Museum of Korea	
국립중앙박물관	3 D4
Seoul Land Amusement Park 서울랜드	4 E6
Seoul Racecourse 서울경마공원	5 E6
World Cup Stadium & Mall	
월드컵주경기장	6 C3

ENTERTAINMENT (pp99–116)

National Centre for Korean Traditional	
Performing Arts 국립국악원	7 E5
Seoul Arts Centre 예술의전당	8 E5
Sheraton Grande Walkerhill Casino,	
Swimming Pool & Kayagum Theatre	
쉐라톤 그랜드 워커힐	9 G3

CENTRAL SEOUL

1

▲ Inwangsan
(338m)

Ⓜ Muakjae

Seoul Fortress Wall

3 ●

2

5 ●
Dongnimmun
Park

Ⓜ Dongnimmun

*Gumhwa
Tunnel*

3

Ⓜ Seodaemun

GYEONGBOKGUNG

Jongno-gu

CHANGDEOKGUNG

CHANGGYEONGG

Anguk

Yule

Yuleolno

UNHYEONGUNG

JONGMY

Ⓜ Gyeongbokgung

Sajik
Park

Sejongno

Gwanghwamun

GYEONGHUIGUNG

Saemunangil

Daegyeongno

Samiro

Ujeongguggno

Namdaemunno

Insadong

Jongno 3-ga

Jonggak Jongno Jongno 3-ga

Line 1

Samiro

Suppyodaggil

Donghwamunno

Euljiro 1-ga Euljiro Euljiro 3-

See Gwanghwamum Map (pp202-3)

See Myeong-dong & Namsan Map (pp206-7)

1 🏛

DEOKSUGUNG

Ⓜ City Hall

Seosomunno

Euljiro

Seosomunno

Daegyeongno

Jilpaegil

Sogongno

Namdaemun
Market

Line 1

Mareunna

Myeong-donggil

Ⓜ Chungmuro

Ⓜ Myeong-dong

16 🅿

Ⓜ Chungjeongno

Ⓜ Hoehyeon

Banporo

4

Line 4

Ⓜ Ahyeon

Seoul
Station

Ⓜ Seoul

Namsan Park

Jung-gu

2nd Namsan Tunnel

Ⓜ Aeogae

Maporo

Mallijaegil

Namsan
(262m)

2nd Namsan Tunne

Namdaemun

5

Line 5

Namsan Pa

Ⓜ Gongdeok
Baekbeomno

Hyochang
Park

Sookmyung
Women's
University

Line 6

Namyeong Ⓜ

14 🏨

See Itaewon Map (p209)

6

Ⓜ Hyochang Park

15 🏨

7 ●

Yongsan US
Military Base

37

8 🏛 Ⓜ Samgakji

SIGHTS & ACTIVITIES (pp43–66)
Agriculture Museum 농업박물관 1 B3
Apple Tours 애플투어 ....(see 7)
Dongdaemun 동대문 2 E3
Guksadang 국사당 3 A2
Jangchung Gymnasium 장충체육관 4 E4
Seodaemun Prison
  서대문형무소역사관 5 A2
Seonnongdan 선농단 6 H1
United Service Organizations (USO)
  주한미연합봉사기구 7 B6
War Memorial & Museum 전쟁기념관 8 C6

EATING 🍴 (pp85–98)
USO Diner ....(see 7)

SHOPPING 🛍 (pp117–128)
Cheongdaemun & Cinemas 청대문..........9 E3
Doota Mall 두타......................................10 F3
Hello apM 헬로에이피엠.........................11 E3
Migliore Mall 밀리오레 12 F3

SLEEPING 🛏 (pp129–44)
Euljiro Co-op Residence
  을지로 코업레지던스 13 E3
Hotel Rainbow 호텔 레인보우 14 B6
Kaya Hotel 가야호텔 15 B6

INFORMATION
French Embassy 프랑스대사관 16 B4

GWANGHWAMUN

A **B** **C** **D**

1

2

3

4

5

6

Samcheong Park

Samcheong P.

● 6

Main Entrance
to Cheongwadae

🏛 28

24 🍴 🍴 25
🍴 20

34 🏛

🏛 11

Hyangwonjeong

Jagyeongjeon

Amisan

GYEONGBOKGUNG

Jongno-gu

Gyeonghoeru
Pavilion

Jaseondang

Samcheongdonggil

Jusaro

Geunjeongjeon

Byeolgundaegil

38 🏛

Hyoja-ro

🅿

🏛 35

See Insadong Map (p205)

12 🏛

7 ●
49
51 🏛 🅿

52 🏛

🏛 31

Line 3   Gyeongbokgung

Gwanghwamun ●

Dongsipjagak

Ⓜ

😊
Yulgok

Naejadonggil

56 🏛

Uljongungno

Insadonggil

Sejongno

Insadong

30 🏛

14 🏛   Gwanghwamun

19 🍴

Line 5

Gyeonghuigung

22 🏛   Ⓜ

Kyobo
Building

Jonggak

Jongno

48 🏛

42
23 🏛 🍴   26 🏛

1 🏛

36 🏛   Line 1

Ⓜ

16 🏛

17 🏛

Saemunangil

55 🏛
33 🏛

50 🏛

Cheonggye
Plaza

Namdaemunno

37 🏛

15 🏛   8 ●

54 🏛
44 🏛   27 🏛

Cheonggye Stream

53 🏛

Seoul Finance
Centre

Daepyeongno

46 45 🏛

202

🏛 32   29 🏛

See Myeong-dong & Namsan Map (pp206–7)

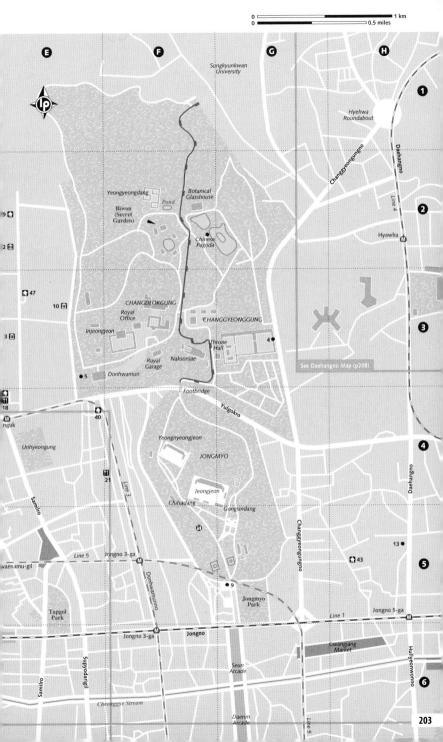

Sungkyunkwan
University

Hyehwa
Roundabout

Changgyeongungno

Daehangno

Line 4

Hyewha Ⓜ

Yeongyeongdang

Biwon
(Secret
Garden)

Pond

Botanical
Glasshouse

Chinese
Pagoda

9 🏠
2 🏛
47
10 🏛

CHANGDEOKGUNG

Royal
Office

Injeongjeon

3 🏛

Royal
Garage

Naksonjae

Donhwamun
5

CHANGGYEONGGUNG

Throne
Hall

4

See Daehangno Map (p208)

18
🏠
Ⓜ
nguk
40
🏠

Footbridge

Yulgokro

Unhyeongung

Yeongnyeongjeon

JONGMYO

Daehangno

Samilro

Line 3

21
🏠

Jeongjeon

Chilsadang   Gongsindang

13

Changgyeongungno

43
🏠

5

Line 5   Jongno 3-ga Ⓜ

waenamu-gil

Donhwamunno

Tapgol
Park

9

Jongmyo
Park

Line 1   Jongno 5-ga Ⓜ

Supyodari-gil

Samilro

Jongno 3-ga Ⓜ   Jongno

Seun
Arcade

Gwangjang
Market

Hullyeonwonno

6

Cheonggye Stream

Daerim
Arcade

Line 5

0 ▭▭▭▭▭ 1 km
0 ▬▬▬▬▬ 0.5 miles

INSADONG

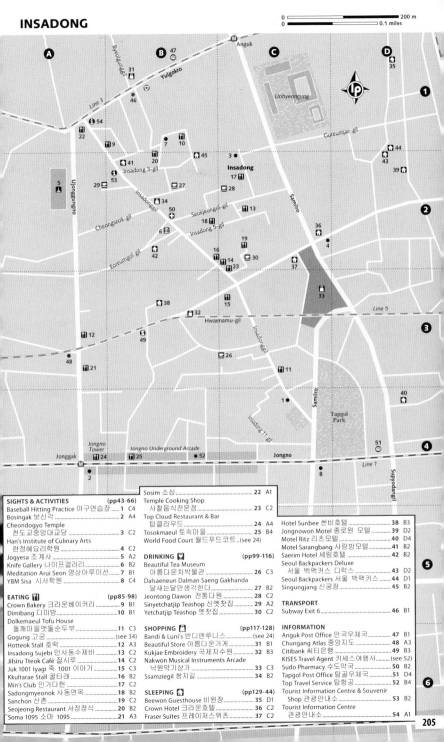

MYEONG-DONG & NAMSAN

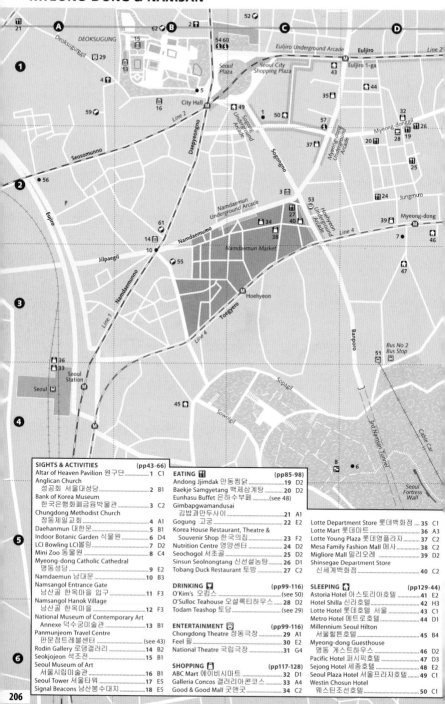

See Gwanghwamun Map (pp202–3)

Daerim Arcade
Euljiro 3-ga
Euljiro Underground Arcade
Euljiro 4-ga

Suyodarigil
Sampung Arcade
Jungbu Market
Hullyeonno
Line 5

Dorihwamunno
Mareunnaegil

Line 3
Shinseong Arcade

Samiro
Line 4

Chungmuro
Toegyero

Bus No 2 Bus Stop

Line 3
Dongguk University
Bus No 2 Bus Stop

Dongguk University

Jangchung Park

Time Capsule Square

Namsangongyongil

Namsan Park

Jung-gu

1st Namsan Tunnel
2nd Namsan Tunnel

Changjungdangil

Bus No 2 Bus Stop

Bus No 2 Bus Stop

Namsan (262m)

Namsan Park

Beotigogae

Line 6

207

DAEHANGNO

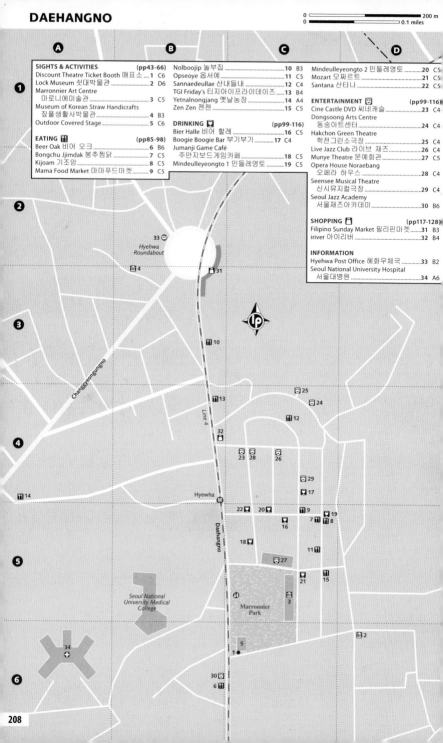

ITAEWON

0 ———————————— 300 m
0 ———————————— 0.2 miles

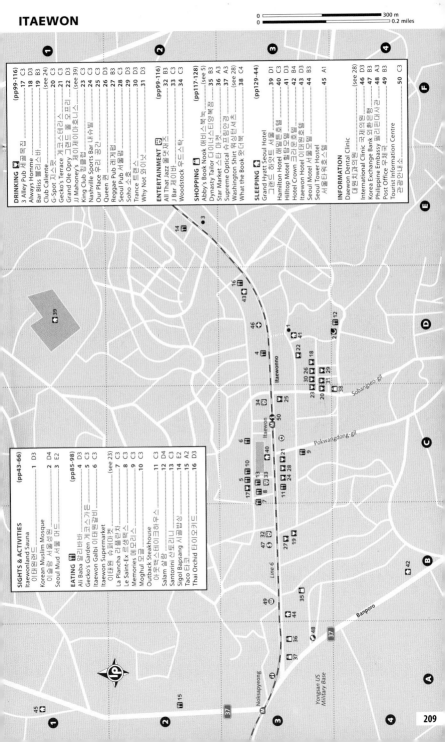

SIGHTS & ACTIVITIES (pp43–66)
Itaewonland Sauna 이태원랜드	1 D3
Korean Muslim Mosque 이슬람 서울성원	2 D4
Seoul Mud 서울 머드	3 E2

EATING (pp85–98)
Ali Baba 알리바바	4 D3
Gecko's Garden 게코스가든	5 C3
Itaewon Galbi 이태원갈비	6 C3
Itaewon Supermarket 이태원 슈퍼마켓	(see 23)
La Plancha 라 플란차	7 C3
Le Saint-Ex 르 생펙스	8 C3
Memories 메모리스	9 C3
Moghul 모굴	10 C3
Outback Steakhouse 아웃백스테이크하우스	11 C3
Salam 살람	12 D4
Santorini 산토리니	13 C3
Sigol Bapsang 시골밥상	14 E2
Taco 타코	15 A2
Thai Orchid 타이오키드	16 D3

DRINKING (pp99–116)
3 Alley Pub 세뤼목집	17 C3
Always Homme	18 D3
Bar Bliss 블리스바	19 B3
Club Caliente	(see 24)
G-Spot 지스팟	20 C3
Gecko's Terrace 게코스테라스	21 C3
Grand Ole Opry 그랜드 올 오프리	22 D3
JJ Mahoney's 제이제이마호니스	(see 39)
King Club 킹클럽	23 C3
Nashville Sports Bar 내쉬빌	24 C3
Our Place 우리 공간	25 C3
Queen 퀸	26 D3
Reggae Pub 레게펍	27 B3
Seoul Pub 서울펍	28 C3
Soho 소호	29 D3
Trance 트란스	30 D3
Why Not 와이낫	31 D3

ENTERTAINMENT (pp99–116)
All That Jazz 올댓재즈	32 B3
J Bar 제이바	33 C3
Woodstock 우드스탁	34 C3

SHOPPING (pp117–128)
Abby's Book Nook 애비스북눅	(see 5)
Dynasty Tailor 다이너스티양복점	35 B3
Star Market 스타 마켓	36 A3
Supreme Optical 슈프림안경	37 A3
Washington Shirt 워싱턴셔츠	(see 28)
What the Book 왓더북	38 C4

SLEEPING (pp129–44)
Grand Hyatt Seoul Hotel 그랜드 하얏트 서울	39 D1
Hamilton Hotel 해밀톤호텔	40 D3
Hilltop Motel 힐탑모텔	41 D3
Hotel Crown 크라운호텔	42 B4
Itaewon Hotel 이태원호텔	43 D3
Seoul Motel 서울모텔	44 B3
Seoul Tower Hostel 서울타워호스텔	45 A1

INFORMATION
Daewon Dental Clinic 대원치과의원	(see 28)
International Clinic 국제의원	46 D3
Korea Exchange Bank 외환은행	47 B3
Philippine Embassy 필리핀대사관	48 A3
Post Office 우체국	49 B3
Tourist Information Centre 관광안내소	50 C3

Itaewonno

Sobangseo-gil

Itaewon

Pokwangdong-gil

Banporo

Line 6

Noksapyeong

Yongsan US
Military Base

209

0 |———————————| 1 km
0 |———————————| 0.5 miles

A **B** **C** **D**

1

22

Yonsei University

3

32

Ewha Womans University

2

Mangwondonggil

Seogoyo

Yeonheuro

Seongsanno

13

8

11 12

14

7

17

34

Hongik University

33

15

10 21

18

25

Line 2

16

Ewha Womans University

Donggyoro

Hapjeongno

Line 6

Hapjeongno

2 Mangwon

Yanghwaro

19

30

Sinchon

Sogang University

24

Hongik University

Hapjeong

Line 2

Daeheung

Seogangno

Sangsu

Line 6

Daeheungno

Gwangheungchang

Seoul Foreigner's Cemetery

4

Tochonggil

Taeheungno

Line 5

3 Yanghwa Bridge

See Hongik Map (p213)

Gangbyeon Expwy 77

Mapo

Bamseom Island Bird Sanctuary

Seogang Bridge

Han River (Hangang)

57

Riverside Park

Yeouiseoro

5

4

23

6

27

26

29

Mapo Bridge

Wonhyo Bridge

Usadangno

Yeouido Park

Yeouinaru

Yeouido

Yeouiseoro

5 Yeongdeungpo Market

Yeongdeungpo Market

31

28

Line 5

Yeouido

35

Yeouidongno

Usadangno

Yonghoro

Saekang Ecology Park

Singil

Cherry Blossom Park

6 Yeongdeungpo

Yeongdeungpo Park

Seoul Bridge

88

20

Noryangjin

Noryangjin

Daebang

0 |—————————————| 1 km
0 |—————————————| 0.5 miles

See Central Seoul Map (pp200–1)

See Jamsil Map (pp214–5)

211

SINCHON & YEOUIDO (p210)

SIGHTS & ACTIVITIES (pp43-66)
63 Building 63빌딩 **1** D6
Ewha Womans University Museum
 이화여자대학교박물관 **2** D1
Food & Culture Academy
 푸드앤컬처 코리아 **3** D1
Jeoldusan Martyrs Museum &
 Chapel 절두산순교박물관 **4** A3
National Assembly 국회의사당 **5** B4
Yeouido Hangang Swimming Pool
 수영장 **6** C2

EATING (pp85-98)
BSD Dubu House BSD 순두부 **7** D2
Chuncheonjip 춘천집 **8** C2
Happy Table 해피테이블 **9** D2
Hwedra Ramyeon 훼드라 라면 .**10** C2
Noryangjin Fish Market Restaurants
 노량진 수산시장 횟집 ....(see 20)
Plaza Fountain Buffet ....(see 1)

DRINKING (pp99-116)
Beatles 비틀즈 **11** C2
Blue Bird 블루버드 ....(see 11)

Mu 무 **12** C2
Wallflowers 월플라워스 **13** C1
Woodstock 우드스탁 **14** C2

ENTERTAINMENT (pp99-116)
Rolling Stones 롤링스톤스 **15** C2

SHOPPING (pp117-128)
Ahyeon-dong Wedding Street
 아현동 웨딩거리 **16** D2
Crow 크로우 **17** D2
Gajukgongyebang
 가죽공예방 ....(see 17)
Hyundai Department Store
 현대백화점 **18** C2
Indoor Market
 신다주종합상가 **19** C2
Noryangjin Fish Market
 노량진 수산시장 **20** D6
Synnara Record 신나라레코드 ... **21** C2

SLEEPING (pp129-44)
Guesthouse Korea
 게스트하우스 코리아 **22** B1

Hotel Benhur
 호텔 벤허 **23** B4
Kims' Guesthouse
 킴스 게스트하우스 **24** A2
Prince Hotel 프린스호텔 **25** D2
Yoido Hotel 여의도호텔 **26** B4

TRANSPORT
Bicycle Hire 자전거대여소 **27** C4
Bicycle Hire 자전거대여소 **28** D5
Cycleway Tunnel 터널 **29** C5
Sinchon Bus Terminal
 신촌시외버스터미널 **30** C2
Yeouido Ferry Pier
 여의도선착장 **31** D5

INFORMATION
International Clinic
 (Severance Hospital)
 세브란스병원국제진료센터 **32** D1
Medipharm 메디팜 **33** C2
Post Office 우체국 **34** D2
Yeouido Post Office
 여의도우체국 **35** C5

GANGNAM (p211)

SIGHTS & ACTIVITIES (pp43-66)
Baseball Hitting Practice
 야구연습장 ....(see 8)
Hyosung Golf 효성 골프 **1** D2
Kukkiwon 국기원 **2** C4
Museum of Korean Embroidery
 한국자수박물관 **3** C3
Thai Spirit 타이스피릿 **4** C3

EATING (pp85-98)
Berries Café 베리스 카페 ...(see 26)
Bonjuk 본죽 **5** D2
Familia Buffet ....(see 34)
Hanmiri 한미리 ....(see 33)
Hard Rock Café 하드락 카페 **6** D2
Mad for Garlic 매드포갈릭 **7** C1
Noodle X 누들엑스 **8** C5
Pho Bay 포베이 **9** C5
Pulhyanggi 풀향기 **10** C2
Sinsun Seolnongtang
 신선설농탕 **11** C5
Songtan Budaejjigae
 송탄부대찌개 **12** C4

DRINKING (pp99-116)
Dublin 더블린 **13** C4
Igloo 이글루 **14** C2
Juju Tent Bar
 주주실내포장마차 **15** D2
O'Sulloc Teahouse
 오설록티하우스 **16** C5
Platinum Microbrewery
 플래티넘마이크로브루어리 **17** C5
Rock'n'Roll Bar 락앤롤바 **18** D2
Tea Museum Café
 티뮤지엄 카페 **19** D2

ENTERTAINMENT (pp99-116)
DVD Cinetique 씨네틱 **20** D2
Once in a Blue Moon
 원스인어 블루문 **21** D2

SHOPPING (pp117-128)
Boon the Shop 분더샵 **22** D2
Central City Mall
 센트럴시티 **23** A4
Galleria (East)
 갤러리아백화점 **24** D2
Galleria (West)
 갤러리아백화점 **25** D2
Huckleberry Farms
 허클베리팜스 **26** D1
Hyundai Department Store
 현대백화점 **27** C2
Shinsegae Department Store
 신세계백화점 ....(see 23)
Synnara Record 신나라레코드 ... **28** C5
Taste Maximum
 테이스트맥시멈 **29** D2

SLEEPING (pp129-44)
Best Western Premier Gangnam
 베스트웨스턴 강남호텔 **30** C4
Dormy in Seoul 도미인서울 **31** C4
Hotel Dynasty
 호텔 다이내스티 **32** C4
Human Touch Ville
 휴먼터치빌 **33** D4
Imperial Palace Hotel
 임페리얼 팰리스호텔 **34** D3
Jelly Hotel 젤리호텔 **35** C5
JW Marriott Hotel
 JW 메리어트호텔 **36** A4

M Chereville 엠쉐르빌 **37** C5
Novotel Ambassador
 노보텔앰배서더호텔 **38** C4
Popgreen Hotel 팝그린호텔 **39** C2
Princess Hotel
 프린세스호텔 **40** D2
Ritz Carlton Hotel
 리츠칼튼호텔 **41** C4
Samjung Hotel 삼정호텔 **42** C4
Sunshine Hotel 선샤인호텔 **43** C2
The Ville 더빌 **44** C3
Youngdong Hotel 영동호텔 **45** C3

TRANSPORT
Bus Stop for Everland
 Amusement Park
 버스정류장 (에버랜드 행) **46** C5
Korea Air Terminal (Central City)
 도심공항터미널 ....(see 23)
Nambu Bus Terminal
 남부시외버스터미널 **47** B6
Seoul Express Bus Terminal
 (Gyeongbu-Gumi-Yeongdong
 Terminal)
 서울고속버스터미널
 (경부선, 구미선, 영동선) **48** A4
Seoul Express Bus Terminal
 (Honam Terminal)
 서울고속버스터미널
 (호남선) **49** A4

INFORMATION
Yeoksam Post Office
 역삼우체국 **50** C4
Yeong-dong Post Office
 영동우체국 **51** C3

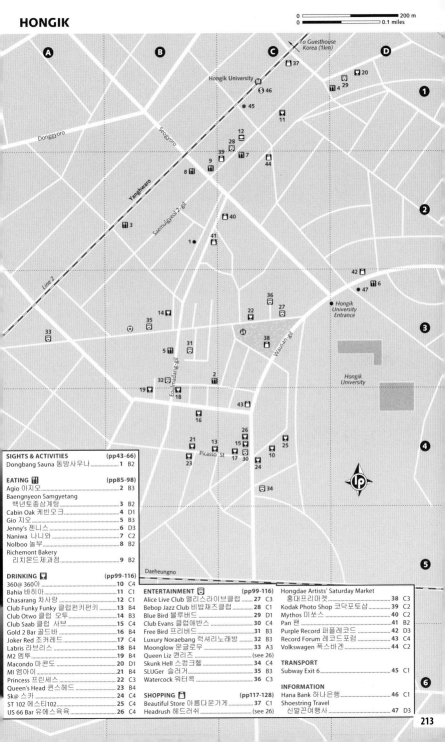

HONGIK

SIGHTS & ACTIVITIES	(pp43–66)
Dongbang Sauna 동방사우나	1 B2

EATING	(pp85–98)
Agio 아지오	2 B3
Baengnyeon Samgyetang 백년토종삼계탕	3 B2
Cabin Oak 케빈오크	4 D1
Gio 지오	5 B3
Jenny's 젠니스	6 D3
Naniwa 나니와	7 C2
Nolboo 놀부	8 B2
Richemont Bakery 리치몬드제과점	9 B2

DRINKING	(pp99–116)
360@ 360아	10 C4
Bahia 바히아	11 C1
Chasarang 차사랑	12 C1
Club Funky Funky 클럽펀키펑키	13 B4
Club Otwo 클럽 오투	14 B3
Club Saab 클럽 사브	15 C4
Gold 2 Bar 골드비	16 B4
Joker Red 조커레드	17 C4
Labris 라브리스	18 B4
M2 엠투	19 B4
Macondo 마콘도	20 D1
MI 엠아이	21 B4
Princess 프린세스	22 C3
Queen's Head 퀸스헤드	23 B4
Sk@ 스카	24 C4
ST 102 에스티102	25 C4
US 66 Bar 유에스육육	26 C4

ENTERTAINMENT	(pp99–116)
Alice Live Club 앨리스라이브클럽	27 C3
Bebop Jazz Club 비밥재즈클럽	28 C1
Blue Bird 블루버드	29 D1
Club Evans 클럽에반스	30 C4
Free Bird 프리버드	31 B3
Luxury Noraebang 럭셔리노래방	32 B4
Moonglow 문글로우	33 A3
Queen Liz 퀸리즈	(see 26)
Skunk Hell 스컹크헬	34 C4
SLUGer 슬러거	35 B3
Watercock 워터콕	36 C3

SHOPPING	(pp117–128)
Beautiful Store 아름다운가게	37 C1
Headrush 헤드러쉬	(see 26)
Hongdae Artists' Saturday Market 홍대프리마켓	38 C3
Kodak Photo Shop 코닥포토샵	39 C2
Mythos 미쏘스	40 C2
Pan 팬	41 B2
Purple Record 퍼플레코드	42 D3
Record Forum 레코드포럼	43 C4
Volkswagen 폭스바겐	44 C2

TRANSPORT	
Subway Exit 6	45 C1

INFORMATION	
Hana Bank 하나은행	46 C1
Shoestring Travel 신발끈여행사	47 D3

A **B** **C** **D**

1

Gangbyeon Expwy

Line 7

Ttukseomgil

77

47

Ttukseom Resort

M

● 1

45

Yongdong Bridge

26

Ttukseom Riverside Park

Olympic Expwy

88

Brand Name St

32 Dosandaero

2

Samseongno

Cheongdam Park

41

Han River (Hangang)

Hakdongno

M Cheongdam

Line 7

Cheongdam Bridge

43

M Gangnam-gu Office

88

20

7

Jamsil Sports Complex

Seolleungno

3

Bongeunsaro

2

● 4

35

COEX Mall

5

6

8

9

Sports Complex

M Asian Park

Sinche

22

11

44

28

36

31

M Samseong

Samseong Bridge

10

Seolleung Park

● 25

50

Teheranno

Line 2

38

Yeongdongdaero

Tancheon 2 Bridge

M Seolleung

Yeoksamno

Samseongno

4

Seolleungno

Dogokdonggil

Hangnyeoul M

Yongdong 6gyo

47

Daechi M

Daecheong M

5

Nambusunhwanno

Yongdong 5gyo

Line 3

Daecheong M

See Gangnam Map (p211)

99 Dogok

Line 3

Maebong M

Yangjaedaero

M Irwon

6

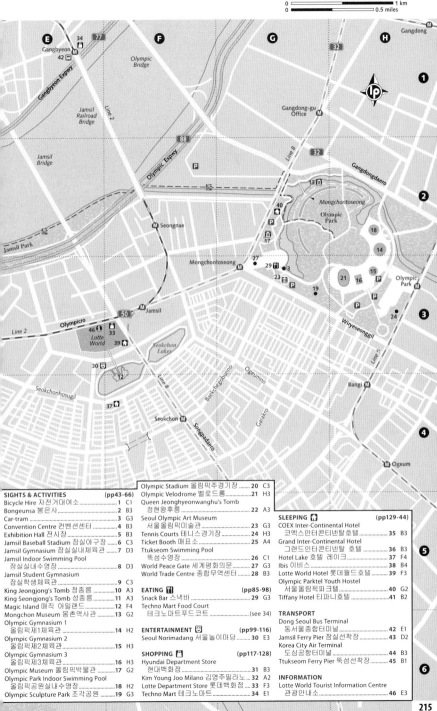

BUKHANSAN NATIONAL PARK

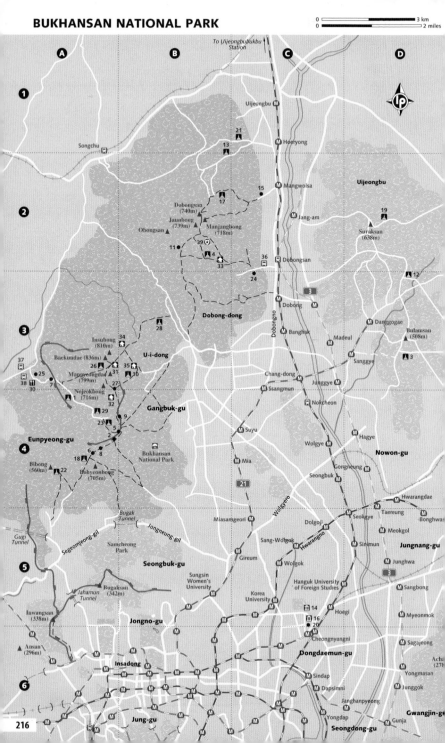

0 — 3 km
0 — 2 miles

To Uijeongbubukbu Station

A **B** **C** **D**

1

Songchu
Uijeongbu
Hoeryong

2

21
13
Mangwolsa
Uijeongbu
17
15
Dobongsan (740m)
Jaunbong (739m)
Manjanghong (718m)
Jang-am
19
Suraksan (638m)
Obongsan
11
39
4
33
Dobongsan
36
24
Dobong-dong
3
Dobong
12
Dobongno
Banghak
Madeul
Danggogae
Bulamsan (508m)

3

28
Insubong (810m)
34
U-i-dong
37
Baekundae (836m)
26
35
Sanggye
3
Mangyeongdae (799m)
31
25
10
Chang-dong
38
27
Ssangmun
Junggye
30
7
Nojeokbong (716m)
1
32
Nokcheon
29
Gangbuk-gu
9
Suyu
23
5
Eunpyeong-gu
2
Bukhansan National Park
Wolgye
Hagye

4

6
8
Mia
Nowon-gu
18
Seongbuk
Gongneung
Bibong (560m)
22
Bohyeonbong (705m)
21
Hwarangdae
Miasamgeori
Wolgyero
Dolgoji
Seolgye
Taereung
Bonghwa
Bugak Tunnel
Jongneung-gil
Sang-Wolgok
Hwarangno
Meokgol
Gugi Tunnel
Segeomjeong-gil
Gireum
Sinimun
Jungnang-gu

5

Samcheong Park
Seongbuk-gu
Wolgok
Junghwa
3
Sungsin Women's University
Hanguk University of Foreign Studies
Sangbong
Jahamun Tunnel
Bugaksan (342m)
Korea University
Hoegi
Myeonmok
Inwangsan (338m)
14
Jongno-gu
16
Sagajeong
Acha (278
Ansan (296m)
20
Cheongnyangni
Yongmasan

6

Dongdaemun-gu
Insadong
Sindap
Dapsimni
Junggok
Gwangjin-gu
Janghanpyeong
Jung-gu
Yongdap
Gunja
Seongdong-gu

216